CARTOGRAPHIC MEMORY

Genoveva,

Thank you for engaging
with my book!

— Juan

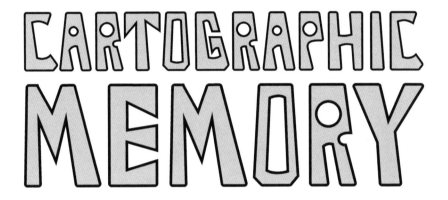

CARTOGRAPHIC MEMORY

SOCIAL MOVEMENT ACTIVISM
AND THE PRODUCTION OF SPACE

Juan Herrera

DUKE UNIVERSITY PRESS
Durham and London
2022

Printed in the United States of America on acid-free paper ∞
Designed by A. Mattson Gallagher
Typeset in Chaparral Pro and Eurostile LT Std
by Westchester Publishing Services

Library of Congress Cataloging-in-Publication Data
Names: Herrera, Juan, [date] author.
Title: Cartographic memory : social movement activism and the
production of space / Juan Herrera.
Description: Durham : Duke University Press, 2022. |
Includes bibliographical references and index.
Identifiers: LCCN 2022005740 (print)
LCCN 2022005741 (ebook)
ISBN 9781478006077 (hardcover)
ISBN 9781478006749 (paperback)
ISBN 9781478007494 (ebook)
ISBN 9781478092735 (ebook other)
Subjects: LCSH: Chicano movement—California—Oakland—
History—20th century. | Mexican Americans—Political
activity—California—Oakland—History—20th century. |
Mexican Americans—California—Oakland—Social
conditions—20th century. | BISAC: SOCIAL SCIENCE / Ethnic
Studies / General | SOCIAL SCIENCE / Human Geography
Classification: LCC E184.M5 H442 2022 (print) | LCC E184.M5
(ebook) | DDC 305.868/72079466—dc23/eng/20220315
LC record available at https://lccn.loc.gov/2022005740
LC ebook record available at https://lccn.loc.gov/2022005741

Cover art: Malaquias Montoya, *Día del Barrio*, 1982.
Silkscreen, 24×16.5 in. Courtesy of the artist
(malaquiasmontoya.com).

This book is freely available in an open access edition thanks
to TOME (Toward an Open Monograph Ecosystem)—a
collaboration of the Association of American Universities,
the Association of University Presses, and the Association
of Research Libraries—and the general support of Arcadia,
a charitable fund of Lisbet Rausing and Peter Baldwin, and
the UCLA Library. Learn more at the TOME website, available
at: openmongraphs.org.

Para Carlos y Elsa Herrera—mi mama y papá—por su amor y apoyo. Y por siempre aceptar y celebrar mis diferentes formas de ser.

And for Fruitvale. A place that grew me up.

CONTENTS

ACKNOWLEDGMENTS

The book that you hold in your hands is my love letter to the Bay Area. It represents my coming-of-age story and the first time I fell in love with a place. First and foremost, I thank Oakland and especially Fruitvale, a place that taught me so much about how human beings produce space. It was through the social relations that I built in Fruitvale and the entire Bay Area that I came to understand the geographic imperatives to our experiences in this world. I also learned about the historical and power-laden process through which all spaces are produced.

The fact that this book occupies space in this world is a testament to the collective endeavor that it takes to write a book. I am indebted to all the people who allowed me to come into their lives and accepted me as a colleague in various nonprofit and community projects. This book is not a full testament to the relationships of trust, love, and struggle that I built with Fruitvale residents and nonprofit leaders. As with all forms of writing, this book describes but a small sliver of the depth of experiences I was blessed with. I thank Mara Chavez for being the first person who welcomed me to Centro Legal de la Raza and enthusiastically took me on as a volunteer. She introduced me to Fruitvale and its numerous nonprofit organizations and political action groups. I am also immensely indebted to Laura Perez—a tremendous human being, activist, leader, and friend. I have never met a person so dedicated to an organization and to the community it serves. I learned so much from working with my fellow members of the board of directors at the nonprofit Street Level Health Project, and I thank them all for allowing me to be a part of the organization. I am especially grateful to all the activists who shared their tremendous stories of struggle with me. These activists continue to inspire me through their dedication to community care and their efforts to raise awareness about the history of social movement struggle in the neighborhood. I especially thank the activists who form part of the Fruitvale History Project and whose stories animate the chapters of this book: Andres Alegria, Regina Chavarín, Mariano Contreras, Lenor De Cruz, Joel Garcia, Judi Garcia, Connie Jubb, Selia Melero, Elizabeth Meza, Annette Oropeza, and Beatriz M. Pesquera.

My path on this journey began when I was an undergraduate at UCLA through my participation in the McNair Research Scholars Program. I thank La'Tonya Rease Miles (LT) for being such an inspiring mentor and for instilling in all of us McNair scholars a profound insight into the politics of research and academic knowledge production. I thank my fellow McNair scholars for being great friends and colleagues throughout this journey, especially Kency Cornejo, Claudia Sandoval, and Romeo Guzman. I also thank Maylei Blackwell, who took me under her wing when I was a young undergrad and has supported me ever since. Maylei has shown me so much about the power of community-building in academia and has been the most amazing mentor and friend. I am eternally grateful for her teachings and support.

The seeds of this book were first sown through my graduate training in the Department of Ethnic Studies at UC Berkeley. My experience at UC Berkeley was shaped by the support I received from fellow students, mentors, and on-campus institutions. One of the most rewarding experiences was my two-year fellowship through the Center for Research on Social Change Graduate Fellows Training Program. I was fortunate to engage with amazing scholars and build long-term friendships I continue to cherish to this day. I thank my all-star cohort: Tamera Lee Stover, Becky Alexander, Emily Gleason, Nate McClintock, Carmen Martinez-Calderon, Eric Pido, and Nicol U. I have never been a part of a more thoughtful group of scholars. My experience as a fellow would not have been the same without the support of a remarkable team of mentors: Christine Trost, David Minkus, and Deborah Lustig.

I was fortunate to participate in many working groups throughout my time at UC Berkeley. I learned immensely from other colleagues and benefited from their thoughtful engagement with my work. I thank the entire team of the Afro-Latino Working Group, who welcomed me into the space even though my research did not entail work with Afro-descendants: Petra Rivera-Rideau, Ryan Rideau, Jennifer Jones, Vielka Hoy, and Tianna Paschel. I especially thank Tianna Paschel, Petra Rivera-Rideau, and Jennifer

Jones for their mentorship throughout the years. The Center for Latino Policy Research hosted another working group that helped me fine-tune my training in immigration studies. My colleagues there included Heidy Sarabia, Abigail Andrews, Fidan Elcioglu, Becky Alexander, and Kevin Escudero.

I am eternally grateful for the support of my faculty advisers at UC Berkeley. Ramon Grosfoguel was a great advocate and chair of my dissertation committee. I thank Thomas Biolsi for believing in my project and helping me bridge my ethnic studies training with the fields of anthropology and geography. Jake Kosek was a remarkable mentor who always knew how to ask the tough questions and pushed me to identify the "so what" of my arguments. I would not be the scholar I am today without the foundational support of one of the most incredible mentors and human beings in academia, Donald Moore. Through him I also met some of my most inspiring colleagues and friends, who each contributed to the development of this project in one form or another: Krystal Strong, Jenny Greenburg, Katy Guimond, Maryani Palupy Rasidijan, Jodi Rios, Diana Negrín, Catalina Garzon, Megan Ybarra, and Lindsey Dillon. I am eternally grateful for Donald's mentorship, *apoyo*, and friendship.

My experience at UC Berkeley was deeply shaped by the Department of Ethnic Studies. I owe a special thanks to my cohort members Jason Oliver Chang, Annie Fukushima, Alejandro Pérez, Dalida Maria Benfield, Eric Pido, Thomas Swensen, Jenn Reimer, and Kim Murphy. Other students made my years in the department productive and enjoyable: Yomaira Figueroa, Tacuma Peters, John Dougherty, Janey Lew, Jason Kim, Joshua Troncoso, Sara Ramirez, Alma Granado, and Leece Lee. I was blessed to teach alongside these colleagues and learned from stellar professors. I have nothing but admiration for Nelson Maldonado-Torres as a scholar and teacher. I learned so much from teaching Asian American studies with Professor Michael Omi, whose scholarship and pedagogy have been extremely influential in my training. By far, one of my favorite teaching experiences was working with Professor Carlos Muños Jr. in Guanajuato and Mexico City. It was such a blessing to learn from Carlos's passion for teaching and his commitment to his students. I also learned much about life and compassion through his remarkable *compañera*, Chela Muños. Other professors in the department provided crucial encouragement throughout the years. Laura Perez was always available to answer questions. Professors Beth Piatote and Shari Huhndorf offered tremendous support and professional development by carefully reading over chapters, research proposals, and cover letters for job applications.

Many other people and institutions provided crucial assistance through-out different phases of the project. I am indebted to numerous librarians who helped me during the research process, especially those at the Stanford University Archives, New York Public Library's Schomburg Center for Research in Black Culture, the Rockefeller Archive Center, the Oakland Public Library, and UC Berkeley's Bancroft Library, Ethnic Studies Library, and Environmental Design Library. The Department of Chicana/o and Central American Studies at UCLA was an incredible intellectual home during my UC President's Postdoctoral Fellowship from 2013 to 2015. Leisy Ábrego and Maylei Blackwell were instrumental in helping me throughout my postdoc years. I especially benefited from the collegial and robust intellectual environment at the Chicanos Studies Research Center at UCLA. I am especially grateful to Maurice "Mauricio" Rafael Magaña, my cubicle buddy and dear friend as a postdoc at UCLA and fellow interlocutor regarding space and social movements. While at Oregon State University I also benefited immensely from the Center for Humanities Fellowship, which provided a quarter off from teaching to focus on writing. This book would not have been possible without the financial support of the California Institute for Mexico and the United States (UC-MEXUS), the University of California Office of the President, the UC Berkeley Office of the Chancellor, and the Institute for the Study of Societal Issues.

At Oregon State University, I thank my colleagues in the Ethnic Studies program and the entire School of Language, Culture, and Society for providing such a collegial and supportive environment. Marta Maria Maldonado, Robert Thompson, and Patti Sakurai were excellent colleagues who taught me much about the power of ethnic studies in a small-town university. I am especially grateful to Natchee Barnd and Charlene Martinez for welcoming us into their family and allowing us to be uncles to their beautiful girls, Nube and Moana.

At the UCLA Department of Geography, I have been blessed with being a part of one of the most collegial departments in all of academia. I thank all my fellow colleagues and the amazing staff for welcoming me and always supporting me along the way. I owe tremendous gratitude to the main motor in the department, Kasi McMurry, for always having my back and guiding me through the administrative minutiae. I am eternally grateful for my fellow colleagues and especially Adam Moore, Jamie Goodwin-White, Lieba Faier, Helga Leitner, Eric Sheppard, Judy Carney, and John Agnew for always being available to chat and supporting my intellectual growth in the department. I was fortunate to be a part of a cluster hire, and it has been incredible to share this experience with Kelly Kay and Shaina Potts. I thank them for being such amazing friends and interlocuters and for the support they have offered throughout this process. Outside the department, I am grateful for so many friends and colleagues: Ananya Roy, Hannah Appel, Amy Ritterbusch, Leisy Ábrego, Gaye Theresa Johnson, Genevieve Carpio, Amada Armenta, Efrén Pérez, Carlos Santos, Chris Zepeda-Millan, Kian Goh, Liz Koslov, Chon Noriega, Rebecca Epstein, Karina Alma, Floridalma Boj Lopez, Maylei Blackwell, Celia Lacayo, Joshua Javier Guzman, Mishuana Goeman, Vilma Ortiz, Ju Hui Judy Han, Shannon Speed, Sherene Razack, Kelly Little Hernandez, Laura E. Gomez, H. Samy Alim, Gary Segura, Matt Barreto, and Sonja Diaz. I am eternally grateful to my graduate advisees, who have shown me the power of collective thought and have demonstrated the energy it takes to change a predominantly white discipline such as geography: Zoe Malot, Maritza Geronimo, Nushy Golriz, Flavia Maria Lake, Nohely Guzmán-Narvaez, and Sara Moya.

This book has been improved through the generous feedback of many amazing people. I thank the Relational Poverty Network Summer Institute for providing generous feedback. The fabulous Sarah Elwood and Vicky Lawson have been immensely supportive since then, and I thank them for their continued mentorship. The Latinx Geographies Specialty Group of the American Association of Geography has also been a huge source of support and encouragement. Thank you all for all your work in helping to validate Latinx people and lives in the field of geography. Natchee Barnd and Adam Moore read my entire manuscript, and I thank them for their excellent feedback. I also appreciate the feedback I received from numerous presentations, including at UC Berkeley's Department of Geography, the Institute for the Study of Societal Issues, the University of Oregon's Department of Geography, UC Davis's geography program, and UCLA's Department of Anthropology. At Duke University Press, I thank Gisela Fosado for believing in this project very early on and seeing it through. I also thank the two incredibly generous reviewers who found important ways to improve the book.

I am especially thankful to my life partner, who has been instrumental in helping me complete this book. Rich Holub came into my life as I reached a monumental turning point and I had to literally re-create the way I navigated the world. This cathartic transition allowed me to take greater risks in my own life and especially with this book. It allowed me to think more creatively (and more authentically) about my relationship to geography and the social-spatial processes of learning to live in the world as a proud Latino gay man. Rich introduced me to a whole new world of social relations and taught me how to re-create my understandings of love, family, and community. I owe so much to Rich's labor of love, care, and partnership, and I look forward to continuing to build our sense of family and community together. So many other people were instrumental in helping me learn to navigate new landscapes of belonging. Jann Ronis and Anthony Lucas were crucial in providing support. Tamera Lee Stover and Mara Chavez have also been tremendous sources of help, and I truly value their unconditional friendship and love. I thank Joseph Cooper and Milton Nimatuj for being important friends and family in Los Angeles and for always welcoming us into their homes and friendship circles.

I am the first of my family to attend and graduate from a four-year university. I am also the first to complete a PhD program. This is not an honorific claim but rather sincere gratitude for all those who supported me when I was in school for what appeared as a never-ending number of years. After that entire period of schooling, I remained behind a desk working on my book while others of the family were being immensely productive in so many other ways. I thank my family for understanding and valuing the difficult terrain that this journey has entailed. Though my parents, Carlos Herrera and Elsa Herrera, only completed some years of elementary school, they always endeavored to understand and support the many years I have dedicated to my postsecondary education. My mom and dad sacrificed so much to come to the United States to offer our family a better life. They inspire me every day through their hard work and passion for life. I also appreciate the support I received from my siblings in both Los Angeles and Guatemala. They always provided intrigue and helpful doses of encouragement over the many years it has taken me to complete this journey.

No other person deserves my sincere gratitude more than Rachel Cruz. She relocated to the Bay Area and left her family to allow me to follow my graduate school career. Rachel fundamentally taught me how to love. She also taught me that the ability to love entails learning how to let go. This is a foundational skill for a geographer—places that we study are always under production and therefore always changing. Geographers must learn to love those places despite the fact that they can never fully be returned to.

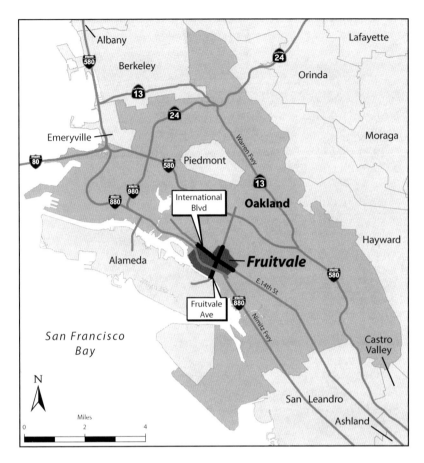

Map of the East Bay emphasizing how the neighborhood of Fruitvale is part of the broader San Francisco Bay Area. Map created by Matt Zebrowski.

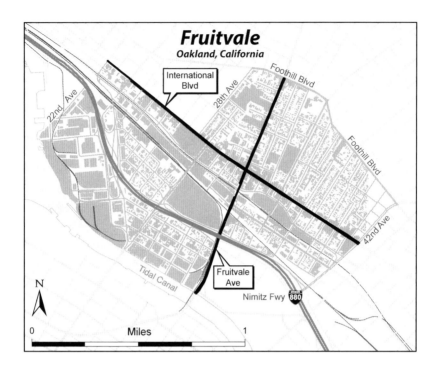

Map of the Fruitvale neighborhood with the intersection of Fruitvale Avenue and International Boulevard highlighted. This is the intersection from which many activist organizations emerged. Map created by Matt Zebrowski.

INTRODUCTION
PUTTING FRUITVALE
ON THE "MAP"

Geography—in its various formations—is integral to social struggles.
Katherine McKittrick, *Demonic Grounds*

Place is an axis of power in its own right. As a basis for the construction of difference, hierarchy, and identity, and as the basis of ideologies that rationalize economic inequalities and structure people's material well-being and life chances, place is a vehicle of power.
Jacqueline Nassy Brown, *Dropping Anchor, Setting Sail*

Loose ends and ongoing stories are real challenges to cartography.
Doreen Massey, *For Space*

My first encounter with Fruitvale happened by accident when I moved to Oakland, California, in 2005. I got lost on the circuitous roads of the Oakland hills and drove west into the flatlands, winding up at an intersection with a colorful set of buildings. An arched entryway welcomed me into a quaint village-like plaza where a sign stood marking it simply as Fruitvale. The architectural design created a pedestrian pathway where families strolled along the plaza, reminiscent of towns in Latin America. The plaza appeared like a cultural center or a set from a movie studio—somewhat surreal at

I.1 Fruitvale arch along International Boulevard at the entrance to Fruitvale Village. Image courtesy of visitoakland.com.

first. It reminded me of an idealized home, a more polished version of the Latino barrio where I grew up.[1]

So this was Fruitvale. Everyone had spoken to me about "Frut-va-le," as Spanish speakers call the region—as a Latino place where I could be involved with "the community" and find "authentic" Mexican and Central American food. It was often described as the classic example of an ethnic enclave, a social science spatial category that erroneously presumes a natural partitioning between immigrant "ethnic" neighborhoods and "mainstream" (read white) spatialities.[2] Having grown up in a predominantly Latino and working-class community in Los Angeles County, I found that the neighborhood had an immediate allure. This automatic conflation of Fruitvale with Latinidad seemed welcoming and inviting and gave me a peculiar feeling of belonging: it beckoned me to return, and I did just that. I revisited the neighborhood the following week to volunteer at Centro Legal de la Raza. At Centro, as everyone called it, I met a group of dedicated lawyers, long-term activists, and middle-class Chicanos all invested in providing free or affordable legal services for low-income and mainly recently arrived immigrants. Centro was created by Chicano law students in 1968, and although it has grown since then and changed physical locations, it continues to be a thriving institution in the neighborhood. Centro's continued vitality demonstrates the sustained traction of 1960s social movement activism. The legal center's name, tethered to the popular term *raza*, which roughly translates to "our race" or "the race," shows the monumental role that race played in helping to cohere 1960s activism.

The neighborhood's charm was not the only thing that attracted me. As a Chicano studies major in college, I learned that education was not merely a project for self-improvement. Education, as student activists mandated in the creation of Chicano studies, is an important tool for the liberation of Chicano communities and other disenfranchised people. Although in my Chicano studies classes I learned to care for "the community," the Chicano movement remained aspatial in my social imaginary. I did not fully understand that it took shape in neighborhoods and that activists mobilized for the defense and care of communities. I understood it as an important historical movement and an epoch that occurred "in the past."

My undergraduate major included a service learning component in which I learned about the importance of working with underserved communities. I joined a team of students that formed part of the Community Programs Office (CPO) at UCLA, an institution created by student activists of color in the 1970s that demanded the university help link students with the struggles of impoverished communities. Students who created the CPO were inspired by Black Power, Chicano, and American Indian movements that established neighborhood projects like Centro in Fruitvale.[3] I assisted a student group sponsored by the CPO called Barrio Youth Alternatives and joined a committed group of CPO students that engaged in transformative experiences mentoring and tutoring youths of color at the Community Coalition in South Central.

Fast-forward five years, when I found myself working with "the community" in Oakland. When I began graduate school, I longed for the kind of community work that I had been trained to do through the CPO. As an ethnic studies graduate student, I was surrounded by peers who equally wanted to connect theory with praxis. I soon came to find out that this "praxis" had a specific spatiality. Friends continually pointed me in one direction, to a space where I could put the ideas I was learning into practice. That space was Fruitvale. It wasn't until I began working in Fruitvale that I fully understood how the Chicano movement literally took shape through space. Put differently, neighborhood improvement projects were both routed through space and productive of spatialities.

This book contributes to a cartographic process of putting Oakland's Chicano movement activism "on the map" of the historical narrative of the 1960s, and Bay Area history more specifically. Fruitvale remains unmapped in the broader geographies of 1960s Mexican American activism. Most accounts of the Chicano movement center places such as Los Angeles, San Antonio, Denver, and other cities in the greater US Southwest. Fruitvale and

Oakland in general seem to have fallen off the map and remain uncharted as a territory touched by the Chicano movement, with little attention being paid to the spaces that activism built and the continued traction of these political forces.

This book offers a geographic examination of how people experience social movements and how social movements produce space. It depicts how activism forges new relationships and intimate kinship networks that deeply transform communities. Oakland's Latino neighborhood of Fruitvale offers a prism through which to understand how social movements produce space. Put differently, this book demonstrates how activism is a process of building diverse forms of spatialized human-environment relationships.

Social movement activism uncovers the power-laden process through which a specific bounding of place takes shape: activists mobilized to care for, defend, and creatively define a specific community called Fruitvale. However, activists' mobilizations also reveal the porosity of place: their relationships involved manifold connections to other regions and centers of power. Finally, their relations fundamentally included a utopic and radical dimension of futurity.

Fruitvale activists were committed to envisioning a different world—a place not yet available to be mapped. Fruitvale became constituted through these multiple sets of interrelations, which included processes of state and philanthropic regulation *alongside* radical utopic dreaming that stretched beyond (both spatially and temporally) the neighborhood I first encountered. This is a book about social movement place-making, a process that is never bounded or fixed—never wholly available to simply point to on a map. [4]

Fruitvale's erasure within the historiography of the Chicano movement is surprising because the San Francisco Bay Area is perhaps one of the geographies most powerfully shaped by 1960s and 1970s mobilizations. Oakland, in particular, is a city etched by the political activism of the civil rights movement and the Black Panther Party (BPP). This activism is memorialized through the popular and academic construction of Oakland as a city of Black protest movements and a place of radical mobilizations. Organized tours allow people to visit the site of the original BPP headquarters or the location of the organization's free breakfast program. The BPP, and African American activism in general, is precisely remembered through the invocation and graphing of the built environment.

The memorialization of Oakland as a site of Black protest and aestheticized Black space has produced historical amnesia about the city's Chicano and Latino mobilizations.[5] We know little about how Mexican Americans mobilized in the city or where they have predominantly lived. Amid Oakland's historical Black and white spatial order lies Oakland's Latino neighborhood of Fruitvale, located in the city's more impoverished sections called its flatlands. It is the area in Oakland with the largest Latino population and a region, as this book reveals, where the Chicano movement forged a broad base of support. Here Chicano movement activists experimented with the creation of community-based organizations that enlisted community members in projects of neighborhood improvement.

How did Fruitvale become such a robust site of activism? One could easily say that as Oakland's neighborhood with the largest Latino population, it would *naturally* hold the greatest number of nonprofit organizations. But demographics alone do not tell the story of the making of Fruitvale as a focal point of activism. In the early 1960s, Fruitvale was not yet a predominantly Latino neighborhood. It had slowly become Latino as Mexican Americans flocked to new jobs in canneries that dotted the neighborhood. The construction of Interstate 880 through portions of West Oakland sent thousands of Mexican American Oaklandites to find alternative inexpensive places to call home. Many congregated in Fruitvale, where they took over homes and businesses vacated by Italian and Portuguese white ethnics who moved to more affluent suburban spaces. And in the late 1960s, some of the first generations of Mexican American students to attend college en masse, including at UC Berkeley and Merritt College, gravitated to Fruitvale, where cheap rents and a growing Spanish-speaking population welcomed them. By the late 1960s, it was a space where students, community members, and activists carved out new community resources. Its proximity to California's Central Valley also quickly connected the region and its leadership to one of the most important movements of workers in recent history—the United Farm Workers (UFW).[6] Galvanized by farmworker movements and the opportunities and resources they attained through civil rights gains (including greater access to postsecondary education), a new generation of activists worked alongside long-term community leaders to shape neighborhood resources.

The effects of this activism continue to shape the neighborhood. From the community-based organizations that animate neighborhood politics, to the murals on the streets and the architectural design of restaurants and shops, it is a region that has come to signal Chicano and Latino identity. It is also a place with the greatest density of nonprofit and political action groups committed to caring for neighborhood residents. Fruitvale is an ever-shifting site of resistance and the epicenter of present-day immigrant rights activism in the East Bay.

Empirically, this book focuses on 1960s and 1970s Mexican American oppositional politics that cohered to form the Chicano movement. The movements that consolidated in the 1960s—including the Chicano movement, Black Power, the gay liberation movement, and the American Indian Movement (AIM)—were anchored by the goal of transforming aggrieved communities into vibrant and self-sufficient places. Social movement actors made specific arguments about the very geography of racism and inequality in the United States. These movements made visible, for example, how state and municipal governments normalized racial segregation and naturalized the unequal distribution of resources for nonwhites (and their respective spatialities). Additionally, activists asserted that racism and white supremacy worked through processes that disciplined space: converting the contiguous landmass of the United States—once under the sole guardianship and care of Indigenous people—into compartmentalized white (and privileged) spaces and nonwhite pathological ghettos/barrios/reservations. Activists also critiqued urban planning policies that disinvested in the inner city and therefore rendered nonwhite and impoverished spaces as dangerous and deserving of overpolicing and punishment. In sum, this social movement activism can be read as a kind of cartographic endeavor that reinterpreted how race and settler colonialism was understood in the United States and how new generations would come to understand the connections between race, place, and colonization.[7] It is this very dynamic that this books centers, examining how 1960s and 1970s social movements deeply remapped race in the United States and detailing these movements' long-lasting spatial and political effects.

Space as Archive of Social Movement Activism

Through my experiences in Fruitvale, I became attuned to how social movements mobilize to make changes in actually existing places. But far more than space being just a surface on which social movements evolve, this book argues, movements *produce* space. Bridging the fields of human geography and ethnic studies, the book reconceptualizes the study of social movements by focusing on how movements produce landscapes shaped out of the reconfiguration of social relations and the meeting of multiple historical trajectories—down to the materiality of transformations in the built environment. Some of these changes escape visual registers. Instead, they are embedded in intricate webs of social relations, institutional networks, and ways of being in the world that are passed down from one generation to the next.

Utilizing rich oral histories, ethnography, and meticulous archival research, I detail how movements transform places, route places to other regions, and mobilize to create an egalitarian futurity. I underscore how in their recollections of the past, activists constructed a politics of activism, race, and social movement struggle forged through productions of space. Activists evidenced parks, institutions, and urban redevelopment projects as a product of their labor. They also detailed educational projects, political consciousness-raising practices, and solidarity movements that were specific to Fruitvale but were also linked to areas beyond this specific neighborhood. By seriously considering cultural politics *rooted* and *routed* through place, I elaborate a theoretical and methodological understanding of space as archive of social movement activism.

I analyze the political nature of these productions of space, with a focus on how activists and institutions marshaled changes to the built environment to make claims to power. I ask how and why a broad constellation of activists and institutions, representing a spectrum of political postures, deploy spatial productions to serve particular functions. As Jacqueline Nassy Brown (2005, 9) has argued, "The materiality of a place lies not merely in its physical, visible form (and visibility itself is a moving target) but in its identity" as a particular place. One example can be seen in the way that activists will point to an empty storefront and label it as the original site of a health clinic constructed out of social movement struggle. In these practices, activists reconfigured the urban landscape to show the materiality of social movement activism, a practice that Brown (2005, 11) refers to as the "use of place-as-matter to explain the social."

For activists and institutions featured in this book, social movement activism took shape through neighborhood-level projects of community improvement and protection. In fact, activists' claims to power were anchored in how they had appropriately cared for different sectors of the community or for the improvement of neighborhood infrastructure and resources. The care of the community was both the object of 1960s political struggles and the subject of contentious debates.[8] By reading space as an archive of social movement struggles, I learned that activists' participation in any form of activism stemmed from their desire to graph a different kind of world. Fruitvale was the locus through which they would envision a more spatially just and egalitarian world. The revolution was literally right around the corner, and its spatiality was desperately waiting to be mapped.

Activists' mobilizations represented a project of, as the title of this chapter suggests, literally "putting Fruitvale on the map." Activists worked collectively to build a new sense of community and graphed a different place imbued with a sense of urgency for change. They envisioned a new sense of place that was fervently politicized and committed to caring for and building social networks with fellow human beings and places near and far. The process of creating and imagining a "new" sense of place only happened through intense political action.[9] For many activists, their vision of this "new" place never fully materialized.

By focusing on the political stakes of activists' endeavors, this book is also about how activists and scholars define the political. Most scholarship on the Chicano movement defines the political as radical attempts to remake US society in which rallies, boycotts, moratoriums, and marches on the streets became the privileged sites of analysis. In most accounts of 1960s activism, political actors were generally framed as those who took center stage, leading marches, delivering speeches, and attending public meetings. Furthermore, political actors were overwhelmingly framed as male due to the sexism and misogyny of many movements.[10]

Cartographic Memory maps activism through a more granular neighborhood-level analysis, bringing into focus the day-to-day quotidian practices through which activists' struggles reshaped urban communities. It highlights a broader constituency of political actors, including women, children, youths, and multigenerational alliances.[11] Collectively they took part in simple acts like helping a neighbor or more complex maneuvers like setting up a free health clinic, establishing arts organizations, and creating youth educational programs. More important, they took part in processes of place-making, building community and creating supportive kinship networks. The materiality of these institutions not only reshaped the urban landscape but also animated contentious politics about the nature of community, Chicanismo, Latinidad, and belonging.

The Materiality of Activism

I would like to further explain what I mean by the social movement production of space. To get to my volunteer job at Centro, I would take Bay Area Rapid Transit (BART), bringing me into almost daily contact with the architectural site I stumbled upon on the first day of encountering Fruitvale.

That structure was the newly completed Fruitvale Village. I remember walking into the collection of buildings and thinking that it was simply created by BART. After months of volunteering, however, I learned that Fruitvale Village was constructed entirely by the Spanish Speaking Unity Council, a 501(c)(3) nonprofit organization that emerged out of 1960s activism (see chapter 4). My encounter with this architectural site, and my subsequent volunteer experience at Centro, propelled me to think more about the role of space in social movement activism. It was as if Fruitvale Village and Centro became agentic interlopers of sorts. Like a conversation that comes out of interviewing a human subject, these encounters set in place a number of questions, lines of inquiry, and years of research with neighborhood institutions.

My quest for answers to the making of Fruitvale Village took me to the remote town of Galt, California, located between Sacramento and Stockton, to interview a central figure from my archival research. Herman Gallegos was involved with just about every Mexican American political action group in the Bay Area, long before the category of Mexican American or Chicano even existed.[12] In his lifetime of work, Gallegos helped to establish numerous nonprofit organizations; served as one of the original founders of the National Council of La Raza (NCLR); and became the first Mexican American to sit on the board of a major philanthropic foundation.[13] Now retired, Gallegos prefers to live outside the spotlight in a town far removed from the geographies of his past activism.

A kind and humble man, Gallegos is devoted to his Catholic faith and to the principles of caring for fellow human beings. I started our conversation by thanking him for his lifelong work of serving as an unofficial movement historian. His careful notes, I told him, were invaluable for helping me understand the formation of Mexican American politics in Oakland (see chapters 2 and 3). I forget exactly how I happened to mention the 2003 construction of the Fruitvale Village. I knew that Gallegos had been involved with the formation of the Unity Council, and during his time as the leader at the Southwest Council of La Raza (SCLR), he helped that organization with the first applications for Ford Foundation funding. I expected him to continue to expand on the work of the Unity Council and to speak about how the organization had single-handedly rebuilt the subway station. Instead, Gallegos took me back in history. He explained that the activism that made possible present-day redevelopment schemes in Fruitvale had origins in turn-of-the-century activism in the entire Southwest. As Gallegos told me: "It is very easy for someone to look at the Transit Village and say what a marvelous project, without fully understanding that we had very strong mobilizations that led to projects like this. Fruitvale Village was possible as a result of some great leadership." He continued, "To think of the Fruitvale Transit Village, you have to go back to the long generations of Mexican American activism, to the post–World War II period when we organized the Community Service Organization (CSO) to bring services to the Spanish-speaking population in Oakland, to the formation of numerous Mexican American institutions" (see chapter 2).[14] Fruitvale Village, Gallegos asserted, would not exist without this earlier social movement activism. "Remember that in the early fifties there were no nonprofits, no Latino groups to speak of, and one wonders how did the Latino community survive?" Gallegos continued. I was struck by the fact that in order to talk about the recent redevelopment project in Fruitvale he had to summon up the past and connect this new production of urban space to a longue durée of social movement struggles.

Social movement activism did not exclusively produce material landscapes. Other activists evidenced the kind of social relations and worldviews that activism set in place: the dynamic networks of solidarity with other geographies and struggles that helped to produce a distinct neighborhood identity. Tina Flores, for example, became politicized through the Chicano movement and centered her work in Fruitvale since her high school years. She is a self-proclaimed radical activist who has worked tirelessly for a more socially just society. I first met her at the annual Cesar Chavez Lifetime Achievement Awards ceremony in 2012, a celebration in which the community honored its activists.[15] Flores seemed to be in charge of the event—she was dressed in her UFW regalia and worked the crowd like a professional organizer. In addition to being a social butterfly (and therefore constantly being in and out of multiple conversations), Flores was always on a mission. She underscored that she had important stories to tell me but was too busy to sit down for a formal interview, despite the fact that it generally took her twenty minutes to tell me so. During our brief and intermittent conversations, she told me much about her uninterrupted identity as an activist. When I first met her, she was getting ready to travel to Cuba to deliver medical supplies. The people of Cuba, she told me, were incredibly dear to her, and she had been making trips to the island since the 1960s. When I reconnected with Flores in 2016, she was leading a campaign to support low-wage workers. She invited me to a demonstration in the neighboring city of Alameda, where workers were demanding a living wage of fifteen dollars an hour. Decades after first being politicized through the

Chicano movement, Flores is still working to care for the poor. Many things have changed since the 1960s—including the very constitution of the Latino population itself—but the kind of social relations that gave coherence to Chicano movement activism are still alive and embodied by figures like Flores. These social relations do not necessarily materialize in a specific shape or form. However, they help form an enduring commitment to social justice and egalitarian milieus that are routed through Fruitvale.

Gallegos and Flores problematize both the spatial and the temporal scope of the Chicano movement. Gallegos, for example, is not the militant activist that one can picture marching in a demonstration with an upraised fist. He would also not characterize himself as one of the Chicano movement activists, who in his view were a bunch of youths who became too militant. Whereas these activists are emblemized by their mobilizations on the streets, Gallegos labored through institutions. He worked to ensure that philanthropic and state agencies paid attention to Mexican Americans' growing needs. Yet Gallegos was active within the Chicano movement, and he advanced some of the major cultural and contentious politics that shaped youth mobilizations. Gallegos shows us that Chicano movement activism was co-constituted with a long tradition of prior Mexican American activism, and that we need to think of the movement as part of a long civil rights struggle.[16] As Gallegos detailed, one can point to architectural sites such as Fruitvale Village and institutions such as the Unity Council as "proof" of the longevity and the power of social movements so often relegated to the past. Gallegos never lived in Fruitvale, yet his activism in places like San Francisco, and the entire Southwest, as this book will show, made the neighborhood a powerful epicenter of activism.

Furthermore, leaders like Gallegos urge us to expand our definition of what counts as "activism." In so much of social movement scholarship, the label "activist" is glued to a singular conception of activism and most closely associated with radicalism and militancy. Yet moderate leaders like Gallegos were also activists, challenging inequalities and mobilizing to gain greater services, protections, and resources for disenfranchised groups.

Flores, on the other hand, embodies the revolutionary fervor of the 1960s. She has mobilized her entire life in Fruitvale, yet her activities were never bound to that particular spatiality. She made connections to faraway geographies of struggle such as Cuba and neighboring places such as the city of Alameda, downtown Oakland, and San Francisco. Together, Gallegos and Flores help to tell a different kind of story of the Chicano movement, helping us expand our analysis of social movement spatialities more broadly.

This book grapples with a fundamental question: How do we measure social movement impacts? Gallegos's and Flores's provocations stand in stark contrast to how scholarship frames social movement activism—as episodic mobilizations with a birth, climax, and subsequent death. Analysts usually label movements as "successful" if they, for example, result in legislative or constitutional changes. Activists who I learned from, like Gallegos, however, pointed to urban space for proof of social movement impacts and to the continuity of spatialities built out of movement organizing. Flores pointed to the longevity of the fight for social justice that animated 1960s radical politics, which she continues to embody. By situating these effects in place, both Flores and Gallegos called for an analysis of the ongoing nature of social movements through a spatial reading of activism. Together, they asserted that Mexican American social movement activism that consolidated in the aftermath of World War II and the Chicano movement of the 1960s are not historical artifacts. They represent an ongoing struggle.

My call for an analysis of social movement continuities echoes what activists I interviewed incessantly proclaimed: "La lucha continúa!" (The struggle continues!). This is not a statement devoid of politics. It is a call to action and a condemnation of the deep-seated racism that continues to structure inequality in the world and produced spaces of resistance like Fruitvale. The race-based inequalities that animated contentious politics of the 1960s are still with us today. Taking stock of these enduring inequalities, and the existence of places like Fruitvale, can help us better understand why and how the contemporary immigrant rights and Black Lives Matter movements continue to challenge a racist and unjust capitalist ordering of the world. This is most important given the way that the United States constructs itself as a postracial egalitarian state (Bonilla-Silva 2018).[17] As geographer Katherine McKittrick (2006) so powerfully demonstrates, racism and sexism are spatial acts. So too is the struggle against these modes of oppression. McKittrick asserts that we must always recognize the geographic imperatives in the struggle for social justice. Activists' struggles are therefore attempts to (re)spatialize a new form of existence that signals more egalitarian, more just geographic stories. Viewed in this way, Fruitvale becomes one locus in the plurality of resistances, strongly connected to other geographies such as Boyle Heights in Los Angeles, Barrio Logan in San Diego, and the revolutionary fervor of the country of Cuba. As the late Doreen Massey (2005, 9) so eloquently argued: "Thinking the spatial in a particular way can shake up the manner in which certain political questions are formulated, can contribute to political arguments already under way, and—most deeply—can be an essential element in the imaginative structure which enables in the first place an opening up to the very sphere of the political."

Cartographic Memory: Analytical and Methodological Framework

A key objective of this book is to think critically about space as an archive of social movement struggles. I came to this conceptualization by paying attention to how activists, such as Gallegos and Flores, remembered the past. These activists' memories emphasize place rather than chronology.[18] Their memories created intricate mappings of the organizations and new community spaces their work helped to construct. In other words, memory served as a central device to materialize and bring into focus the transformative and experimental aspects of the Chicano movement. I contend that the fact that activists remembered their work in geographic form opens up a larger metric for how we measure social movement impacts.[19]

To draw attention to this concept of space as archive, I employ cartography to highlight how activists and institutions viewed the gains of their work through productions of space and how they advanced these projects toward claims to power. Historians have linked cartography and power in their critiques of how maps are typically conceptualized as objective representations of space (Craib 2009; Edney 2005; Harley 1988, 1992). As Raymond Craib (2004, 6–7) observes, "Modern cartography, founded upon some geometric and mathematical principles as perspectival space, took form as a supposedly objective science mediating between spatial reality and human perception of that reality. Its products—maps—acquired a disembodied purity, functioning as transparent windows onto preexisting space." Eschewing the presumed objectivity of maps, historians of cartography have demonstrated the centrality of mapmaking in statecraft and the accumulation and reification of state and imperial power. Maps, therefore, are never apolitical, and their production, even in the form of memory, is filled with contradictions and contestations.

Historically, maps have been used to dispossess nonwhite and Indigenous people throughout the United States. Consider, for example, redlining maps that defined which neighborhoods would be available exclusively to white and non-white residents, serving as a form of what McKittrick (2006) calls georacial management. Geographer Laura Pulido (2006, 23) and other scholars have shown that as a consequence of this organization of space, Black-owned property is less desirable and therefore worth less than white-owned property (see also Lipsitz 2006; Rothstein 2017). Historical and present-day processes that map racial divisions contribute to the making of racial inequalities. As Mishuana Goeman (2013, 16) reminds us, "Maps, in their most traditional sense as a representation of authority, have incredible power and have been essential to colonial and imperial projects."

Goeman's powerful intervention, *Mark My Words*, argues that colonized and racially marginalized groups have continually contested mappings that produced dispossession and erasure.[20] Her study centers native strategies to (re)map native space, which she believes "challenge the seemingly objective and transparent forms of Western mapping by including narrative experiences and cultural systems that tell and map a story of survivance and future" (23).[21] Maps, in other words, can also be used to tell alternative histories *and* futures. I contend that Chicano movement activists employ mappings toward the same logic. Confronted with a context in which the scholarly community erases their contributions in the region, and most neighborhood residents don't remember their labor, activists retold their stories to lay claim to their organized acts of neighborhood care.

In my definition and utilization of the concept of cartographic memory—a practice activists deployed and a framework for understanding how leaders defined their activities though the invocation and graphing of space—I borrow from Maylei Blackwell's (2011) theorizing of "retrofitted memory." Retrofitted memory functions as a form of "countermemory that uses fragments of older histories that have never been disjunctured by colonial practices of organizing historical knowledge" (Blackwell 2011, 2). As Blackwell's term suggests, it is possible to draw from these discarded and suppressed forms of knowledge to understand how, as these leaders defined it, they mobilized to construct "new forms of consciousness customized to embody material realities, political visions, and creative desires for societal transformation" (2). I build on Blackwell's concept by emphasizing the geographic nature of activists' memories.

Cartographic memory is not just an act of remembering. It is a political remaking of urban geography and therefore a *selective* mapping to emphasize the contributions of certain groups, while rendering others less visible. This is precisely the political nature of activist mappings. Their impartiality shows how activists marshaled their selective mappings to emphasize their unique contributions to community change. Activists' cartographic memories, for example, performed the important function of summoning to life some of the places and organizations that no longer exist.[22] I analyze how activists' cartographic memories stabilized space toward various political means and how competing cartographic memories revealed the multiple conflicts and contingencies that characterized movement activism. Moments of coherence also demonstrated the negotiations and compromises that defined the movement. Cartographic memories expose the political nature of place-making and the centrality of space in negotiations of power.

Cartographic memory is also a methodological tool for thinking and writing about place. Although this is a book about a place called Fruitvale, it also charts geographic connections forged through social movement activism. I too explored some of these faraway places. I went to Stanford University, for example, where Dr. Ernesto Galarza donated his extensive files that chronicle the formation of numerous Mexican American organizations. Galarza was one of the first Chicano PhDs who supported multiple movements and helped to bridge academia with community needs. Next, I traveled to the Schomburg Center for Research in Black Culture in New York City, where I was reminded how racial minorities are understood in a relational fashion: I went to a library and research center on Black culture—located in Harlem—to learn more about Chicano organizations in Fruitvale.[23] It was during one of those trips that I was hailed as comedian George Lopez by a Black Harlemite while I enjoyed lunch at a neighborhood restaurant.

My research also took me to the Rockefeller Archive Center in upstate New York, where I analyzed how the Ford Foundation worked to fund and transform social movements. I literally retraced the steps many of the leaders I interviewed took as they attended Ford Foundation meetings in New York City and brokered connections with other agencies and social movements. I asked myself how these leaders must have felt entering these predominantly white centers of power. Many of them, like myself, were first-generation college graduates who grew up in mainly Spanish-speaking immigrant communities. I wondered: How did they represent neighborhood projects in order to make them legible to these people? What silences were created through this process, and how was this a product of the unequal power relationships? These power differentials manifested themselves in the archives: I combed through reports written by disparate reporting agencies and Ford Foundation monitors or program officers about neighborhood-level projects. It was not just the most prominent leaders who had connections with Ford Foundation representatives; instead, the foundation's agents often descended on the communities that were funded (like Fruitvale) and wrote about these spaces in reports and diverse forms of correspondence. In these reports (which were also representations of space), there was rarely any mention of Fruitvale. I had to re-create Fruitvale through specific references to organizations, names, and geographic locations from a collection of project reports about "Oakland."

Mapping Fruitvale's geographies of activism also entailed reading the archives and oral histories alongside my own ethnographic research in the neighborhood. I created my own space-time analysis that helped me discern how historical trajectories influence contemporary dynamics. Just like activists' cartographic memories, my ethnography also mapped the social relations I built with community residents and different nonprofit and political action groups. For six years I worked closely with the Street Level Health Project, a free health clinic and community resource center that works predominantly with recently arrived immigrants. First, as a volunteer I had to get to know the lay of the land. I learned the locations of agencies where people could go for housing assistance, health care services, legal aid, tenants' rights assistance, shelter, and other resources. I also befriended members of those agencies. Later, as president of Street Level's board of directors, I worked closely with representatives of 1960s organizations like Centro Legal de la Raza, Clínica de la Raza, and the Unity Council, who all helped the emergent Street Level gain a better institutional footing. My ethnography revealed that because space is an archive of social movement activism, the contemporary experience in the neighborhood is equally shaped by many of the organizations whose historical formation this book chronicles. I quickly learned to map neighborhood power relations in order to understand how and why certain organizations held more political and economic clout. Just as activists used geography to tell their stories of activism, keeping a spatial focus on history and the present was essential for the telling of this story.

My final point regarding cartographic memory is that it also highlights a perspectival approach to writing about place. This book offers a graphing of Fruitvale and Oakland that differs prominently from previous ethnographic and historical representations. As a geographer, I study how places are a product of heterogenous social relations that occur in space in a contemporaneous plurality.[24] What this means is that spaces like "Fruitvale," and "Oakland" more broadly, do not represent a homogeneous set of social relations. Fruitvale, for example, has been previously described as a part of a larger violent geography of Oakland where youths encounter heavy policing through what sociologist Victor Rios (2011) refers to as the "youth control complex." Similarly, Marie "Keta" Miranda (2003) portrays the violence found in Fruitvale but also captures a long history of activism in the neighborhood and shows how it is also a place where female gang members

1.2 Entryway to the most recent location of the Street Level Health Project. It is a block away from the main intersection of Fruitvale Avenue and International Boulevard. Photograph by the author.

have reinterpreted their identities. Geographer Margaret M. Ramírez (2020) similarly describes Fruitvale and other Oakland neighborhoods as specific borderlands where gentrifying forces violently grate against long-term Latinx and Black inhabitants. Historian Robert O. Self's (2003) magnum opus regarding racial politics and spatial conflicts in Oakland showed how the city was shaped by struggles for power between white and Black political forces, referring to Mexican American/Chicano politics on only a few scattered pages.

I mention these previous works not to discredit them or to reveal their intellectual or methodological blind spots. I do so to show that places like "Fruitvale" and "Oakland" are shaped out of a multiplicity of social relations and therefore are subject to different kinds of renderings. These scholars followed particular peopled (and place-based) stories that were available to them in the archives or that they encountered through their social relations and research practices. Like maps that are viewed as objective representations of space, academic studies of a "community"—or of a place—are often viewed as truthful and comprehensive, with the result that other stories or sets of social relations are not available. A perspectival approach urges us to question an analytical desire to produce comprehensive and truthful representations of place. Any account of the production of a space, such as a city or a town, is never all-encompassing. It just tells a specific rendering or a perspectival—and ongoing—story about a particular place. Loose ends and ongoing stories, according to Doreen Massey, are real challenges to cartography. They are also perplexing to historical accounts of place.

Toward a Space-Time Analysis of Social Movements

Although much of my fieldwork entailed discovering the different spaces that historical and present-day activists constructed and traversed, it was surprising that the bulk of social movement theory has largely ignored the spatiality of contentious politics. As Ulrich Oslender (2016, 13) observes, before 1990, "there was a deafening silence in the existing literature on social movements regarding the relevance of place in its theorizations." Since the mid-1990s, however, geographers have attempted to show how geography matters in social movement literature.[25] These accounts have undertheorized two fundamental issues that I seek to address: (1) how social movements actually produce space (as opposed to how geography matters in the making of contentious politics), and (2) the issue of time and temporality, or what I refer to as *social movement continuity*.[26] I construct a spatial reading of contentious politics that creates a register of the *continuities, legacies,* and *lingering* social movement effects routed through place.[27] This kind of longue durée accounting of social movements requires an understanding of how social movements in fact produce space.

Social Movements and Their Spatialities

Much of social movement scholarship has prioritized questions regarding process in analyzing contentious politics.[28] Debates first wrestled with queries about what constitutes a social movement.[29] Scholars also asked questions along the following lines: How and why do social movements emerge? How do movements make claims to states? How do states respond? And what leads to the fall of movements? I chose to focus on how people experience social movements. Experiences happen in and through space, and experiences shaped out of human relations also produce space. This is precisely why geographers have analyzed how geography shapes social movement imaginaries, practices, and trajectories.[30] Paul Routledge (1993) was one of the first scholars to think critically about the role of "place" in shaping social movement politics, namely, showing how geography informs why social movements occur where they do. Laura Pulido's (2006) pathbreaking book *Black, Brown, Yellow, and Left* offers the most explicitly geographic reading of 1960s radical movements in Los Angeles. As Pulido so poignantly reveals, racial geographies impacted how activists were politicized and how they worked together across racial and spatial differences. Cohabitation between different groups, for example, led to the cross-pollination of mobilizing strategies and framed the international orientation of race-based leftist groups. Oslender (2016) reaches a similar argument regarding Black land struggles in Colombia. As his work reveals, we cannot understand identity-based movements without accounting for the specific places where social movements evolve and where identities are constructed and physically carried out (Oslender 2016, 25).

More recent work has focused on how social movements take shape in an increasingly globalized world. Scholars have wondered if in this era of space-time compression, place and locality matter as much as in the past. Instead of pressuring at the local level for changes in neighborhoods, many movements will jump scales and make claims at the level of the federal government or in the arena of international courts. This has been the case for many Indigenous social movements in the Americas that pressure international agencies and courts to make demands in their own countries. It is therefore not surprising that in the late 1990s analyses of scale and scale jumping became the craze in social movement literature, leaving analyses of place or "the local" by the wayside (Leitner, Sheppard, and Sziarto 2008). Geographer Helga Leitner (2008) and colleagues have critiqued this privileging of one spatial register over another.[31] They assert that it is necessary to pay attention not only to the relevance of particular spatialities in specific contexts but also to their co-implication. Why wouldn't social movements utilize both local and international arenas to demand changes?

Against Episodic Conceptualizations of Movements

My approach to the study of contentious politics adds to these analyses by emphasizing how social movements produce material spaces and networks of social relations that alter the built environment (see also Magaña 2021). In other words, instead of thinking of geography simply as context (or surface), I emphasize how social movements reshape geographic communities. That is, because the very terrain of struggle is place, the landscape becomes a subject of politics and is therefore transformed. Social movements advance new cultural formations, politics, and ways of being in the world that reconstitute material landscapes. Although some of the spaces might no longer exist, they form a central part of how activists remember their activism. Take, for example, the institutionalization of grassroots struggles. As activism moved from the streets into institutions, activists constructed new organizing spaces, which shifted the social relations and how resources were routed to the neighborhood.

I am not suggesting that places in which social movements take root—like Fruitvale—do not change, or that these places do not represent the effects of other social and political processes such as transnational migration or capitalist restructuring. Fruitvale has transformed tremendously, and its residents now are mainly undocumented workers who find solace in the concentration of businesses and organizations that cater to their needs. It is now also a prime destination for upwardly mobile homebuyers hoping to secure cheaper prices in the San Francisco Bay Area housing market. However, the existence of 1960s organizations such as Clínica de la Raza anchors the traces of Chicano movement activism in the neighborhood. It is not just a reminder; it exists in its materiality and its ability to shape the urban landscape and how people experience the neighborhood. Clínica de la Raza is one of the major tenants of Fruitvale Village. Once a volunteer-run clinic that took over the space of an old bakery and restaurant, it is now a state-of-the-art medical facility with beautiful offices. Additionally, it has a network of clinics throughout the East Bay. Recently arrived immigrants will probably never know that Clínica was created by social movement activism. They may, however, feel welcomed by seeing the words *Clínica* and *Raza* and believe that the facility's services were designed for a Spanish-speaking population. Clínica's services, and the social relations that it enables, allow us to see the social movement continuities and to understand that this process is equally ripe with politics. In this way, Chicano movement activism, and prior forms of contentious politics, contour Fruitvale's terrain of resistance and undoubtedly affect contemporary forms of activism.[32]

The bulk of social movement literature, however, stresses an analysis of the conditions that create the context for the rise and fall of movements. Doug McAdam, Sidney G. Tarrow, and Charles Tilly (2001), for example, write about contentious politics as "moments" or "episodes" of mobilization—a kind of language that narrows analysis to movement life cycles. As they detail: "We stress sorts of contention that are sporadic rather than continuous, bringing new actors into play, and/or involve innovative claim making" (8). They admit that the combination of conflicting claims and episodic action attracts their attention because it "leaves a residue to consider their commitments and allegiances, and practices and political identities in the name of which future generations will make their claims." This idea of a "residue," I believe, requires greater theoretical elaboration. I suggest we rethink this concept, which implies that this "left- behind" material lacks agency and is incapable of shaping politics in the present day.

In a similar vein, Chicano movement historiography privileges the rise of 1960s and 1970s youth mobilizations that eclipses all other previous histories of activism (Acuña 1972; E. Chávez 1994; Gómez-Quiñones 1978, 1990; Muñoz 2007). Chicano movement historians acknowledge the existence of reformist policies that fit into what ethnic studies scholar Carlos Muñoz (2007) calls the Mexican American generation, or what historian Ernesto Chávez (2002, 42) calls "inadequate forms of protest for securing the plight of Chicanos in the late 1960s and 1970s." These studies fundamentally argue that with the rise of Chicano militancy in the late 1960s, prior reformist forms of political engagement effectively ceased. This episodic conceptualization of Chicano history overly emphasizes activism as a temporal process—with different stages that replace one another—as opposed to employing a place-based analysis that is attentive to the multiple modes of activism within a particular space-time.[33]

As a result of this temporal reading of social movements, the Chicano movement was declared dead by the late 1970s.[34] Prior to that, a movement that consolidated as the Mexican American generation was allegedly eliminated by the birth of the Chicano movement. No formal eulogy could be found for the fall of these movements, but analysts proclaimed that the visible parameters of what constituted each mobilization were no longer visible. This was most extreme for the professed death of the Chicano movement: gone were the marches and the large-scale moratoriums. The central culprits for the movement's demise included the policing of activists;[35] the incorporation of movement leaders into government and nonprofit leadership positions (E. Chávez 1994, 119); and, finally, the rise of conservative politics ushered in by the Nixon and Reagan administrations.[36]

Maylei Blackwell's (2011) brilliant critique of Chicano historiography, ¡Chicana Power!, demonstrates how this temporal analysis produced significant erasures. Blackwell argues that this politics of periodization locates "women's and feminists' interventions outside of movements instead of including them in a larger agenda for social justice integral to the legacy of the Chicano movement" (29). As she reveals, Chicano historiography has produced a monolithic portrayal of the movement organized around "epic male heroes rather than the multi-sited local community and labor struggles that coalesced into a national movement" (28). The reduction of multivariant movement organizing into a single lens flattens our understanding of Chicana and Chicano political actors. This framing of Chicano movement activism also obscures an analysis of social movement continuity. It does not allow us to see the impacts of Chicano movement activism on the built environment or the constitution of geographic communities, or the continued traction of such activism in shaping politics.

The Politics of Community Improvement

Chicano movement activism entailed the construction of a vast safety net of organizations and services. Through this process, activists ensured not just the provision of goods and services but also the longevity of the movement goals and its ethos of community improvement. Activists expanded on a long tradition of underserved communities of color constructing their own resources as state welfare policies significantly overlooked non-white populations. They effectively built their own safety net, creating welfare where the state had abandoned it, and in the process forging a collective sense of community. This unleashed political debates about what constituted community needs, who and what constituted "the community," and how neighborhood improvement projects would be funded and maintained.

Social movement projects of neighborhood improvement were a response to what activists referred to as state abandonment. Postwar race-based social movements in Oakland and elsewhere in the United States asserted that the welfare state was never created to benefit people of color (Self 2003). Activists asserted that the welfare state emerged precisely when Jim Crow segregation and separate but "equal" were cornerstones of US imaginaries. However, segregation never resulted in equality. The establishment of the welfare state was framed through these segregationist and unequal policies: whereas whites were conferred privileges that included new mortgage loans that subsidized their movement to the suburbs, people of color were overwhelmingly excluded from those benefits. This bifurcated welfare state also lacked fair employment and full employment provisions, and excluded hundreds of thousands of Black workers and other people of color from the protections of labor laws (Self 2003, 11). Not coincidentally, redevelopment policies overwhelmingly privileged white people and their spatialities as state policies "helped to develop some places and underdeveloped others" (3).[37] Postwar spatial developments accelerated processes of what Ananya Roy (2017) calls racial banishment.

Throughout the United States, debates among activists regarding how to ensure community welfare were contentious. In Fruitvale, activists continually conducted various needs assessments. They wrestled with the reality of multiple and often competing community needs. A multigenerational and diverse set of actors mobilized to advance their own visions of which community needs were most salient. What one activist group deemed as necessary to care for may have differed from what others considered important. Some activists staunchly believed in community autonomy: resources, moneys, and direction would be taken from the community and organized by residents. Others were willing to work with distinct entities (both state and nonstate) from outside the community in order to expedite projects of neighborhood improvement.

Neighborhood projects took place in Fruitvale but drew from multiple connections to other spaces of resources. These connections to the outside were of course a subject of contentious politics. Activists, for example, were connected to a national movement of US minorities and an international third world agenda against colonialism and imperialism. These international struggles mapped how Fruitvale was interlinked with other revolutionary geographies of struggle (see chapter 5). Another feature of these connections concerns philanthropic and state projects. In order to enact community projects, some groups prioritized building relationships with funding streams that included federal and philanthropic grants. The nature of activist connections reveals the politics of community improvement: the competing approaches regarding the reality of community needs and desires, and how such projects would be funded, executed, and maintained.

A key political fault line was the division between activists who viewed themselves as radical and those who took a much more moderate or conservative approach to achieving community change. In my engagement with archival sources and in interviews with key Bay Area leaders of the 1960s, I was attentive to how they represented these heterogeneous approaches to struggle. Though many 1960s activists I interviewed were often dubbed conservative *vendidos*, or "sellouts," because they chose an institutionalized path of nonprofit mobilizations, they never considered themselves as having been duped into taking a particular path.[38]

Just as these more reformist activists were branded as sellouts, they also pejoratively constructed a constituency of radicals who engaged in what they deemed as inappropriate forms of mobilization. I found that neither archival sources nor interviewees revealed a clear definition of what constituted radicalism or militancy.[39] Activists who fought for greater state resources and electoral opportunities for Mexican Americans viewed radicalism and militancy as the constitutive outside of their ideals of democratic integration. To be clear, even the more reformist activists varied in what they conceived as appropriate engagements with state institutions and private foundations. Some of the radical activists also dabbled in some form of electoral politics. Thus *radicalism* and *conservatism* were elastic terms that shifted in relation to spatial and historical contexts.[40]

My intent is not to argue that one form of activism was better than the other. Instead, my purpose is to show the complexity of Chicano movement organizing. By situating their social movement participation in space, activists revealed that radical spaces stood in proximity to more moderate organizations and therefore signaled moments of convergence between groups traditionally seen as mutually exclusive. Many activists' recollections emphasized the spatial cohabitation, and therefore the mutual constitution, of competing political ideologies. In other words, you cannot talk about one form of activism in isolation. They were informed by one another and, in fact, were situated in the same neighborhood. Some were adversaries, but more often than not, they were residents or caretakers of the same neighborhood motivated by a shared (but often contested) agenda of community improvement.

Institutionalization of 1960s Social Movements

In order to show the complexity of different kinds of Chicano movement approaches to activism and neighborhood improvement projects, this book makes a slightly controversial move regarding contentious politics. I find that institutionalization of grassroots activism does not end movements. Most social movement analysts, as Tianna Paschel (2016) points out, argue that institutionalization leads to movement death. Institutionalization, read primarily as affiliations with the state, is in fact the premier kind of "proof" that a movement has failed or has been co-opted. This is especially the case for movements that took shape in the 1960s and 1970s, decades that are often assumed to be a high-water period for global movements articulating a revolutionary reshaping of the world. Put simply, institutionalization is the antithesis of revolution.

Paschel's work shows how Brazilian activists mobilized state channels to advance their demands as Black political subjects. These activists framed themselves as "militants of the state" and mobilized as part of a national social movement. Paschel's findings have profound implications for the study of Mexican American social movements in the Bay Area. As noted earlier, the region is widely known as an epicenter of 1960s activism. Numerous books, for example, detail the role of the Black Panthers in reshaping Oakland politics. If so much attention has been paid to racial Black politics in Oakland, why does no book-length monograph exist on Mexican American politics? I think the answer is linked to how scholarship measures social movement mobilizations.

The literature on race-based 1960s organizing has primarily privileged the most radical and most visible features of organizing. Mexican American activism in Oakland took multiple routes. In addition to militant street protests and boycotts, many Chicano activists chose the path of institutionalization. In order to maintain the organizations, many activists forged strong alliances with state and philanthropic institutions. Here lies the key to why these activities have been overlooked in the literature on Bay Area social movements: in social movement literature, the creation of alliances and collaboration with state and philanthropic forces have been equated with co-optation, which leads to social movement death.

The Nonprofit Industrial Complex

Readers might already be asking about the ominous entity that haunts 1960s social movement activism—the nonprofit-industrial complex (NPIC). In fact, this book provides a genealogy of the emergence of the NPIC, or a form of state and philanthropic regulation over political ideology and leftist social movements. For many critics, the NPIC represents a $1.3 trillion industry and the seventh-largest economy in the world, whose extreme profitability proves the co-optation of 1960s mobilizations (Allen 1970; Rodriguez 2017). As Dylan Rodriguez (2017, 30) argues, "The NPIC thus serves as the medium through which the state continues to exert a fundamental dominance over the political intercourse of the US Left, as well as US civil society more generally."[41] In these analyses, the state (and by proxy the demands of capital) shackles the nonprofit sector and deadlocks radical political mobilizations. Throughout the following chapters, I offer in-depth analysis of how the state and foundation complex did surveil and control organizations at critical moments. And, not coincidentally, the organizations that received the most funding were those that have made the most impact over time. I find that although they are indeed a product of state and philanthropic regulation, these organizations also demonstrate the importance of longevity. They highlight that the provision of ongoing systems of care matter, and that holding on to space over time is important and requires a tremendous amount of work.[42]

As someone who has worked in nonprofits and studies their historical formation, I am uncomfortable with how most nonprofit work is written off as ineffective or counterintuitive because it forms part of a larger NPIC. Despite the reality of poverty and crime in Oakland and the different forms of violence that shape so many urban experiences, in Fruitvale I was surrounded by a diverse constellation of people and agencies that genuinely cared for the well-being of the community and its residents. Throughout my fieldwork, I saw how care enveloped the historical and present-day work of a number of actors, including nonprofit workers, state public health nurses, and immigration attorneys. Nonprofit leaders also described many Fruitvale redevelopment plans as fundamentally about caring for the neighborhood and its future. I believe that we not only have to acknowledge this work but also seriously consider the political power it holds (notwithstanding its limitations). Furthermore, there are multiple ways of caring for a neighborhood or ensuring its improvement, which also means there are multiple approaches to enacting and achieving social change. Instead of completely discrediting the efficacy of one approach over another, I believe it is important to see their simultaneity and co-implication.

I hope this book can help us add greater nuance to the literature on the NPIC. I highlight some of the political debates regarding state and philanthropic regulation that activists and nonprofit leaders wrestled with and show how this impacted the built environment. The nonprofit organizations that I study acknowledge that they emerged from social movements, and in fact this history serves as a mode through which they secure legitimacy in the community. The social movement nature of the organizations also ensures that other organizations and movements actively monitor these institutions, albeit within a constrained set of options.[43]

Architecture of the Book

This book uses historical methods, including archival research and oral histories, and blends this form of knowledge with ethnography to analyze how people and institutions make sense of social movement activism and deploy it toward various political means. It is also fundamentally about how we memorialize social movements and the forms of evidence we summon up to remember them. This type of analysis requires thinking of the production of space in a nonlinear fashion. Toward this end, the book switches between the past and the present to show how historical and present-day activists and institutions utilize this social movement legacy to advance their own claims to power.

I follow social movement actors and the institutions they built. I especially analyze the Spanish Speaking Unity Council, the nonprofit organization that frequently gets framed as the neighborhood's principal steward. This exercise of following institutions requires making connections across space, scale, and history. Furthermore, I trace the political processes contoured by state and philanthropic institutions and how they impact social movement formations. I demonstrate how the Unity Council became an institutional powerhouse due to state and philanthropic funding, turning itself into a community development corporation (CDC) in 1969. Instead of funding grassroots politicizing projects, the Unity Council now had to produce what were dubbed "measurable" results. This included services such as Head Start or educational or job placement opportunities for residents. The core of these measurable results was the actual production of brick-and-mortar buildings—such as senior housing, apartments, and other community improvement projects.

Although the Unity Council became the principal organization charged with a mission of developing urban space, in chapter 1, I show how a multiplicity of political actors and organizations helped to produce the neighborhood as a geography of activism. I demonstrate how in their recollections of the past, activists constructed a geographic framework by which to account for the social movement production of space and crafted deep emotional bonds with themselves and the neighborhood. Drawing from oral histories with 1960s and 1970s Chicano activists, I argue that activists' cartographic memories show us how they built robust cultural politics of place that shaped how they understood the movement's impacts on community formation. I show the multiple and often competing approaches to neighborhood improvement.

How do we understand the making of a diverse set of organizations located in one particular place and responsible for making changes to the built environment and often represented as rightful neighborhood stewards? In order to do so we must go back to the development of post–World War II organizing in the Bay Area and the making of Oakland as a geography ripe with social movement activism. Chapters 2 and 3 offer a window into understanding how postwar Mexican American mobilizations provided the blueprint for the formation of the Chicano movement. The movement can thus be reconceptualized not as a heroic stage but rather as a continuation of Mexican American movements that reshaped postwar California.

In chapter 2, I argue that institutionalization of grassroots activism respatialized 1960s mobilizations, taking activism from the streets and into professionalized nonprofit organizations. I show this by analyzing how the federal War on Poverty created the architecture for the making of Mexican American nonprofits. In addition, this chapter sets up the important framework through which to understand the unique position of Mexican Americans in a Black/white city. I show how the federal War on Poverty resulted in greater state and philanthropic oversight of urban racialized neighborhoods. Subsequently, the care and management of racialized inner cities becomes a contested terrain of struggle involving social movement actors, state agencies, and private philanthropy.

Chapter 3 shifts scales to examine the national scope of race-based 1960s organizations. This was a time in which the entire spatiality of power in the United States was being challenged—from changes to voting rights that promised to reshape the electorate, to the effects of desegregation policies. Activist struggles in Fruitvale were connected to other geographies of resistance and the effects of federal and philanthropic regulation. Although most scholarship of this era has focused on the policing of radicalism, moderate Mexican American organizations were also targeted. I illustrate this by following the formation of the Southwest Council of La Raza, which became one of the first 501(c)(3) Mexican American nonprofit organizations and a subgrantee organization that channeled Ford Foundation moneys to grassroots organizations like the Spanish Speaking Unity Council. Federal regulation of Ford Foundation projects resulted in a catastrophic antipolitical mandate for its nonprofit grantees. Although the federal government strictly linked "politics" with electoral processes, in practice the antipolitical mandate deradicalized nonprofit projects because leaders feared that their actions would be prohibited. A newly created nonprofit entity—the CDC— sought to redirect energy from challenging inequalities to productions of space. It also shifted the responsibility for maintaining inner cities from the scale of the federal government to local-level organizations like the Unity Council.

Chapter 4 examines the 2003 construction of the Fruitvale Transit Village, a project that put Fruitvale on the map as a nationally recognized model of transit-oriented development. It explores how the Unity Council used its social movement origins to justify its ability to properly care for the neighborhood to advance its redevelopment plans, thereby securing its position as a rightful community steward. As a CDC, the Unity Council joined a national movement led by African American CDCs that saw the transformation of the built environment as a social justice issue equally important as educational access, equal opportunity job placement, and the fight against housing discrimination.[44] I argue that the Unity Council deployed its commitment to community improvement in order to normalize its urban redevelopment projects.

Chapter 5 provides another approach to mapping the social movement production of space by showing how Fruitvale was interlinked with other geographies of resistance. The core of the chapter examines the international nature of 1960s activism, showing how activists connected their struggles to geographies outside the neighborhood, including Cuba, Mexico, and beyond. Activists' recollections of their activism entailed a process of mapping the interlinkages to that "beyond." These connections were political claims to the powerful role the Fruitvale neighborhood played in the making of national Chicano movement struggles. The chapter wrestles with the issue of mapping Fruitvale as a distinct geography of activism in the context of the multiple routes and flows in and out of the neighborhood.

In the conclusion, I examine the unfinished nature of social movements. I argue that present-day and historical activists perform the important work of maintaining and reinterpreting this social movement mandate of neighborhood improvement. I do so by foregrounding my own experience working with the Street Level Health Project to reveal how historical Chicano organizations such as Clínica de la Raza and Centro Legal de la Raza helped the emergent organization gain an institutional footing. This shows us how the Chicano movement and prior forms of mobilization never fully died but are ongoing. Furthermore, activists I interviewed are organizing to preserve the history of their Fruitvale-based activism. In this way, 1960s and 1970s activism continues to shape neighborhood politics, resources, and conditions of possibility for activism today.

Finally, I consider how an analysis of the social movement production of space can help us rethink how we conceptualize the study of inner-city space, or how we come to understand the connections between, race, space, and politics. Social movement activism did indeed help to produce a place that is now known as the Latino neighborhood in Oakland. But what social movement actors really sought to produce was an ephemeral space of social justice, a spatiality of freedom and justice that perhaps gestured more toward the future than toward an actually existing place. Social movement activism from the past, as in our contemporary period, sought to produce a space that was not yet in existence. The activist mappings that I detail in this book can be read not just as a way of remembering the past but also as a methodology for envisioning an alternative future. And this future, not unlike social relations in the present day, is also a subject of politics contoured by a multiplicity of ways of caring for a world that is peopled by manifold ways of being.

1

MAKING PLACE

One day I will pack my bags of books and paper. One day I will say goodbye to Mango.... Friends and neighbors will say, What happened to that Esperanza? Where did she go with all those books and paper? Where did she march so far away? They will not know I have gone away to come back. For the ones I left behind. For the ones who cannot out.

Esperanza in Sandra Cisneros, *The House on Mango Street*

All utopias require mapping, their social order depends upon and generates a spatial order which reorganizes and improves upon existing models.

Denis Cosgrove, *Mappings: Critical Views*

"I have lived on this street since 1959," declared Regina Chavarín as we began our conversation about her lifetime of social movement activism. At sixty-six, Chavarín has charm and charisma that make her appear years younger. She welcomed me to her home, where I realized that our conversation would also include her then husband Roger Chavarín.[1] They felt compelled to share their memories together and worked in sync with one another. When one forgot the details of a particular event, the other filled them in. Like their joint retelling of their activism, their shared memories were connected by a sense of collectivity, by the fact that their activism was not singular but part of a larger neighborhood project. In the midst of their recollections an argument emerged about the different landscapes that social movement activism produced. Regina Chavarín's face brightened with enthusiasm as she described how just about every corner of the community was transformed, even a space right in front of their house. She escorted me outside, pointed across the street, and began to explain:

> So across the street, there was an acre of vacant land. There were homes that had fallen in a bad storm and so when I got here it looked pretty bad. In 1970 the neighbors and I started organizing. We would meet to discuss neighborhood issues, and we always wanted to do something around that vacant lot. Well we incorporated it as a land trust—it's an acre of open space, so on my street there's a hundred-foot drop to the other street. We planted over a hundred trees and shrubs after we stabilized the field. It is known as Jungle Hill in the community.[2]

As she pointed to different features of Jungle Hill, Chavarín proudly narrated how the community organized and forged connections with a San Francisco–based nonprofit that helped it solidify the land trust. Chavarín's memories of her activism produced an affective milieu filled with love, passion, and care. Furthermore, her retelling of this activism was a call to be acknowledged for the labor she and other activists performed. By linking the formation of Jungle Hill to community activism, she challenged conceptions of parks as simply the good deed of the state, or apolitical and ahistorical places. The park called Jungle Hill, Chavarín asserted, was built through struggle.

Chavarín ushered me back into her home, where my attention shifted to its museum-like quality. The walls were adorned with countless Chicano movement posters, certificates of recognition, photographs, United Farm Workers (UFW) flags, and other movement ephemera. This collection demonstrated her own and her husband's curatorial prowess in the way they historicized their participation in many organizations. As they described the various items, their attention shifted to the people they had met and worked with. Pointing to one of the walls, Regina Chavarín, showed me a photograph of then governor of California Jerry Brown declaring Jungle Hill a park. Above that was a poster of Cesar Chavez's commemorative stamp from 2003. To the right was a Crusade for Justice poster signed by famed Chicano activists Jerry and Corky Gonzales.[3] And in the middle was a letter addressed to Mr. and Mrs. Chavarín by Corky Gonzales, writing on behalf of the Crusade for Justice in 1994. It read: "Corky, Jerry and the Crusade for Justice Family told me to tell you that we all love you. No matter what they say about you. Que viva la raza! Que viva Aztlán! Que viva el movieno!" Right below that letter were a UFW flag that marked the first celebration of Cesar Chavez Day and a picture of Roger Chavarín during one of the UFW boycotts. The Chavaríns' tribute to Jungle Hill's creation—situated on their wall alongside ephemera from other Chicano movement struggles—was an argument about the localized effects of the Chicano movement. Fruitvale emerged not as an isolated Chicano community but as a powerful interlinkage of sorts—robustly connected to a national movement. Fruitvale and its multiple landscapes of activism became agentic—serving as a kind of archive of Chicano movement struggles and as proof of the blood, sweat, and tears of the community's struggles. Although Fruitvale is never historicized as a geography of Chicano movement activism, activists like Chavarín emphasized not only how the neighborhood was *itself* a geography of activism but also how it was interconnected to other places of struggle throughout the United States.

Activists remembered their social movement participation by emphasizing their deep emotional connections with neighborhood projects. They intricately mapped their contribution to neighborhood improvement. I contend that the fact that activists remembered their work in geographic form opens up a broader register for how we measure social movement impacts and the power-laden processes through which activists created a distinct sense of place. The other major goal of this chapter is to show how social movement activism has continued traction in the neighborhood, but which I mean both the longevity of a social movement mandate to protect and care for the community and the continued political power that this exerts on the neighborhood. In their recollections of the past, activists constructed a politics of activism, race, and social movement struggle forged through productions of space. I specifically analyze how competing cartographic memories show the perspectival nature of history and memorialization of the past. Notwithstanding these perspectival renderings (which sometimes even constituted feuds), mobilizations cohered in remarkable ways to create a unique neighborhood identity. My analysis extends to how historical and present-day activists experienced the results of this activism.

Activists' memories were central to how they constructed cultural politics of place. Through their activism, they fashioned a collective community identity that differentiated Fruitvale from other Oakland districts. It also resituated the neighborhood as one that was intimately linked to the national Chicano movement. By recollecting this work, they created complex mappings of the organizations and new community spaces their work helped to construct. Most of the organizations dotted the main streets in Fruitvale and were concentrated at the intersection of Fruitvale Avenue and East Fourteenth Street. As Annette Oropeza, a 1970s activist and former educator and counselor in Oakland, told me:

You know, the focal point was in general in that corner: Fruitvale and East Fourteenth. There was the Street Academy that was in that corner. If you go south from there in Fruitvale there was the original Centro Legal. Right next to Centro Legal was a taller *gráfico* [community graphics and arts studio] that Malaquías Montoya ran. If you crossed the street on Fruitvale, crossed East Fourteenth Street, and started going toward the hills, on that side of the street there was a barrio youth center. I think they changed buildings, but they stayed in the general area. Geographically that's where everything was happening.[4]

Oropeza's memory mapped how residents and activists experienced the neighborhood and shows how organizations were spatially embodied. The organizations, including youth centers, arts organizations, and legal services, were clustered in the center of the neighborhood's major trafficways. Oropeza asserts that this network of organizations structured residents' interactions with one another and their relationships with the social movements of the time. In addition, Oropeza's memories also highlighted the very grassroots nature of organizing, meaning that many of the activities were localized in the community: "We did not have computers back then, so we couldn't put that information on the internet so we did it all door-to-door. Grassroots, door-to-door talking to people about the propositions and why we need to vote against this if we had our Dia del Barrio we'd make flyers and pass them out." Her cartographic memory reminds us that actors' day-to-day experience of the movement took on an urban form, which informed how they remembered the past. In addition to mapping geographic locations, their memories also brought forth the emotional attachments to place that social movement activism set forth.

These recollections were far from mere memories. They represented a set of embodied practices and experiential repertoires of organizing that continued to guide activists' participation in neighborhood projects. Collectively, activists' recollections made an important argument that had a temporal dimension. The Chicano movement forged a collective identity for the neighborhood and built spaces, some of which remain today. By spatializing their movement activism through cartographic memory, they constructed powerful rationales for the longevity of the Chicano movement. In the decades following the 1960s and 1970s, activists experimented with the grounded practices of organizing, the institutional frameworks, and repertoires of resource mobilization and engagement with community residents. This ongoing experimentation also included a commitment to social justice and the valorization of cultural difference rooted in the appreciation of different languages, traditions, and ways of being in the world.[5] Through their deployment of cartographic memories, activists challenged conceptions of the movement's declining significance by pointing to space and institutions as proof of its continued traction.

To fully explore these ideas, I first demonstrate how these spatial productions and cartographic memories defined how activists recollected their activism. For many activists, transformations of the urban landscape served as an archive of organized practices of community care. I argue that activists' cartographic recollections were fundamentally political claims to power that operated through space. Activists deployed these cartographic memories to defend the appropriateness of their struggle and to argue for the longevity of Chicano movement mobilizations. I then define how activists detailed the ways in which Chicano movement mobilizations built community by establishing a robust constellation of neighborhood organizations.

Graphing Social Movement Space

Movement institutional formations were essentially part of a community-building endeavor. The function of cartographic memory in this chapter is to emphasize how social movement activism built community. Despite internal contradictions, or the dynamic simultaneity and multiplicity that define any space (Massey 2005), cartographic memory shows us how activists made concessions, built institutions, and consolidated a shared sense of community identity. Activism was not aspatial. It was spatialized in actually existing neighborhoods, and despite the various ways in which activists defined "the political," all represented collective attempts to improve the neighborhood and the world at large.

I explore the kinds of lived experiences of social movement activism that happened in and through a relationship to space. This is a process that geographers call the making of "place." Activists constructed deep emotional and experiential bonds to these specific geographies and developed a profound sense of place.[6] The cartographic inflections in activists' memories reveal not just the political nature of their memories but also their affirmations of the deep emotional connections they had to the community where they labored. It was as if these geographies became mapped onto their bodies, creating what the late Chicana theorist Gloria Anzaldúa called "geographies of selves." Through this concept, Anzaldúa highlights the often undertheorized relationship between geography and the construction of self. According to Anzaldúa, the experiences that human beings have in specific geographies have a way of marking the psyche and "every cell" of the body. In her theorization, spaces become constituted by the human connections with the spirit world, nature, and ancestors, and by the dynamic simultaneity of all these connections. "The places where I've lived have had an impact on my psyche, left a mark on every cell in my body" (2015, 68), wrote Anzaldúa. This beautifully captures how just about every activist I met carried Fruitvale with them wherever they went. When I mentioned Fruitvale, their eyes brightened and their smiles widened. Fruitvale, and its geographies of activism, was integral to the making of their subjectivity.

Furthermore, activists' sense of place was also linked to a particular coming-of-age period in their lives. This underscores the importance of keeping space and time together. Most of the activists I interviewed were young adults when they took part in this activism, which means they came of age in this era of Chicano movement activism. Their memories of place-making corresponded to their experiences learning to navigate the world as adults. The bulk of the activists were in their early twenties, and they were learning to be proud of being Spanish-speaking, Mexican American, and/or Chicano. One way for them to do so was to care for the spaces where minorities were quickly becoming a numerical majority, such as Fruitvale. However, as adults coming of age in the 1960s and first-generation college students, they were also learning that the world was a massive place composed of different cultures, economic systems, and ways of caring for fellow human beings. As much as they learned to see the particularities of their experiences-in-place, they also came to understand the diversity of the world at large. They came to consciousness about international struggles against white supremacy and imperialism and questioned the role of the United States in setting in place global inequality. One of the major causes of the time, for example, was the fight against the war in Vietnam, which activists found as another iteration of the imperial growth of the United States. Activists' intimate connections to Fruitvale were therefore always already networked, with a sense of coming to consciousness about the world at large.

If space is constructed out of social relations (Massey 2005), it would be impossible to think that these forms of sociality ever totally vanished. Indeed, social movement activism helped to produce social relationships, material landscapes, and forms of being in the world that do not automatically disappear from one day to another. Instead, they are passed down from generation to generation, maintained in some form through institutions and activists' cartographic memories, which, according to Anzaldúa, are mapped onto their bodies. My endeavor is to highlight that these memories are alive, remembered, and still curated by these activists. This means that we as scholars and analysts have to reckon with social movement continuity in a more profound way.

Spatial Practices of Remembering

On April 27, 2014, I attended the annual ceremony for Fruitvale's Cesar Chavez Lifetime Achievement Awards. The crowded meeting hall was adorned with UFW flags and posters from the 1960s that commemorated boycotts and marches. Attendees cheered as award recipients gave speeches about their life's work. At the core of their recollections was an argument about how their activism had transformed the neighborhood. What struck me most about the award recipients was that they were not grand, widely recognized leaders. They also were not recognized for some grandiose action or event. One of the recipients, for example, was an African American man who was celebrated for having dedicated his life to his work as a safety crosswalk guard at a busy intersection near a school. His lifetime achievement was making sure that children crossed the street safely on a daily basis. He was recognized for ensuring the well-being of school kids as they navigated through space.

Another award recipient was Alfredo Cruz, who arrived in Fruitvale in the early 1970s from Colorado and quickly began to work with groups based in the Catholic Church. He was recruited to work in the UFW and thereafter was involved in a multiplicity of projects, including at one time operating a printing press that produced movement materials in the Bay Area (see chapter 5). At the ceremony, Cruz recalled how in the early 1970s he and other neighborhood residents converted an unsightly vacant lot into a vibrant urban farm. During our interview later that month, Cruz explained how they "took three truckloads of garbage out of there, because it was a mess."[7] He also helped to repurpose other vacant lots into neighborhood parks. Cruz remembered:

> At the end of my block there was a creek and there was an elderly woman who couldn't control the weeds. Every year she would set a fire to burn the weeds. We converted that space into Foothill Park, and it still exists today, except that now its name is Cesar Chavez Park. There was also an annex to the park that came about, a playground for kids across the street. That was between Thirty-Eighth and Thirty-Ninth Avenues, and

the community garden was on Thirty-Ninth Avenue. The park is located on Thirty-Seventh Avenue.[8]

Cruz's recollections of movement activities were geographic claims to the production of space. He did not talk about an abstract park, instead remembering the park's location and the process by which neighborhood activists worked to bring these kinds of material changes to the neighborhood. He described how the park had changed over time, acquiring new sections and even a change in name. According to geographer Doreen Massey (2005, 105), current Western-type maps give the impression that "space is a surface—that it is the sphere of a complete horizontality." In contrast, according to Massey, space "presents us with a heterogeneity of practices and processes" and is an "ongoing product of interconnections," meaning that "it will always be unfinished and open" (105). Cruz's mapping was an examination of the present and past, indicating how the park's formation was an ongoing process and that the social movement activism that shaped it was unfinished, and therefore not a historical artifact. Cruz continued to participate in different neighborhood projects, and he lived in and owned rental properties in the community. Efforts of the Chicano movement, he asserted, still had traction in the neighborhood; he pointed to the existence of places like Cesar Chavez Park, which he and other community activists built. The neighborhood's geography and the memories associated with it brought into focus the gains made through movement mobilizing.

Annette Oropeza also told me how neighborhood activism transformed geographies often viewed simply as recreational, such as parks, into spaces of politicization. Her favorite example of this was the annual community celebration that occurred at a neighborhood park once called Sandborn Park:

> The Dia del Barrio was a huge celebration. I still have a lot of the posters: it was an event we put on every summer, and it was meant to be fun and bring people to the park. We had music and speakers and dancers, performances, but we also had all the community agencies out there with booths and talking about what they did, and this brought out the families. The event was held at Sandborn Park, which is now called Josie de La Cruz Park and Carmen Flores Culture Center. Carmen had a lot to do with that, the things that were going around with the community.[9]

Like other activists, Oropeza asserted the crucial role of neighborhood public spaces, such as parks, in people's experience of movement organizing. In addition to showing the very spatiality of activism, Oropeza's memories, similar to Cruz's recollections, reveal the unfinished legacies of Chicano movement activism in the neighborhood. The park is now beautifully manicured, with ample playground space and a recreational center that bears the name of a long-term activist, Carmen Flores. Furthermore, Flores's daughter, known to everyone as Twinkie, runs the recreational center.

Annette Oropeza's passion was working with youths, and thus the bulk of our conversation pivoted on the different educational spaces she either worked at or helped to construct. Throughout the interview, she described the energy and activism of the time: "We always had something going on. We were always either at the park, or doing a march, or getting together, taking our contingents from Fruitvale to a bigger march that was maybe happening in downtown Oakland or San Francisco. People were always mobilizing."[10] These mobilizations occurred through the network of organizations that brought people together and built a broad base of support. Furthermore, she mapped her activism by illustrating her participation in neighborhood educational projects for youths: "There was also a school ... the Emiliano Zapata Street Academy and it was right on the corner of Fruitvale and East Fourteenth. It was in an old furniture warehouse. Then a second Street Academy opened in East Oakland that ended up combining and years later moved into a space that was once a library. . . . The school was really important. It was a focal point. You had people that had worked with the UFW farmworkers that had become teachers there."[11] Oropeza's memories, like Cruz's, spoke about community formation through the projects that social movement activism helped to construct. For Oropeza, educational spaces were at the core of her experience as an activist and of the neighborhood's geography. The Street Academy recruited students who had either dropped out of Oakland Unified School District or were on the verge of dropping out. Instead of viewing these students as failures, Street Academy equipped them with culturally relevant education and a pedagogical system based on building community among the student body. She also detailed how the Street Academy forged translocal linkages between Fruitvale and the UFW solidarity movements occurring throughout the United States. The Street Academy ultimately relocated closer to downtown Oakland and became part of the Oakland Unified School District. Yet for Oropeza, it would always be tied to her memories of the Fruitvale neighborhood. Oropeza's story and the spaces and experiences she graphed through memory illustrate how individual mappings are situated forms of knowledge. Yet when viewed together, they create a latticework of places that construct the neighborhood's geography of activism.

1.1–1.3 Posters of annual Dia del Barrio celebrations originally produced by Malaquias Montoya and now part of activist Annette Oropeza's personal archive. Photographs by the author.

Activists' cartographic memories were essentially perspectival renderings of geography and admittedly were unstable. In fact, my citing of their
mappings is not intended to demonstrate accuracy. Many times activists
admitted they did not remember the exact locations of some organizations. In other instances, different activist mappings contradicted one
another. Maps, according to Michel de Certeau (1984, 97), are "fixations"
that "constitute procedures of forgetting." As Raymond Craib (2004, 91)

observes, "In presenting a smooth façade of clearly marked lines, estab-lished plots, and definitive borders, the map obscures the social process of its own production." A map comes to represent certainty and fixity, in-stead of revealing the contested process by which territory is measured and given an artificial form. Activists' cartographic memories defied the fixity inherent in the production of maps. In contrast to the erasures that maps typically present, activists' memories operated fundamentally as a form for remembering. Viewed in concert, these mappings offered a more expansive and robust understanding of how the Chicano movement shaped the neighborhood, and its continued effects.

The Proof Is in Space!

By situating their social movement participation in space, activists also made a critical intervention regarding the breadth and scope of the Chicano movement. The Chicano movement is primarily conceptualized as a radical uprising spearheaded by a new generation of youths who revolted against previous moderate or reformist political postures—known in the scholarly literature as the integrationist Mexican American generation. The activ-ists I interviewed, however, represented a wide spectrum of mobilizing strategies that were not reducible to protest and militancy. This led me to conclude that labels such as *radical* and *conservative* obscure the complexities of movements and the social actors who participate in them. In their mem-ories, radical spaces stood in proximity to more moderate organizations and therefore signaled moments of convergence between groups traditionally seen as mutually exclusive. Alfredo Cruz, for example, was a member of the militant Brown Berets and served as a security guard for protests and street demonstrations. He simultaneously participated in a church-based nonprofit, Oakland Community Organization, which helped to establish Fruitvale's first urban farm in the late 1970s. Similarly, many other activ-ists' spatial recollections of the movement emphasized the cohabitation, and therefore the mutual constitution, of competing political ideologies.

Many activists' cartographic memories brought back to life the fleeting landscapes of organizations that no longer existed. Elizabeth "Liz" Meza began our conversation by handing me a neighborhood map that she had drafted. It was a simple sketch of one central intersection that other activ-ists had discussed previously: Fruitvale Avenue and East Fourteenth (now called International Boulevard). The map was not to scale, and it showed only a few streets and detailed only a few organizations. Despite the im-

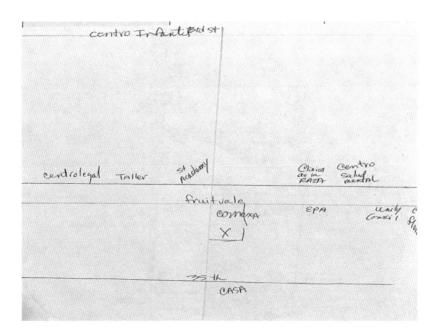

1.4 Map by Elizabeth "Liz" Meza, one of the key founders of COMEXAZ, that graphs some of the major community organizations and political action groups. Photograph by the author.

precision of Meza's map, it made important heartfelt arguments. It fundamentally spatialized and institutionalized the 1960s and 1970s Chicano political mobilizations by transforming abstract streets into geographies of activism. It also demonstrated the cohabitation, and therefore the mutual constitution, of various types of organizations. Meza later classified some of these organizations as "conservative" and others as more "radical." She was a self-proclaimed radical who organized many protests and developed a news service agency called the Comité de México y Aztlán, known as COMEXAZ, which collected and distributed radical news about Latin America and Chicanos in the United States (i.e., Aztlán).[12] The COMEXAZ offices were located at the famed intersection of Fruitvale and East Fourteenth and also served as a meeting place for radical activists.

Meza's cartography principally referred to defunct organizations to reclaim the powerful work they had performed despite no longer being in operation. These radical organizations were especially important, according to Meza, because they did not rely on funding from the state and therefore operated under fewer political constraints. Meza affirmed that COMEXAZ

1.5 Activist Eberardo Hernandez entering the COMEXAZ office. Photograph by Lenor de Cruz.

could therefore be a truly political space. "People used our offices for organizing, meetings, or fundraisers," she recalled. "We became a central point for organizing because we didn't have state funding, so we didn't have any chains or strings to limit our politics." The very radical possibilities of COMEXAZ rested on refusing the "chains," or "strings," of state and philanthropic funding. However, this refusal also stipulated its limitations for survival. Unlike organizations that Meza categorized as "conservative" that received state and philanthropic funding and continued to operate, most "radical" organizations, she acknowledged, had disappeared. As she clarified: "Nonprofits ... were more conservative and I think they had to be. They got money from grants. They were smart enough to sustain themselves and to grow and have a positive effect in the community while we [the radical groups] just disappeared." As many of the radical leaders faded into obscurity, so did the valorization of the organizations they had developed. Meza's mapping of one of these organizations, COMEXAZ, revealed the function of memory in conjuring what no longer exists and what has largely been forgotten in neighborhood recollections. Through this narrative process, she retold her involvement with COMEXAZ, which summoned up recollections of other activists, how they had come to the organization, and their unique contributions to the neighborhood. According to Meza, COMEXAZ was organized to serve a more radicalized or bolder political purpose:

> Gilberto, me, and Freddy; the three of us were sort of streetwise, we were a kind of different breed. When we got here we were thinking Malcom X, we weren't thinking Martin Luther King! We were thinking in terms of militant organizing. We were more street-smart, *trucha*, we were on point. I am not saying that the other people weren't either. We just had a harder edge to us. We were a little more militant. My major in college had been political science, and I had started to read a lot of Marx, Hegel and stuff. I studied like crazy, but a lot of it was over my head or didn't make sense to me. That's the kind of thinking that we came in when we were more into the theory. We wanted to have the "correct political line."[13]

The COMEXAZ office became a meeting place for radical groups and a laboratory for experimentation in different forms of activism and political theory. Activists involved in the organization studied Marxism and could avail themselves of radical news from Latin America and beyond. To clarify, activists met in Fruitvale and read Marx's work together in the COMEXAZ office facilitated by the organization's membership. They then connected Marx's works to the struggles they saw around them. The power of COMEXAZ rested in its ability to be both a meeting place and an educational space, where critical learning and thinking would occur. Yet the organization's influence went beyond its brick-and-mortar existence. As a political action group, COMEXAZ had clout throughout the neighborhood and beyond. According to Meza: "We developed that ability to demonstrate political power by organizing dozens and hundreds of people. We were trying to show the people that they had political clout if they organized." In addition to its news monitoring service (see chapter 5), COMEXAZ also housed a small office of the Third World News Bureau, which was an extension of the radio station KPFA. Furthermore, COMEXAZ ran a multi-leaf offset printing press that had been donated to the organization, and leaders such as Liz and Gilberto learned how to operate it. The organization therefore became a hub for publicizing activist events. "We would do leaflets for people at low or no cost—depending on the issue," Meza proudly recalled.

1.6 COMEXAZ members. *Left to right:* Gilbert Gonzalez, Pancho Rodriguez, Liz Meza (holding daughter Xochitl), Andres Cisneros Galindo, George Singh, Ana Rojas, and Antonio Rios. Photograph by Lenor de Cruz.

Meza lamented that more radical organizations dissolved primarily due to activist burnout and lack of funding. Moreover, many of these self-proclaimed radical organizations became targets of police and FBI infiltration. As she further explained: "There were a lot of police infiltration in most of the political orgs at the time, and we discovered it because we did the Freedom of Information Act, but we already suspected folks. The FBI also came, and they invaded our office one time and took our typewriters."[14] Meza's cartographic memories detailed the projects these radical organizations engendered, which were at once local, national, and international. In these memories, Fruitvale came to represent an interlinking of different movements that spanned distant geographies. Her recollections were political and selective cartographic memories that give meaning to those fleeting landscapes of past radical organizations. The political nature of her memories rested on bringing to life the organization that she helped to run for years, and that she lamented no one really recalled. By recentering COMEXAZ, and literally drawing it on a map (therefore locating it in the neighborhood), she pulled herself and others who had formed part of the organization out of obscurity.

Leaders of what Meza referred to as "conservative" organizations similarly deployed space to give power to the work they had done. Self-proclaimed radical groups critiqued organizations that had become too institutionalized due to state and philanthropic funding, branding the leaders of these organizations as "sellouts" and "conservatives."[15] By the 1980s, organizations such as Clínica de la Raza and Oakland's premier community development corporation (CDC), the Unity Council, had developed into corporatized agencies that radical activists argued had corrupted their initial grassroots political agenda. Radical activists alleged that the conservative organizations had been able to survive because they aligned themselves with the goals of private philanthropy and state agencies. In my interviews with those leaders, I noticed how they, like the "radicals," deployed cartographic memories to emphasize their work. These individuals did not draw maps for me, but they nevertheless retold their activism in cartographic form. Their recollections wielded space to bring into focus the new opportunities and social relations their activism had achieved.

In the summer of 2012, I interviewed a leading Bay Area activist, Herman Gallegos, in his home in a remote town near Sacramento. When the Chicano movement came up in our conversation, he offered a loud critique of militant forms of organizing, stating, "I think that some of the students got into this supernationalistic mentality and I had a problem with that."[16] Furthermore, he explained his frustration with Chicano movement scholarship that did not accurately portray mobilizations as existing in areas like Oakland before and after the temporal framework assigned to the movement. Finally, Gallegos asked, "What was left behind by that kind of militant activism?" In contrast, he eloquently recalled the material legacies left behind by nonprofits and nonmilitant organizations: "You can look at the Unity Council, you can go to the barrios where we organized throughout California. East San Jose is a good example of where we had no streetlights, no stop signs, the creek would overflow. Today the streets are paved, there are sidewalks, there are streetlights, there are soccer fields, youth agencies, Head Start programming in cities. You *can physically see* the changes. I am not saying that there are no problems, but you can go to other barrios and *there are physical changes*."[17] For Gallegos, these material legacies show the "progress" made in urban barrios and the appropriateness of nonmilitant forms of activism. As he argued, the fact that a person could walk through a neighborhood and point to specific services, buildings, or other infrastructural changes offered proof of the effectiveness of this mode of activism. Gallego's cartographic memories, like those of other leaders, clarify the role of nonprofits in crafting geographies of opportunities by providing social services and infrastructural improvements. By linking these nonprofit-mediated improvements to a long tradition of Mexican American organizing, he highlighted the social movement production of space.

In contrast to what they deemed as the efficacy of an institutional approach to mobilizing, nonprofit leaders like Gallegos claimed that radical approaches to community improvement were ineffective. Dr. David Hayes-Bautista of Clínica de la Raza, for example, argued that many of the "radical" and "revolutionary" approaches to community empowerment were not effective and failed to translate into much more than rhetoric. As he described it: "There was a lot of posturing going on. We at Clínica de la Raza had things to do, so we didn't really have to be supermilitant. In fact, every so often we got some undergrads from UC Berkeley who said they want to revolutionize the community and we would tell them: 'Here is a broom … let's get started with that.' That's the way to revolutionize a community."[18] Fruitvale's community-based organizations were a meeting point of divergent approaches to political mobilization. As Dr. Hayes-Bautista believed, more radical groups had unrealistic plans to "revolutionize" or radically transform and politicize the community. La Clínica's leadership, which was dubbed as "not sufficiently" Chicano or not radical enough, found that mobilizations needed to be more practical and concerned with meeting the most critical community needs, such as easy access to health care.

Despite ideological differences between radical and more moderate institutional sectors of the Chicano movement, these groups shared neighborhood spaces and converged around projects of community care. Self-proclaimed radicals admitted that educational centers were major sites of convergence, especially the Centro Infantil elementary school, a bilingual and bicultural alternative educational center. As Liz Meza described it: "What was so critical about it was that everybody's kids went to that school. So you had people from Centro Legal, people from Educación Para Adelantar, the Unity Council. … Centro Infantil had a board of directors that was political and progressive."[19] As Meza's description of this collaborative project reveals, activists labeled "radical" and "conservative" shared these politicized educational projects and worked with one another. For these activists, community mobilizing entailed securing the well-being of family and children, and they consequently cooperated to create alternative forms of education. Labels such as "conservative" and "radical" therefore obscure the points

1.7 Offices of Centro Infantil. The school remains in the same location, but new additions have been built. Photograph by Annette Oropeza.

of collaboration and negotiations that characterized Chicano movement community projects. In contrast to the Chicano movement historiography that places "radical" protest organizations in perpetual opposition to reformist or "conservative" modes of activism, Meza's cartographic memories reveal how neighborhood institutions fostered moments of convergence. The fact that radical and conservative organizations were located in the same neighborhood meant that they often engaged with one another. Thinking through activists' cartographic memories allows us to see the grounded complexities of social movement activism.

These moments of convergence between competing political postures also shaped the very physical appearance of buildings. In my interview with Jose Arredondo, one of the original Oakland-based activists whose family history goes back to when Mexican Americans were located in West Oakland, for example, he described the controversy about the mural that envelops the exterior of the Spanish Speaking Citizens Foundation. The Citizens Foundation was created as a community resource center in the 1960s, and the mural was commissioned in 1989 to celebrate the continued importance of the organization. The mural looks like a coherent commemoration of Chicano culture: a celebration of indigenous ancestry with Aztec iconography throughout, portraits of important leaders such as Cesar Chavez and Dolores Huerta, UFW flags, and depictions of street protests and boycotts. What appears like a coherent and unitary portrayal of the Chicano movement, however, is actually a divided and contested depiction. As Jose Arredondo explained:

> I chose two very good artists that were both still here in the area. They had a disagreement between them on what should go in the mural. I met with them on a Saturday and two beautiful sketches rolled up. They said that I had to choose between them, that they wouldn't work together. I told them no. So they had to work together. I have pictures of them working side by side. We had kids working with them too. So they decided to draw a line down the middle and one of them covered the ancient history and the other covered the contemporary, and they come together and it worked out.[20]

Arredondo explained that the disagreement had to do with how each of the artists characterized the Chicano movement. The process of creating the mural shows the contested nature Chicano movement organizing. However, it is also possible to see how activists and artists made important concessions, which allowed the movement and its institutions to cohere as a project.

Activists' recollections of Chicano movement organizing were principally a mapmaking process. They demonstrated how the Chicano movement changed the urban landscape, and their memories, operating in cartographic form, brought into focus the day-to-day experience of organizing. Their spatial technologies of remembering were a method by which to render visible their contributions to place-making. These cartographic memories defied contemporary mappings of the neighborhood that overlook how social movement activism shaped the community.[21] They also brought into focus the rich history of Mexican American/Chicano activism that is overlooked in the Black/white historiography of the city of Oakland. Furthermore, activists lamented that present-day neighborhood residents

1.8 Mural that envelops the Spanish Speaking Citizens Foundation building. Photograph by the author.

(many of whom are recently arrived migrants) do not acknowledge the history of social movement struggle that built contemporary neighborhood resources. Within this context, activists' cartographic memories valorized the achievements of their activism and justified the appropriateness of their organizational practices.

The Social Relations of Community Care

In addition to mapping their struggles through their memories, activists argued that their work helped to forge a collective community identity. Fruitvale did not always symbolize a Mexican American neighborhood. Historically, it had been an Italian and Portuguese community and began to change at the height of World War II–fueled industrialization and the postwar movement of ethnic whites into more suburban areas of the East Bay. The creation of Fruitvale as a Mexican American place with a shared politicized identity occurred through social movement organizing. Activists experimented with diverse techniques of building community and created political solidarity among different constituents. Many of these new relationships were intergenerational partnerships between an older generation of grassroots organizers and a new group of politicized youths. Activists further explained that these dense networks of activism constituted long-term friendships, partnerships, and even romantic ties. These forms of sociality continued long after what is perceived as the decline of the movement.

Building Community

The Chicano movement routed first-generation college students to develop neighborhood projects. As one of the founders of Centro Legal, Jose Martinez, described his fellow law students: "They had the rhetoric, the connections, the ideology of community involvement and representation for poor people, increased civil rights and participation by Hispanics and Chicanos, and that kind of thing."[22] Another activist, Regina Chavarín, emphasized how even as a high school student she began to learn of the political work occurring at the time. As she described the student energy: "[With] the Third World Strike that was going on in San Francisco [State University] and UC Berkeley, I started paying attention at the time I was still in high school. That really helped open up my ears that there was more going on and it was exciting. The work of Cesar Chavez really hit close to my heart. I couldn't read enough (which was very little at the time); everything I could find, I read."[23] Chavarín was in one of the first cohorts of Mexican American students to enter UC Berkeley after the formation of the Third World Liberation Front, a movement that fought for ethnic studies on campus and greater opportunities for students of color. In 1969, she began her studies and was quickly recruited into different on-campus and community projects. As she remembered, "I was in MEChA [Movimiento Estudiantil Chicano de Aztlán] my first year; I was a secretary or something, because that's what the girls did back then, you know." Once out in the community, Chavarín experimented with other forms of leadership through institution-building projects. Student organizations helped to broker relationships with Mexican American neighborhoods and to grassroots organizing occurring beyond the campus. Chavarín recalled that when she was an undergraduate at UC Berkeley, there was a community projects organization "which gave grants to students to do things in the community. So a lot of funding for projects in Oakland was start-up grants from there." In this fashion, students experimented with the movement's goal to help "the community." This all happened in a context in which, after the Third World Strike and the enactment of affirmative action programs, students of color were actively recruited to enter the university. Many of the improvements that student activists fought for as part of the Third World Strike in the Bay Area were for greater diversity in admissions. By 1969, university officials responded, and that year resulted in one of the most diverse undergraduate and graduate student classes that higher education campuses in the Bay Area had ever seen. This development also included law school admissions. Joel Garcia, then a first-year student at Berkeley's Boalt Law School, told me that in 1969 a total of twenty-one Chicano law students were admitted. The first Chicana ever admitted also enrolled that year. These new first-year law school students were quickly recruited by second- and third-year Chicano law students to go work out in the community. One of them, Albert Moreno, continues to be the chair of the board of directors at Centro Legal de la Raza. As Joel Garcia, one of the founders of Centro Legal de la Raza and Clínica de la Raza, told me:

> I came to Berkeley in the fall of 1969 and in the spring the second- and third-year law students organized Centro Legal. They got the funding for it, they got the location. It was on Thirty-Eighth Avenue and East Fourteenth Street. So guess who gets to be the law students to serve the community? I think all twenty-one of us at different times to different degrees got involved. They just said: "Get in the car and we are going to Oakland." I had never been to Oakland. And I remember going from Berkeley we went to Oakland on the Warren Freeway, and we are all thinking these are hills, there are mansions, what do you mean these people need services? So then we descended into the flatlands, and that showed me that topography reveals a literal stratification of society starting from the flats to the Oakland hills. We get down there and they let us out of the car and they said, you guys are gonna work this. They didn't ask us if we wanted to. They told us to get to work.[24]

As Garcia reveals, students were literally mandated to engage in neighborhood improvement projects. Garcia was one of the founding members of both Clínica and Centro. He grew up in the small town of Tehapachi, California, and went on to attend UC Santa Barbara, where he was one of the founding members of Movimiento Estudiantil Chicano de Aztlán. Among his many accomplishments, he helped to write the founding documents for Chicano studies, including the Plan de Santa Barbara. Once he was at Boalt Law School, Fruitvale became the site where he put many Chicano movement lessons into practice. For many students like Garcia, Fruitvale-based projects introduced them to Oakland and the Bay Area at large, where they forged social relations that helped to shape neighborhood resources and connections to the community.

The 1960s mandate of Chicano community improvement jump-started preexisting neighborhood organizing endeavors in Fruitvale. As described in chapter 2, since the late 1950s, progressive sectors of the Catholic Church had helped to organize neighborhood residents to forge a united voice for Mexican Americans in Oakland. Furthermore, organizations such as the Community Service Organization (CSO) developed local neighborhood politicization projects (see also Herrera 2012). Many of these projects linked Spanish-speaking residents to state services that were not available in Spanish and had a major focus on citizenship campaigns. They also advocated for the creation of state programs designed for Mexican Americans. These neighborhood organizing hubs, composed mainly of parents and an older generation of leaders, helped to guide neighborhood projects in the 1960s and 1970s. As Dr. David Hayes-Bautista, one of the founders of Fruitvale's Clínica de la Raza, recalled: "I got a phone call one night from one of the moms who I was working with. She said that the parents' group could not depend upon the county, so they needed to develop their own health center. Then of course she started telling me, 'We don't know anything about it. And you are the only person that knows anything about it. So we would like to ask you to direct us.' So I said, 'Eleanor, I haven't even started [medical] school yet.'"[25] Dr. Hayes-Bautista's recollections demonstrate relationships of collaboration between a new generation of Chicano youths and an older Mexican American generation. There was a specific gendered component to this work, as mothers who organized to improve community resources spearheaded neighborhood-level forms of organizing. Many of these initial organizing hubs occurred at members' homes and grew into more institutionalized projects. The central goal of these joint efforts was the care and protection of the neighborhood and its residents.

Movement institutional formations were fundamentally part of a community-building endeavor. Chavarín remembered that "when El Centro Legal and La Clínica's first site was identified, it used to be an old restaurant or bakery.... We went there and cleaned it up. I put a crew together which consisted mostly of women, my brothers, sisters, students."[26] This work proved to be a multigenerational project that enlisted the help of all sectors of the neighborhood population. Chavarín's recollections of the formation of Clínica and Centro Legal demonstrate the collaborative labor required to build these institutions.

1.9 First location of Clínica de la Raza. Photograph courtesy of Joel Garcia.

Once formed, nonprofit projects channeled future generations into neighborhood-building efforts. For many first-generation students, nonprofits became their first paid employment opportunities. Chavarín said of her involvement with Centro Legal that she "applied and my roommates and I worked there that summer. It was in my neighborhood on Thirtieth Avenue. I kept volunteering during the year. . . . It kept me in touch with the neighborhood and it kept me connected."[27] As a Fruitvale resident, Chavarín was able to work in the community where she was raised and to build new relationships with neighbors. Nonprofit projects rerouted students like Chavarín back to their neighborhoods and ensured that there were spaces to put into practice the movement goals of social change and justice for the Chicano community.[28]

Centro Legal de la Raza emerged in 1969 when a group of law students at UC Berkeley created a neighborhood Chicano legal center due to frustrations over the absence of county legal services for the Spanish-speaking population. Jose Martinez recalled: "Alameda County Legal Aid had neighborhood law offices and obviously there was one in downtown, there was one in the Black community, but no office directed toward the Chicano community. And our view of Alameda County Legal Aid at the time was [that it was] favoring the Black community and not spending enough resources on the Hispanic community."[29] Parents and students understood that Oakland antipoverty officials concentrated their efforts on African American institutions and that little information existed on Mexican Americans as a group with shared interests (see chapter 2). As a founding member of Centro, Joel Garcia, told me: "We started from scratch at Centro Legal. We got people together that wanted to serve the community, and whoever walked in the door got taken care of and we didn't charge anything. We saw everything: tenant rights issues, immigration, a lot of unemployment insurance, fair employment hearings for people denied unemployment benefits or workers comp."[30] Dr. Hayes-Bautista elaborated: "We were undergraduates, graduates, we tended to be a little bit extreme, and we all thought since [antipoverty programs] are not doing what they are supposed to do and clearly there are needs in this community, why don't we address the needs?"[31] Jose Martinez, then a student in UC Berkeley's law school, told me a similar story about the resourcefulness of students and the support from UC Berkeley:

> We managed to get the Alameda County Legal Aid to pay the ground lease on the office space. It was an old storefront, and they contributed desks, paper, they maybe paid the phone or something. I remember we got the dean of the law school to contribute surplus file cabinets, desks, and broken chairs. We went down to the storefront and opened it up, it was kind of like an unsponsored program from the law school. [Although] it was a branch office of Alameda County Legal Services, it was important to us that there would be Chicano community control.[32]

Community efforts to build institutions were guided by the Chicano movement's mission of establishing programs and services that were built for and by Chicanos. Joel Garcia remembered:

> What we found in [Fruitvale] or the Colonia Mexicana [the Mexican Colony] was a smaller scale of what the neighborhood is today. The community consisted of people who had been there for generations, back from when the land grants were created. And then there were recently arrived migrants, and everything between. There weren't as many undocumented, there weren't that many day laborers. They were all our clients, they were the people that came to us. And then the other people who came to us were the *pintos*, the people who had been in jail and got released into the community and had nowhere to go, but they had a legal need, so they would show up at Centro Legal. You had an incredible mix of people, and the door was always open.[33]

Instead of waiting for state services to come to the barrio, activists created their own. They challenged state-sanctioned modes of community development and maintained their integrity as agencies based in and directed by the community. These were inclusive spaces that were focused on bringing all sectors of the Chicano population together to build community. As Garcia reveals, this also meant welcoming formerly incarcerated Chicanos and helping them get back on their feet after being released from jail.

The formation of Central Legal de la Raza and Clínica de la Raza reveals how the Chicano movement was spatialized in Oakland. It also demonstrates how activists and community residents deployed multiple tactics to create and maintain neighborhood resources. These organizations were crafted to represent and reconstitute the meaning of community. Activists and community residents utilized the concept of "community" as a mechanism in claims-making processes. They created a new politics rooted in the redefinition of the needs and mechanisms through which the Chicano community would create its own resources. This was significant in a period when city and federal agencies overlooked the expanding Mexican American population in Oakland. Chicano movement organizations were initially independent institutions that received no assistance from state agencies. As the organizations grew, they began to work with particular state institutions, such as the university, to bring about change in Mexican American neighborhoods. They also pressured city officials and other state agents to channel resources to the Mexican American community. As such, the formation of these institutions demonstrates the contested process of state and nonprofit incorporation of movement activism. However, activists remembered with a sense of pride that their projects were initially independent from state and philanthropic funding.

The Chicano Movement as Boot Camp

Movement activism was not just about joining a street protest or action; it occurred primarily through the kinds of neighborhood-level social relationships activists developed. Through their commitment to the neighborhood, they participated in a "boot camp" of sorts where they developed enduring social networks that were committed to making positive changes in the community. The ideas of *comadrazgo* and *compadrazgo* describe these kinds of political kinship networks, which revolved around community protection and care.[34] The activists argued that the social relations they built through their movement activism endured and shaped how they interacted with the neighborhood in the following decades.

Both Roger and Regina Chavarín began their activism as students. They met through their work in the neighborhood and shared the experience of working on various community projects. Through these mobilizations, they forged lasting relationships with other activists. These relationships constituted a boot camp where activists experimented with different modes of organizing and relationship-building. As Roger Chavarín recalled, "Everyone came to boot camp together, and the next generation is in line and there's going to be better services because you won't have to deal with the racism and the alienation. You were literally neighbors and you were connected."[35] In Chavarín's view, the Chicano movement built services for the future generation through the collaborative work of different institutions. This occurred through a shared, politicized mission of community improvement. These social networks consolidated future opportunities and charted connections to numerous county and nonprofit resources. Regina Chavarín, for example, went on to direct a nonprofit called the Narcotics Education League (NEL). As its executive director, she relied on the social networks she had built through social movement activism. As she explained: "Help was a phone call away, a handshake away. It was really easy. That was one of the things that I noticed about the years working at NEL. I always kept my connection with everybody. I could walk into county agencies or other nonprofits and get help because I had either worked there or done volunteer work or sat in a committee. It was like going to see your compadres, your comadres."[36] Central to Regina Chavarín's explanation of the importance of these social networks was their longevity. Though the moments of street protest were now in the past, the social relations built through these mobilizations endured. And these lasting relationships represented a set of opportunities that enabled contemporary forms of mobilizations. Similar to Chavarín, other activists like Annette Oropeza spoke about the long-term impacts of movement social relations:

> I still see Andres [from the Third World News Bureau] because he is my comadre's husband and they are still in the area. Norman [also from the Third World News Bureau] I keep in touch with because he is one of my daughter's compadres. And by extension he is my compadre. It is amazing that I am talking to you about the folks that I still stay in touch with, especially Liz from COMEXAZ, we go way back. I am still connected with people from different community organizations, political groups that were working out in these areas.[37]

As geographer Doreen Massey (1994, 154) reminds us, "What gives place its specificity is not some long-internalized history but the fact that it is constructed out of a particular constellation of social relations, meeting and weaving together at a particular locus." Social bonds and forms of sociality developed in the 1960s and 1970s were kept alive through the relationships activists built with one another. These relationships helped to continually produce Fruitvale as a place shaped by Chicano movement activism and an incubator of social movement struggles. These bonds (including romantic and familial relationships) and experiential practices of organizing and working together did not end. They continued and helped activists build new partnerships in the years that ensued.

Conclusion

"I was really lucky to run into you because I wanted to tell this story," remarked Liz Meza as we concluded our conversation in 2012. We met rather serendipitously a week earlier at Fruitvale's Cesar Chavez Lifetime Achievement Awards ceremony. In her statement to me, Meza was not referring just to a retelling of her individual life history. She also referred to the story of COMEXAZ, of social movement activism in Fruitvale, and of activists' labor that helped cohere the neighborhood as a place profoundly shaped by the Chicano movement. "This story should have been written some time ago," she continued. "I'm really glad that . . . whatever part you use, that it's going to be told." How does one respond to such a profound and deeply felt sentiment? I remember that I choked up, and I thanked Meza for her time and for entrusting me with her memories. I have remembered Meza's words throughout the years, and each time I revisit them, I am reminded of the sheer responsibility of writing and producing knowledge. But more than that, I am reminded of the politics that shape writing about the production of space. How does one tell the totality of stories and social relationships that come to produce space, and how does one do justice to the beauty of this process? Meza's parting message to me was enveloped by a weighty sense of nostalgia, a deep feeling of loss due to the invisibility of this history.

This chapter has been an attempt to carry out Meza's wish to tell the story of how social movement activism produced Fruitvale and changed activists' lives. It is also an effort to rethink how we write about and analyze social movements, especially in our present moment in which commemorations of the Chicano movement are now part of the ethnic pageantry of US neoliberal multiculturalism. This is most powerfully performed through the celebration of figures such as Cesar Chavez and, more recently, Dolores Huerta. This kind of incorporation of social movement icons achieves a crucial political function that fashions the United States as a postracial nation where race-based mobilizations are a thing of the past (see Melamed 2006, 2011). It also helps to create a romanticized version of the movement that overlooks the complexities and contradictions that typically characterize mass mobilizations. Similarly, we are left without an assessment of the grounded neighborhood-level changes that social movements helped to construct.

In contrast to the neoliberal multicultural reading of 1960s social movements, in this chapter I have demonstrated how the Chicano movement forged a broad base of support in Oakland and helped to produce new resources that changed the community's political landscape. Activists' recollections of movement participation were not reduced to charismatic leaders or their participation in protests. Instead, they emphasized how Chicano movement mobilizations produced the Fruitvale neighborhood. The bulk of these changes occurred through the creation of neighborhood institutions, which contoured the way in which residents and activists experienced the movement. The institutions spanned multiple types of political postures and represented the diversity of approaches that activists took to achieve community care. Like activists' cartographic memories, analysis of social movement activism must be attentive to the dynamic simultaneity and multiplicity of social relations and organizational practices that give place a social meaning.

By situating their memories in space, and by producing cartographies of their activism, activists asserted the way in which Chicano power was experienced in urban neighborhoods. In so doing, they foregrounded the centrality of place-making to constructions of activism and the Chicano movement. And these places, and the multiplicity of social relations they set forth, are still in formation. Such claims are important given changing demographics of the neighborhood, whereby most residents are now recently arrived immigrants who are unaware of the history of activism that bore fruit for the community. They are also important given that most scholarly analyses frame social movement activism as episodic, with a birth, climax, and subsequent death. These analyses ignore the openness of space and the fact that social relationships that shape movements—and produce space—have long-lasting effects that do not easily die off.

THE OTHER
MINORITY

From my perspective, community describes not a static, place-based social collective but a power-laden field of social relations whose meanings, structures, and frontiers are continually produced, contested, and reworked in relation to a complex range of sociopolitical attachments and antagonisms.
Steven Gregory, *Black Corona*

Fruitvale's grassroots-level mobilizations did not happen in a vacuum. Much of this activism had its roots in post–World War II organizing throughout the United States. In California, this activism blurred the boundaries between the urban and the rural—bringing the farmworker movements taking shape in rural areas of the Central Valley into intimate relationships with cities such as Oakland, San Francisco, and Berkeley. It also put different movements and racial groups into deeper conversations with one another. Mexican American leaders, for example, worked alongside civil rights struggles spearheaded by African Americans. They sought to show that as a minority group in the United States, Mexican Americans were equally worthy of civil rights and poverty alleviation programs.

These various encounters also fortified relationships between social movement activists and a newly constructed federal machinery for poverty alleviation that coalesced by the early 1960s as the War on Poverty. These complex and contested relationships transformed many social movement projects of neighborhood improvement into formalized 501(c)(3) nonprofit organizations. Through this institutionalization process, movement services and programming became even more rooted in place. In fact, funding was predicated on meeting the local needs of a particular community.

Federal poverty alleviation innovations in the 1960s transformed the state's relationship to urban communities and their respective social movements. On one hand, this intervention can be seen as state and philanthropic attempts to quell urban unrest and pacify movements. Scholars have shown that this new programmatic focus on urban issues also helped to pathologize urban youths and justify greater policing of the inner city.[1] At the same time, this historical process created the architecture of race-based nonprofit organizations like the Unity Council, Clínica de la Raza, and Centro Legal de la Raza. Many formerly grassroots organizing endeavors became routed through nonprofits, which differed from previous modes of mobilizing. This unprecedented change provided new opportunities and constraints for social movement activists.

In today's world, the institutional entity of the 501(c)(3) nonprofit organization is a staple in many cities. Community development corporations like the Unity Council, for example, abound in places like Los Angeles, Phoenix, San Antonio, and San Francisco. Community health clinics, legal centers, and even many workers' centers are also run as nonprofit organizations. Admittedly, many contemporary activists, and academics alike, critique this model of service delivery and urban redevelopment because of its level of institutionalization and disconnection from the grassroots. Yet we rarely question how and why the institutional entity of the nonprofit became naturalized as the principle mechanism to bring about social change. To understand this expedited and unparalleled level of social movement institutionalization, I analyze how Mexican American/Chicano nonprofit organizations came into existence.

My use of cartographic memory in this chapter and the next allowed me to better spatialize archival sources. I also supplemented archival materials with oral history interviews, which allowed me to give greater life to the historical actors and the spaces where they labored. As I reviewed memos, policy briefs, newspaper articles, and interview transcripts, I followed the consolidation of disparate organizations into larger and more recognizable institutions. I wasn't just thinking of some abstract place where funding and resources simply descended. In fact, many of the program reports that I reviewed included detailed demographics and characteristics, focusing on the patterns of specific neighborhoods and often showcasing bountiful photographs of program recipients. Grassroots mobilizations deeply rooted themselves in specific places through institutionalization. Activism literally went from the streets to activist homes, to borrowed church spaces, and finally into rented or owned buildings. I paid attention to the relationships that were built and the spaces that activists and community members forged. This is the nature of cartographic memory—the insistence that historical processes, and archival documents by proxy, are spatial. They carry with them the inscriptions not just of historical actors but also of the very spaces and emotional bonds that human beings produce in and through specific locations.

In their negotiations with state and federal agencies, Mexican American community leaders rendered Oakland's Spanish-speaking community legible as rights-bearing subjects and positioned the organizations they created as their stewards. This consolidated an important precedent for the role that Chicano nonprofits and other political action groups would play in guiding and helping to constitute the formation of Chicano communities. These social movement actors came to understand nonprofit organizations—like the Unity Council—as one modality through which they could advance their neighborhood improvement projects.

Oakland and the War on Poverty

Fearing a repeat of the Watts uprising (popularly understood as violent race riots) that occurred in Los Angeles in 1965, President Lyndon Johnson's administration targeted Oakland in the War on Poverty that same year. By 1968, 140 nonmilitary federal programs were spending close to $100 million a year in Oakland, an amount that overshadowed the city's own budget of $57.9 million (Orozco, Austin, and Beale 2008; Pressman 1975; Self 2003).[2] Designed to eradicate poverty, federal legislation between 1964 and 1971 provided generous funding for job, educational, and social service projects—all focused on a new agenda of human development rather than the improvement of decaying urban structures or the elimination of structural inequalities (Katz 1993; Self 2003; Weir 1988). The War on Poverty was fundamentally concerned with the "empowerment" of the poor—a concept that signaled a new understanding of poverty and how to fight it (Cruikshank 1999). Antipoverty experts introduced programmatic innovations such as Head Start, remedial instruction, elementary summer school, and neighborhood legal services to improve the quality of life in inner cities. The federal government's antipoverty agenda relied on empowering local communities to develop, organize, and implement federally funded antipoverty programs and to gradually devolve control for these to local communities (Kramer 1969; Marris and Rein 1967; O'Connor 1996).

War on Poverty policy and planning initiatives shifted the responsibility for poverty alleviation from the federal government to local communities and responsible self-governing urbanites, setting an important precedent in the management of urban racialized communities. They created a new way for a variety of stakeholders committed to the improvement of racial minorities to work together to fix what was deemed the "urban problem." At the height of civil rights struggles, minority communities protested overpolicing and government disinvestment in the inner city. Popularly understood as "riots," these forms of urban unrest brought national attention to racial segregation and economic inequality—a set of conditions that came to be referred to euphemistically as the midcentury urban problem. This led to the development of new and intimate relationships between state agencies, private philanthropy like the Ford Foundation, and social movement actors as these disparate forces worked collaboratively to create and implement antipoverty programs.

Mexican American activists fought to be recognized as a minority deserving of antipoverty programing. On April 15, 1966, for example, Oakland's Mexican American Unity Council held a press conference to present a six-point list of demands to city hall. The manifesto boldly called on the newly elected Republican mayor, John R. Reading, to appoint a representative of the Mexican American community to Oakland's city council. The *Oakland Tribune* (1966, 4) reported that the group also sought the hiring of an expert who could "train the city council and other civic leaders" to better recognize the problems of the Spanish-speaking community.[3] Activists delivered their declaration in a language of urgency that reflected their fierce determination. Collectively, these requests were attempts to secure equal War on Poverty funding for Oakland's Spanish-speaking residents. Mexican American leaders were concerned that federal antipoverty funding would be directed predominantly toward alleviating African American disadvantage, leaving the Spanish-speaking community without monetary support. Activists argued that "Oakland, whose motto is 'The All-American City' should be for all Americans: that the Treaty of Guadalupe [Hidalgo] should be honored to the letter as well as in spirit" (*Oakland Tribune* 1966, 4).[4]

These proclamations by Bay Area Spanish-speaking citizens stand in stark contrast to the traditional understanding of racial politics in Oakland as almost exclusively Black and white (Gregory 1999; Moynihan 1969; O'Connor 2001; Self 2003). In the early 1960s, little was known about the Spanish-speaking population in Oakland, and only a few studies and scattered reports even mentioned its existence. However, Mexican American activism had long existed in the city and flourished in the postwar period. As stakeholders focused on expanding their political influence, Mexican American organizations challenged the conflation of racial inequality and poverty exclusively with African American disadvantage. This coupling of poverty and blackness was in part constructed by an impressive list of poverty studies that focused on urban ghettos and "rendered technical" the needs, desires, and behaviors of the poor.[5] The focus of the War on Poverty as a solution to African American disadvantage also reflected white middle-class fears about the "threat" of Black radicalism and violence.

Like their African American counterparts, Mexican American organizations mobilized to become agents in the rapidly expanding market of federally funded, place-based solutions to poverty. They reinterpreted the War on Poverty agenda and helped guide their community by marshaling a commitment to efficient care of the growing Spanish-speaking population. Although these processes are often explained as an antagonistic competition for scarce resources, my analysis details the collaborative ethos that defined the coalitions Mexican Americans built with African Americans.

The Ford Foundation: A New and Important Stakeholder

Many of innovative features of the War on Poverty stemmed from the increasing role of private foundations in urban affairs. By the 1950s, the Ford Foundation committed itself to issues of racial and ethnic inequality through its efforts to influence public policy regarding the "urban problem" (O'Connor 1996). The Ford Foundation saw itself as activist and interventionist in relation to urban and regional development (Magat 1979; O'Connor 1996). The initial planning for the War on Poverty emerged out of the Ford Foundation's Gray Areas program. Oakland was also the first site where these ideas were tested.

In 1962, the *Oakland Tribune* enthusiastically reported that Oakland had been selected as one of three pilot cities to receive a $2 million grant to help forge an "all-out attack on the social problems of minority groups and the proper assimilation of new citizens into the community" (1). The program targeted the Castlemont district of East Oakland, which was deemed a "transition area" due to the out-migration of white middle-class residents and their replacement by lower-income Blacks, resulting in what analysts of the time called "social disorganization" (Rhomberg 2004, 135; Salzman 1963). The Castlemont neighborhood was rapidly becoming home mainly to African American residents, like many Oakland districts located in and around the inner city. The program's objective was to prevent this neighborhood from becoming a "Negro ghetto" and subsequently falling into decay. The Gray Areas program channeled resources into the Castlemont district and made local community members responsible for the implementation of programing and management of funds. The participation of local residents was required through a formalized citizens' advisory committee, and the coordination of existing city services was also expected through the Oakland Interagency Project. This type of participation from neighborhood residents coupled with the coordinated support of city agencies became the cornerstone of the Gray Areas program. The local community was both the target of intervention and the agent responsible for bringing about the desired change (O'Connor 1996, 1999).

The Gray Areas program, according to Alice O'Connor (1996), signaled the first shift away from structural and economic reform as a way of alleviating poverty. Instead, reform was to come from changes in individuals and their behaviors. The War on Poverty was built on this kind of devolutionary process that transferred the problem of poverty from the federal government to local communities and ultimately to individual subjects.[6] As sociologists Peter Marris and Martin Rein (1967, 9) argue about War on Poverty efforts, the "devolution of power extends beyond any formal jurisdiction to the citizen himself. He is expected, ideally, to be an active promoter of the well-being of his community—his children's school, the amenities of his block, neighborhood affairs." Focused on assimilating formerly rural Black populations to urban life, the object of antipoverty programs was to transform what were viewed as "deficient" Black subjects into self-governing urbanites.[7] Many of these new Black urbanites were part of the Great Migration of Blacks from southern rural areas to industrializing cities such as Oakland. The Gray Areas program and subsequent War on Poverty, explains O'Connor (1996, 617), "perpetuated the notion of poverty as a problem confined to *other* people and diverted attention from its links to economic restructuring, population movements, racial discrimination, and government policies that perpetuated inequality." Black migrants from the South were seen as unfit for urban life because they lacked experience with city dwelling and overwhelmingly struggled to pull themselves up by their own bootstraps. Their impoverishment was their fault and not a result of the legacies of slavery that influenced Jim Crow segregation and unequal distribution of resources and wealth. A shift in focus to individuals and in changing peoples' behaviors required the recruitment of different local agencies—both state and nonstate—to run projects to govern the conduct of the poor and other subjects who were viewed as deficient.

The Community Action Program and the Architecture of Nonprofits

The Community Action Program (CAP), established in 1964 by the Economic Opportunity Act, was the centerpiece of this agenda and mobilized community members through nonstate, usually private nonprofit organizations, known as community action agencies (CAAs) (Cruikshank 1999; Jackson 1993). Instead of sending War on Poverty moneys to states or to municipalities as grants, the federal government allocated them to the newly established, independent CAAs (Clark 2000; Marwell 2004, 268). The CAA theoretically administered a diverse collection of more than a thousand federally funded, local, neighborhood-based antipoverty agencies whose mission was to coordinate existing social services and bring new services closer to the poor. As in the Gray Areas program, the federal government privileged associationalist practices that promoted a new and powerful role for nonstate agencies like CAAs in combating poverty (O'Connor 1999). At the local level, federal policies also encouraged newly formed community service organizations to expand their existing activities by contracting with the Office of Economic Opportunity and to compete for federal grants.

The devolutionary practices of the War on Poverty, however, were fundamentally limited from the onset. Employing the famous motto of "maximum feasible citizen participation," these efforts used an unrealistic language that sought to empower communities and individual citizens to become agents in the development of their own communities (Kramer 1969; Moynihan 1969). According to a workbook prepared by the Office of Economic Opportunity (1965, 10), CAAs were organizations "established at the local community level to direct and coordinate the attack on the complex of poverty problems found in the given community" and were to serve as "catalyst and coordinator, acting to bring about change and to mold diverse activities into a smooth, effective instrument for reducing and eventually eliminating poverty in the local community." This dual role of catalyst and coordinator bestowed individual CAAs with enormous responsibility and required that community members, most of whom had minimal educational and organizational training, act as a cohesive administrative entity (Kramer 1969). This was an unreasonable expectation from the onset and paved the way for enormous challenges for CAAs.

Oakland's CAA was troubled from the start. Its staff was poorly trained, it was unable to act as a cohesive entity, and it was engaged in many disputes with city government. Black middle-class leadership, which dominated the CAA, also came into conflict with working-class Black sentiments and goals (Pressman 1975, 63). As O'Connor (2001, 133) writes, the federal government never fully clarified the meaning of "maximum feasible citizenship participation" or articulated how much decision-making power would be granted to individual citizens. In fact, the idea of mobilizing communities as political and programmatic entities was an ideal without much of a proven record (Kramer 1969; O' Connor 1996; Williams 1975). According to Ralph Kramer's (1969) study of War on Poverty programs in the San Francisco Bay Area, this mobilization of the local community proved to be a disaster in practice. However dystopic the devolutionary practices were, though, they represented a moment of opportunity for community-based organizations and existing leaders to render poverty in Oakland as an identifiable, researched, and necessary target of governmental improvement programs. African American middle-class professionals took control of Oakland's CAA. According to Rhomberg (2004, 139), this "facilitated their own political entry into the new institutional forms of the regime."

Challenging the Coupling of Poverty and Blackness

African American dominance in Oakland's War on Poverty efforts was consistent with national trends. The federal government envisioned the War on Poverty, at its creation in 1964, as a program of empowerment aimed at the "poor" (Cruikshank 1999). While the "poor" brought together disparate racial, gendered, and generational segments of the population, numerous scientific and authoritative studies of the time came to define poverty as synonymous with African American disadvantage (Marris and Rein, 1967; Nichols 1966; Record 1963; Salzman 1963; Wood 1968).[8] Studies overwhelmingly reported that "Negroes" suffered far higher unemployment rates than whites as well as diminishing incomes; these studies employed a culture-of-poverty analysis that justified creating a coordinated front of job, educational, and other skills development programs intended to transform deficient subjects into respectable urban dwellers.[9]

Within these poverty formulations, researchers deemed Mexican Americans a nebulous third group in between Blacks and poor whites. Categorized as "whites with Spanish surnames," by 1960, 6.5 percent of Oakland's population had Spanish surnames and constituted one-fourth of the non-white minority group (Bernardi 1965, 1). Compared with African Americans, Mexican Americans were far more dispersed and not confined to a single geographic region. Gene Bernardi (1965, 4) found that Mexican Americans, like African Americans, were overrepresented among the unemployed and poor and had the lowest levels of educational attainment of any group. A very large portion (80 percent) of the California Spanish surname population in 1960 had been born in the United States, its territories, or possessions. California had a larger Spanish surname population in 1960 than any other state in the Southwest, a total of 1,426,538. [10]

By 1965, prominent Bay Area researchers acknowledged the importance of studying the growth of the Mexican American population and poverty. However, influential studies such as those conducted by Wilson Record of the University of California, Berkeley, and research director of Oakland's Gray Areas program identified "Negro" poverty and disadvantage as most pressing. As Record (1963, 1) wrote, "The Negro population is relatively new to the Bay Area, whereas Mexicans have been a familiar sight for a long time." As new migrants from the South and Southwest, he argued, "Negroes ... have a salient conspicuousness, their semi-rural traits standing out even more sharply against the Bay Area urban backdrop because of their color" (1). Based on his findings, Record recommended that Blacks merited more immediate consideration in poverty studies.

Poverty researchers and program administrators also explicitly over-looked Oakland's Spanish-speaking residents because they were not per-ceived to symbolize the same threat that Blacks did. As early as 1963, for example, the Oakland Tribune reported on Record's study in which he warned that San Francisco Bay Area communities had either to "make room" for Blacks or face the threat of a "growing number of angry black men" (Irving 1963, 8). Estimating a doubling of the Black population by the 1980s, Record (1963) argued that Black-white relations would become the most critical racial tension within San Francisco Bay Area communities. What was par-ticularly worrisome, he noted, was the "social and political militancy of Bay Area Negroes, in contrast to the passivity or mild protest of the Chinese, Japanese, Indians, and Mexicans" (2).

Cities like Oakland with a prominent African American population offi-cially equated poverty with blackness and accordingly funneled antipoverty funds predominantly toward alleviating Black disadvantage. Members of Oakland's Spanish-speaking community quickly understood this and orga-nized to prevent their continued marginalization in the contest over federal War on Poverty resources. They did this by building on a long history of community-based organizing and by allying themselves with important sec-tors of the African American Democratic Party establishment. Organizations such as the Community Service Organization (CSO), the Mexican American Political Association (MAPA), the American GI Forum, and religious groups had represented the Mexican American population for decades, primarily in West Oakland. These organizations came into existence focusing on small-scale, membership-run, neighborhood improvement campaigns aimed at citizenship participation and leadership development. During the War on Poverty era, these organizations accelerated their mobilizations by working collaboratively to fight for greater federal resources.

Post–World War II Mexican American Organizing

Oakland's postwar organizing had its roots in an active Spanish-speaking Catholic movement that focused on developing religious and social services for Mexican Americans. Established by radical priests such as Father Gerald Cox, Father Charles Phillips, and Father John Ralph Duggan, this church-based movement began by hosting Spanish-language masses and fostering self-help projects, including after-school programs for youths and assistance for poor families such as job placement programs and access to legal counsel. Consistent with the liberation theology movement unfolding throughout Latin America, these priests fought for the poor and the oppressed. They did so by linking Oakland's Spanish-speaking residents with Mexican Americans throughout California focused on setting up congregations in rural and urban areas (Cox 2006). Through these activities, Oakland church groups networked with the Spanish-speaking residents of rural towns throughout California, many of whom were farmworkers, and became familiar with their struggles. These church-based mobilizations set forth the organizational base through which secular organizations such as the CSO emerged in Oakland.[11]

Postwar church-based mobilizations inspired an entire generation of leaders who found in the language of liberation theology the tools they needed to expedite community improvement projects. Many of the Mexican American leaders had grown up Catholic, but it was not until the 1950s and 1960s that they were introduced to this new kind of Catholic-based movement. As postwar Mexican American activist Herman Gallegos detailed: "These priests had the courage to talk to us about social change and to deal with the same concepts that basically, Gustavo Gutierrez did in liberation theology. That it's not your place in life to simply pray to God, accept it and say well that's the way it is but to simply get up and do change."[12] The clergy modeled for these emerging leaders how the church could advance social movement causes. Additionally, the clergy's dedication to the Spanish-speaking population taught them valuable strategies for gaining community trust. It is therefore not surprising that priests were generally invited to bless organizations and meetings, and that leaders such as Cesar Chavez often called upon the support of the church. As long-term activist Elvira Rose recounts, the priests "used to go up and down California's Central Valley organizing people in the small towns."[13] The church-based groups, according to Rose, also provided meeting spaces for some of the first CSO meetings: "So in those times we didn't have buildings and so the church ... that's how they allowed us to meet there at their building and gave a lot of support services."[14] By building these localized connections with community members and subsequently linking the struggles of disparate congregations up and down California, these church-based mobilizing strategies demonstrated the importance of collective organizing. This kind of organizing required not just politicizing congregations but also connecting them with the kinds of services they needed. Therefore, service provision was an essential arm of the organizing model that this group of clergy set in place. As Herman Gallegos nostalgically recalled: "They spoke Spanish, they were very caring for our community and ... some nuns started Catholic schools, parochial schools and there was a safety net that was pretty much service oriented."[15]

It is important to situate this organizing in a context of national postwar activism among communities of color in the United States. Throughout the Southwest, organizations such as the League of United Latin American Citizens (LULAC), the American GI Forum, and the CSO emerged in the post–World War II period to safeguard rights for Mexican Americans. LULAC was officially funded on February 17, 1929, in Corpus Christi Texas, with the mission of alleviating the appalling conditions of poverty and civil rights abuses facing Mexican Americans. As historian David Gutiérrez (1995, 77) writes, LULAC's constitution emphasized that the best way to overcome these conditions was to organize as American citizens, even to the extent of excluding unnaturalized Mexican nationals (see also Acuña 2004). The GI Forum was established by a group of Mexican American veterans in 1949; like LULAC, Gutiérrez (1995, 155) reports, it argued strongly that civil rights efforts must be focused on US citizens of Mexican descent. Founded in Los Angeles in September 1947, the CSO was the first organization that promoted cooperation between Mexican Americans and Mexican immigrants. Unlike the GI Forum and LULAC, the CSO had no citizenship requirements for membership and often encouraged noncitizens to join. The CSO made naturalization of noncitizen members a priority and radically expanded its organizing campaigns to incorporate undocumented Mexican migrants, who were viewed by the organization not as sojourners but as integral members of the Mexican American community (Gutiérrez 1995, 170). As David Gutiérrez further argues, developments during the post–World War II period marked "a significant victory for Mexican American activists and organizations that had pursued an integrationist civil rights strategy. These organizations shrewdly manipulated a wartime rhetoric shaped by discussions of human rights and the self-determination of peoples that dominated domestic and international political discourse" (152). This agenda shaped the claims-making process of an expanding collection of organizations, advocacy groups, and mutual aid societies that began to dot the US Southwest.

Building on the work of radical priests in the Catholic Church, the CSO played a large role in organizing Mexican Americans after 1945. Founded by Fred Ross, Antonio Rios, and Edward Roybal with the support of Saul Alinsky's Industrial Areas Foundation, the CSO became the training ground for the first generation of Mexican American leaders, including Cesar Chavez, Dolores Huerta, and Gilbert Padilla (Acuña 2004; Gallegos 1989; D. G. Gutiérrez 1995; Orozco, Austin, and Beale 2008). The CSO attracted a large contingency of wartime veterans who returned home in the postwar period to find that they were subjected to discrimination despite their service. As long-term Bay Area activist Alex Zermeño recalled, the membership consisted of disgruntled veterans: "World War II started CSO. You know, poor Mexicans they went to war and they became sergeants and lieutenants. They came back with self-respect, a whole different opinion of themselves. Then they went back to Salinas and Oakland and they want to treat you like they were treating you before when you went to the service and that pissed them off!"[16] These veterans became involved with the CSO in order to fight against discrimination. They demanded to be taken seriously as rights-bearing citizens who had fought a war for the preservation of freedom.

The CSO grew rapidly in California as a grassroots organization. Acuña (2004, 279) writes that by the early 1960s, it had thirty-four chapters with a total of ten thousand dues-paying members, but as a grassroots organization it had little institutional support and meager funds. Portrayed by reporter G. W. Sherman of the *Nation* in 1953 as the source of the "political awakening" of the Spanish-speaking minority, the CSO endeavored to transform a "relatively voiceless element in the community into an integrated responsible segment of society" (256). It did so by concentrating primarily on the training of local leaders who were taught to engage in self-help efforts such as neighborhood physical improvements, voter registration, education, housing, and other civil rights projects.[17] The CSO believed that community development happened only by first building internal leadership.[18] In a classic integrationist civil rights move, the CSO leadership hoped to enlist its members in a democratic project and to guide them to participate fully in all aspects of American society. The CSO was committed to giving voice to Mexican Americans as virtuous agents of societal change.

In 1954, the CSO became a national organization whose objectives, as reported in the Los Angeles Daily News (1954, 3), were "to coordinate efforts for the common good of the community" and "encourage active participation of neighbors in civic life and to improve relations among all races, nationalities, and religions." Believing in the power of the vote to leverage demands and reap the promises of democracy, the CSO equated voter registration with progress.[19] It maintained that voter registration drives would "build sufficient community bargaining power throughout the Spanish-speaking neighborhoods to command the attention of the public and private officials who [were] in the position to assist in the neighborhood improvement and group advancement."[20] Voter registration and voting, for the CSO, were the conduits to obtaining help. The organization, however, was not in the business of running political campaigns. Instead, it leveraged the Mexican American vote to support demands from government representatives and elected officials.[21]

The CSO is an understudied organization, and scholarly literature on it focuses primarily on its work in Los Angeles. Yet in Oakland, it had a sizable membership and had tremendous power in mobilizing its members to make use of county and state services and to understand the importance of their vote. Education was a prominent component of the organization's activities, which included citizenship classes, basic English as a second language instruction, and Spanish-language classes led by the head of the educational committee, who was a teacher in the Oakland public schools. By 1956, the Oakland CSO chapter had 143 dues-paying members and a regular attendance of about 75 people at general assembly meetings. The chapter's services included a voter registration program that worked with the Voters League of Alameda County.[22] As in other areas of the US Southwest, Oakland's CSO was focused on building the Mexican American electorate. As CSO activist Elvira Rose recalled: "I walked with the CSO in Oakland when they were pushing the Spanish-speaking people to get out and vote 'cause a lot of them were citizens but they didn't vote."[23]

The CSO focused on creating the next generation of leaders by helping to organize community members to advocate for themselves. Leaders like Alex

Zermeño had come to Oakland from Salinas. As a child from a farmworker family, he was eager to escape the challenging life that his parents endured. As a teenager, Zermeño got involved with the CSO, working as what was called a "bird dog"—he would walk ahead of canvassers going from door to door in order to talk to people and make them feel more comfortable to register to vote. Zermeño attended the CSO's first statewide meeting in Monterey in 1954. He and his parents were impressed by the charismatic leaders they met: Cesar Chavez, Fred Ross, Dolores Huerta, Herman Gallegos, Saul Alinsky, and Jimmy Delgadillo. From that time on, Zermeño remained active in the organization and held various leadership positions. As he described: "My greatest satisfaction of CSO was to see a person realize they were in power. To see somebody you were involved with . . . help them look for answers and see them get up in front of a city hall and make their presentation, man, when they walked away from that podium they were ten feet tall!"[24] Although the CSO trained several high-profile leaders, its real mission was to create a sense of leadership among all its members.

Elvira Rose was a CSO leader with a natural skill for working with people. The daughter of a Costa Rican father and a Mexican American mother, she grew up in West Berkeley, where she served as a broker for her parents and community members alike. As one of the few English speakers in her community, she became the unofficial neighborhood translator at a young age. As she detailed: "Ever since I was little the people would come to my parents and say 'Can Elvira go with me to help me translate . . .' I always liked to help in the community. So people would come and ask me to help them translate . . . they trust you if you are part of the community." In the 1940s, Rose attended UC Berkeley and expanded her work with the Mexican American community through her affiliation with Oakland's CSO chapter. As she described: "We really had to start by having meetings in our house. That's how they start trusting you. They don't come into a building and . . . you know, you gotta build in this confidence in them, like, 'Hey, I'm just like you and I'm trying to help' because it is hard to speak a different language and you just don't trust anybody." When I interviewed Rose, she lived in Berkeley and was under the care of a nurse. We sat in her living room, and I could tell it was difficult for her to remember events and details. She evidenced memory loss, often repeating something she told me a minute before. Despite this, her eyes lit up and her face glowed when she spoke about her work with the church and the CSO. I watched as she once again recalled her youth and the work that shaped her political subjectivity. This politicized work demonstrated how organizations like the CSO cultivated in their leadership a commitment to the improvement of the Mexican American and broader Latino community.

The CSO was also concerned with making sure that Mexican Americans were getting elected to positions of power and holding various commissions and agencies accountable. For example, they pressed for interpreters at the local courts, advocating for this to both the Alameda County Board of Supervisors and the district attorney's office. The CSO newsletter of June 1964 featured an open letter to the Alameda County Board of Supervisors questioning why a Mexican American candidate who had scored as the number one applicant was not selected.[25] The CSO's demand to increase the Spanish-speaking electorate also proved to be a way to push its demands for greater representation in city agencies and elected office. Through both its educational programs with youths and adults and its voter registration drives, the CSO had an immense responsibility not just to provide for the Mexican American community but also to direct this community in a particular fashion. It did so by creating relations with already existing city services and by guiding its membership in the use of these services. It also joined other organizations to protect and defend the Mexican American community.

Coalitional Politics

Mexican American groups accordingly navigated a social movement terrain already heavily contoured by African American protest, which influenced Mexican American forms of activism. To effectively speak the language of racial and ethnic rights in the 1960s, Mexican American activists understood they had to ally with African Americans as racialized subjects. They also carefully crafted a history of their experiences of inequality based on an existing language of civil rights and protest that African Americans had codified through negotiations with the state. Mexican American groups celebrated and in fact emulated both the civil rights gains of African Americans and the urgency of the emergent Black Power movement. However, they understood both the potential openings of each movement strategy and the limitations of militant and radical practices. While they supported a direct linkage with African American civil rights struggles and in fact collaborated with certain groups and campaigns, they also saw the limitations of this movement that did not place their own issues of language and immigration at the center of discussion.

In the postwar years, African Americans made tremendous inroads into city offices and the Democratic Party and garnered substantial political clout in Oakland (Rhomberg 2004; Self 2003). According to historian

Chris Rhomberg (2004, 123), this development was symbolized by the 1954 founding of the Men of Tomorrow, a civic service club of Black business, professional, and religious leaders. In addition, as Gallegos (1989, 33) recalls, African Americans had institutionalized groups like the Urban League and the National Association for the Advancement of Colored People (NAACP), which accomplished a plethora of civil rights gains that helped them garner legitimacy among the white establishment. In Oakland, prominent Black businessmen and politicians were committed to ensuring the advancement of Blacks and understood the War on Poverty to be the fruit of their civil rights struggles.

Mexican American leaders who observed examples of African American institutional power were encouraged at the possibility of developing greater clout for their own community. The idea was not to compete with African Americans. Instead, Mexican Americans had little institutional power and were not seen as a major political force in the city of Oakland. Herman Gallegos and other CSO leaders understood that to start building their own institutions, they had to create alliances with African American groups and also make a claim for the special needs of the Spanish-speaking population. As Gallegos told me: "African Americans had an emerging leadership. There was a group called the Men of Tomorrow, and they used to meet at a restaurant in West Oakland called Slim Jacobs; they would meet there once a month. These were guys that became future mayors, judges. I remember going to one of those luncheon meetings and they were very bright, and I kept thinking: Where are we? We are not anywhere! We are not visible!" Invitations to meetings like those described by Gallegos stemmed from long-term relationships between the two communities, given that they shared political circles and even grew up close to each other. Before the building of the freeway system in Oakland, most Spanish-speaking residents lived in West Oakland, which by the 1960s had become a predominantly African American neighborhood.

Mexican Americans in Oakland accordingly turned to African Americans leaders with whom they had worked and whom they considered friends (Gallegos 1989; Grillo 2000). They relied on two key figures in their community—Jimmy Delgadillo and Evelio Grillo—who both had affiliations with the CSO and the City of Oakland.[26] A community leader extraordinaire and a competitive boxer, Delgadillo was born in West Oakland and grew up with many of the Black leaders of the time. As Alex Zermeño described him: "Jimmy Delgadillo was one of the key guys.... [He was] born and raised in West Oakland. You see, West Oakland before it was a Black neighborhood, it used to be a Chicano neighborhood. He talked like he was a Black from West Oakland; he had the street talk, the slang. He went to Saint Mary's Church there in Oakland, which was the center of Chicano activity."[27] Delgadillo worked closely with Fred Ross in Oakland to help with the consolidation of the CSO and became its first chairman. He also was one of the founding members of what would become the Unity Council. He had a long and illustrious politically active career, much of which stemmed from his affiliations with prominent African American political leaders. For example, he was a childhood friend of William Byron Rumford, the first Black elected official in Northern California, and others who represented Black Democratic power. Like Delgadillo, Evelio Grillo was an Afro-Cuban immigrant who spoke Spanish and was well connected with the city's African American elite; he served as assistant to D. G. Gibson, who became one of the foremost leaders of the California Democratic Party (Grillo 2000, 133). These two figures, because of their African heritage and having grown up alongside African Americans, facilitated alliances between the two communities. This, according to Zermeño, entailed learning to marshal the language of civil rights: "Our only power was to join with the Black community, and their agenda was the same as ours. You know, civil rights, civil rights, civil rights!"[28]

Mexican American organizations such as the CSO joined forces with other groups to push for civil rights legislation. In the 1950s, CSO representatives were part of a civil rights coalition that regularly met with Jewish, Black, Anglo, and trade union leaders to frame their collective strategy for public policy involvement in California. This formal coalition was partially responsible for passage of the Rumford Fair Housing Act in 1964 and earlier, in 1958, the establishment of the Fair Employment Practice Commission (Orozco, Austin, and Beale 2008). In 1963 the Oakland CSO chapter publicly aligned itself in a united front with the NAACP and the Congress of Racial Equality (CORE) against discriminatory practices. The CSO formalized this position in 1963 during its executive board meeting in San Jose where it reaffirmed its national policy and openly advised that a violation of civil rights, or the denial of equal protection under the law, was a matter of historical concern to the CSO, both nationally and at the chapter level.[29] As a result of the CSO's work, twelve families received waivers of the citizenship requirement for admission to low-cost housing managed by the City of Oakland Housing Authority. The CSO committed itself to continuing the struggle for the elimination of this type of citizenship requirement, which it claimed served to "intensify the inequitable burdens on minorities who contribute to the growth and progress of the community."[30]

In addition to Mexican American leaders collaborating and learning from African American leadership models, they also took part in educating their membership about the two groups' shared struggles. Oakland's CSO chapter saw civil rights abuses as a priority and justified alliances with African Americans based on their shared experiences with discrimination. A 1963 Oakland CSO newsletter, for example, acknowledged the formal partnership in antidiscrimination claims through a special feature titled "El Momento Actual" (The current moment), written entirely in Spanish.[31] Utilizing the imagery of brutality against African Americans in Mississippi and a language of compassion and urgency, the piece declared that Mexican Americans should be committed to supporting African American civil rights. In 1963, CSO leaders endeavored to convince their constituency that African American civil rights efforts were equally their struggles:

> It should be noted that this is not a struggle of Negroes against whites, although it might appear this way on the surface. This is something that affects all minority groups, and it is fitting that we the members of other ethnic groups also make this struggle our struggle. Because we are all treated alike we must all identify with this struggle. We must not be mute witnesses or insensitive to another group's pain. Their pain is our pain at the same time that their gains are our gains. It is not just that we abandon that brave race.[32]

This is an example of how Mexican American organizations attempted to construct a shared sense of discrimination by a white oppressor, which they hoped would propel their constituents to defend the civil rights of all minority groups. Oakland's CSO chapter argued that in the Southwest, Mexican Americans overwhelmingly benefited from "Negro" antidiscrimination efforts, such as sanctions against housing discrimination and employment discrimination cases. Similarly, it acknowledged that Mexican Americans shared a parallel experience of police brutality and excessive surveillance by law enforcement. Oakland CSO members were encouraged not just to sympathize with African American struggles but also to analyze experiences of disadvantage through the lens of their own civil rights abuses.

Oakland CSO activists were so adamant in their shared civil rights agenda that they ridiculed Mexican Americans from other regions who were allegedly hesitant to ally with African American struggles. A 1964 CSO newsletter featured an essay titled "What Is the Mexican American Doing in the Civil Rights Movement?" that critiqued the statements of an unnamed Mexican American attorney from Los Angeles who worked for the state attorney general's office. The attorney described the sentiments of Los Angeles Mexican Americans regarding civil rights struggles in the following fashion: "With the tremendous Spanish surname population our group could be a potentially powerful force in the civil rights movement. However, in the past there has been a lack of participation by the so-called grassroots. [T]here are some who have stated that the Mexican-Americans have no problems, others who have stated our problems are different from those of the Negro, and finally we have those who state that if we do have problems, that we should be left alone to solve them in our own manner."[33] Members of the Oakland CSO chapter were outraged by the article and declared that it was ridiculous to suggest that Mexican Americans in Los Angeles remained "selfishly concerned with what is or is not Mexican American, Spanish speaking vs. the problem of the Negro." The Oakland CSO newsletter editors declared that these Mexican Americans had truly lost sight of the problem confronting them and asked: "Have they not seen discrimination in Public Housing, Accommodations, Education and Employment?" The editors were so concerned that they jokingly stated: "Perhaps, it is the music from the Mariachis that blinds them."[34]

The scolding tone of these newsletters can also be read as illustrating the reservations some Oakland-based Mexican Americans had about allying themselves with African American movements. It is not at all surprising that Oakland Mexican American organizations would support African American civil rights struggles, given the extent of friendships and formal relations members of these organizations had with prominent African Americans. More revealing are the Mexican American organizers' emphatic and dedicated attempts to convince their constituents that such alliances were not only necessary but also a matter that directly affected them.

Some organizers feared that associating too closely with African American civil rights would render issues of language discrimination, culture, and immigration of less import. Representatives of the CSO agreed that while the problems of Spanish-speaking groups were not as "exacerbated as the Negro's," their concerns were complicated by the additional fact that many spoke mainly Spanish and thus required different kinds of mobilizing strategies and agendas.[35] As former CSO leader Herman Gallegos (1989, 35) noted: "The issue of color discrimination was much more severe for blacks.... Hispanics were an unknown quantity. We had to overcome the language barrier and the citizenship barrier to become a potent political force so as to get attention. It wasn't because blacks didn't want it; it was just simply that we had to do our own development." Although most Mexican

Americans thus did not question supporting a shared civil rights agenda with African Americans, certain sectors were cautious of the organizational means employed.

Emphasizing their rightful participation as citizens in all aspects of American society, these integrationist Mexican American leaders urged their constituents not to embark on a radical separatist approach akin to the Black Power movement. They wholeheartedly critiqued organizational practices that did not respect an integrationist approach centered on active citizen participation through formal political processes. In a 1966 MAPA newsletter, for example, president Eduardo Quevedo cautioned an expanding constituency about engaging in a separatist radical movement: "Much is heard today of Black power, non-violence versus violence or self-defense … for us Mexican Americans and other Spanish-speaking people in California the idea and slogans of Brown Spanish-speaking Mexican American Power [are] being suggested as a new slogan." While welcoming a new militancy in demanding Mexican American appointments to government and policy-making positions, MAPA admonished militant leaders who discouraged voter registration campaigns. As Quevedo warned: "Today we are hearing many well intentioned Mexican Americans shouting 'we are not going to register any voters unless we get money from the party." He warned of the danger of this approach: "MAPA [was formed] because we had not the 'power' to bring about some significant changes about our living conditions and relationships in our society." For Quevedo, change was only possible "through active political participation" and exerting pressure "by the Mexican American community in the area of policy making."[36] True to this integrationist agenda of the post–World War II period, MAPA readily privileged formal political processes and rightful participation in democratic lobbying as the core values of Mexican American organizations. MAPA and other organizations constructed this idealized practice of citizenship, which they argued could only be employed in a manner that respected the democratic and peaceful principles of the movement.

Building a Mexican American Institutional Presence

At the height of federal investment in the War on Poverty, Mexican American organizations sought recognition and compensation for their labors in community development. Mobilizing on the success of their postwar activism, these organizations expanded their sphere of influence. Given that the federal government distributed War on Poverty funds at the local level and encouraged community organizations and local state agencies to vie for these moneys, Mexican Americans were concerned they did not have enough of an institutionalized presence to effectively compete. At that time the existing organizations, like the CSO, were grassroots membership-based groups without state or private foundation fiscal support. They therefore worked together and consolidated to represent a more coherent and organized voice for Mexican Americans.

One of the initial actions was to consolidate existing organizations. As Orozco, Austin, and Beale (2008) quote from an interview with Arabella Martinez, the first executive director of the Unity Council, "The concern underlined the need for [Mexican American] leaders to collaborate and form a united front and build a local movement. The Mexican American Unity Council was designed to bring together activists and groups and build a cohesive agenda."[37] Building a critical mass required transforming groups such as soccer clubs, church congregations, and brotherhood associations into politicized entities that fit the federal requirements necessary to qualify as War on Poverty Community Action Programs. The Unity Council unified a multiplicity of organizations and committed itself to mobilizing Spanish-speaking residents as a group. The partner organizations included the CSO, the Guadalajara Club, the Neighborhood Project, the People's Institute for Education, the Women's Council of the East Bay, the American GI Forum, MAPA, the Women's Auxiliary, the Organización Mexicana y Comite Pro-Fiestas Patrias de Oakland, the Latin-American Library, the neighborhood Advisory Committee, the Oreden Fraternal Hijos de Puerto Rico, the Club Social Puertoriqueño, the Cooperative Puertorriqueña, and the Filipino American Political Association.[38] Some of these organizations were not exclusively Mexican American; they included Puerto Rican and Filipino organizations, given the shared experiences of both groups with the Spanish language. Furthermore, Filipinos labored alongside Mexican Americans, especially as farmworkers.

The idea of bringing together different groups was not completely new. Activists often wore multiple hats and generally supported a number of groups. As described by many of the activists from this period whom I interviewed, they were at once active with the CSO and the Unity Council and employed by a specific state agency. Elvira Rose, for example, was employed by the California State Department of Labor and was also active as a volunteer with different political action groups. Given that most services were becoming concentrated in Fruitvale, it was easy to facilitate this kind of dynamic interaction with different groups. This was a critical strategy for holding state agencies accountable to the needs of the community. Like Rose, other Mexican American leaders "infiltrated" different government agencies in order to guarantee that resources would be channeled to the community.

This collaborative ethos also had roots in proving the importance of Mexican Americans as a rising voting bloc. Representatives from MAPA and CSO, including James Delgadillo, Bert Corona, and Edward Quevedo, organized Mexican Americans to vote and command greater attention from elected officials. MAPA was formed in 1959 and committed itself to providing an environment "through which the Mexican American can channel his political efforts and demands."[39] The organization's leaders envisioned themselves as stewards in the proper political guidance of the Mexican American population. According to James Delgadillo's letter of July 16, 1965, to Anthony Barbieri of the US Department of Labor, MAPA possessed "special resources which consist of organized statewide rank-and-file citizens, who have had useful work experiences within and offer real hope for the progress of a million Americans of Mexican descent in California."[40] MAPA claimed it could mobilize a "million Americans of Mexican heritage," which it argued constituted "organized rank-and-file citizens [which included] . . . a considerable number of young and determined leaders . . . capable of transposing the responsibilities of citizenship to persons of bilingual cultural background and instill in said persons the incentive to contribute to the fullest extent of their abilities in furthering the vitality of our economical and social betterment."[41]

The fact that Mexican American leaders so eagerly mobilized to qualify for War on Poverty funds did not mean they were not critical of federal funding. In fact, groups held different stances regarding affiliations with the federal government, as can be seen in how leaders shaped Mexican American participation in War on Poverty programs. Leaders were strategic in deciding how organizations would be directly affiliated with the federal War on Poverty. First, they created the Spanish Speaking Citizens Foundation to serve as the sole recipient of federal funding. Many leaders feared that federal money would derail organizations from their mission of empowering Mexican American community members. As Alex Zermeño described, the rationale for setting up a single entity to receive federal funding was to protect the movement's autonomy: "[The Spanish Speaking Citizens Foundation] would get antipoverty money, and it was fine, that was their function. Ideally that's a temporary thing [because when you get federal funding] Uncle Sam owns your ass! And the antipoverty agency for the city owns your butt because if you don't play along, you don't get the money, and if you don't get the money, you don't exist."[42] Leaders like Zermeño were critical of the new kinds of relationships with the federal government primarily because they feared that funding would come with strings. Along with these strings came dependency on federal government funding. As Zermeño details, organizations not only would have to "play along" to sustain their daily operations but also would depend on federal funding in order to simply exist. This critique of the potential for federal co-optation had roots in many of these leaders' activism in the CSO. The CSO's main mission was to respect the concerns of the "indigenous-based community organization" and not have any issues be predetermined by the national office organizers.[43] The CSO staunchly refused federal money in order to remain independent.[44] Ultimately, according to Zermeño, "the idea was to be in a position where you could turn down money, because lots of money comes with strings, officially and unofficially."[45]

The farmworker movement is perhaps the best example of where the War on Poverty had a devastating impact on organizing. According to Erica Kohl-Arenas, the War on Poverty brought substantial resources to the Central Valley where Cesar Chavez and the UFW were organizing. However, it also introduced a plethora of "institutional barriers, organizational turf battles, and limited definitions of farmworker self-help" (Kohl-Arenas 2016, 53). Disparate organizations and leaders in the Central Valley had to navigate this new terrain of funding and programmatic restrictions that ultimately failed to achieve transformative social change.

Crafting Mexican American Spaces

Mexican Americans worked to develop their own linguistically and culturally autonomous spaces for community organizing. As early as 1964, the Unity Council encouraged the City of Oakland to create a program for the development of leadership within the Mexican American community. Additionally, it requested a leadership conference for Mexican Americans, followed by weekly seminars to train and develop leaders. As was reported in a CSO newsletter, this form of leadership development validated Mexican American traditions: "One of the methods of bridging the gap between the Mexican American community and the general community is to create pride and confidence in the Mexican cultural background and to use this added confidence in the individual's respective group and in the broader community."[46] The Unity Council encouraged the creation of these kinds of spaces to foster a greater sense of engagement in the Mexican American community. It did not want to create a separatist form of community organizing. Instead, the goal was to create a strong Spanish-speaking citizenry that could be better advocates for their own linguistic and cultural needs.

This type of leadership development created a sense of ownership in democratic processes. By 1966, the Unity Council had created a Spanish-speaking advisory group specifically geared toward War on Poverty negotiations and programing. According to Jack Ortega, then chairman of the Unity Council, "For the first time, the poverty program was explained to these people, and they were made to feel that there was a place in it for them."[47] In a letter to the head of the Oakland CAA, Ortega extolled the success of the newly created meeting space: "The group is expanding rapidly, and wishes to continue on this basis—not because we want to isolate ourselves from other minority groups, but rather because we feel that, in this way, we can best resolve the problems of communication and cultural differences that are peculiar to the Spanish-speaking people of this area."[48] As Ortega detailed, Mexican American community groups understood that their cultural and linguistic differences made it difficult for them to fully participate in the larger society. By representing the Mexican American community and fostering culturally inclusive meeting spaces, leaders sought to address and direct the demands of this population.

In addition to the creation of the Spanish-speaking advisory group, Mexican American organizations pushed the City of Oakland to establish a Spanish-speaking Target Area Advisory Committee (TAAC). This was a significant accomplishment given that Oakland's TAACs were originally designed to represent communities in four geographic areas: East Oakland, North Oakland, West Oakland, and Fruitvale. The fifth TAAC, which became known as the Fruitvale Spanish-Speaking Committee, was the only one defined by language and culture. This committee ultimately challenged the geographic definitions of antipoverty programs and demanded the recognition of Oakland's Spanish-speaking population. Mexican American groups argued that unlike African Americans, Spanish-speaking residents were not confined to one specific geographic location; they were dispersed widely throughout the city and beyond (Brasher 1966; Wood 1968). Although War on Poverty stipulations privileged "community" as the unit of analysis, they emphasized a geographic, place-based understanding of organizing and belonging. For Mexican American leaders, community was far more than geography, uniting an ethnic/racial collective that cohered around a shared agenda of social, cultural, and political improvement throughout the Southwest. Clearly, Mexican Americans and other Spanish speakers were already congregating in Fruitvale, but this was not a bounded, insular terrain.

Mexican American admission into War on Poverty programs quickly transformed organizations like the Unity Council and altered their activities. Oakland's Unity Council started as a political action group. With the advent of the War on Poverty, it became an institutionalized social services provider. As a service-providing organization, it attained antipoverty funding to create various programs, including Education for Advancement, which offered ESL classes. The centerpiece of the Unity Council's transformation was the creation of Fruitvale's Latin American Library, which offered books in the Spanish language and was funded through a direct grant of $100,000 of federal antipoverty funds (Pressman 1975, 59). In fact, most of the activists I interviewed remember the Unity Council's first Latin American Library, which was the first of its kind in Oakland to offer books in Spanish and dedicated to Mexican American culture. It also became an important meeting place for events and gatherings. Additionally, the California Department of Labor established one of its employment service centers in Oakland's Unity Council office, working with the council to ensure that Spanish-speaking residents could access the deluge of job training programs created by War on Poverty funding.[49] The Unity Council became an institutionalized presence in Oakland, serving as both an advocacy group and a meeting point for different community services.

Institutionalization allowed the Unity Council to quickly gain a sense of permanence in the Fruitvale community. In 1967 the Unity Council officially became a 501(c)(3) tax-exempt nonprofit organization. By 1970 it purchased its first building, located at 1470 Fruitvale Avenue, at the heart of the Fruitvale community where Mexican Americans were quickly becoming the majority. This form of institutionalization was therefore a spatial endeavor. Along with the Unity Council, other organizations began to emerge in Fruitvale (see chapters 1 and 5). The Unity Council became a kind of community anchor, setting in motion the creation of other organizations and routing resources into the community.

Given the invisibility of Mexican Americans in government-funded poverty studies, Mexican American organizations also conducted their own research. They leveraged their authority on the needs of Spanish-speaking residents to forge a cohesive programmatic agenda for their constituency and in the process created a distinct target of government—the Mexican American community. As early as 1965, for example, representatives of MAPA, the CSO, and the Unity Council worked together with the City of Oakland to produce a report titled *Staff Report of a Mexican American Community Development Survey and Resulting Proposal*.[50] The report was the product of months of interviews and collaboration between different Mexican American organizations and City of Oakland staff members. It revealed the lack of access Mexican Americans confronted in gaining city services and recommended the creation of bridging programs to connect Mexican Americans to existing services. In this proposal, Mexican American leaders envisioned a comprehensive package of care rooted in cultural revitalization, empowerment, and inclusion in the broader US culture. Their proposal sought to "inculcate in the Spanish surname community a pride in its historical and cultural heritage."[51] To do so, leaders hoped "to create in the people an awareness that their forebears played an outstanding role in the exploration, settlement and development of this country and in contributing to the establishment of its institutions."[52] Mexican Americans did not need to feel excluded from access to civic services; they were entitled to these benefits because they themselves had helped to create them, armed with a sense of pride in their culture and their rightful claims as citizens. In their negotiations with the City of Oakland, leaders thus gave coherence to the term *Mexican American community* for the first time and articulated a set of mutually shared interests, needs, and desires.

The formalization of this designation was at once a valorization of Mexican culture and language heritage and also an homage to the important contributions Mexican Americans had made in the United States. This was a specific response to official US Census use of identifiers such as "whites with Spanish surname" that leaders claimed led to the undercounting of the Mexican American population. In Oakland, Mexican Americans' widespread identification as Spanish-speaking allowed them to ally with other groups such as Puerto Ricans and Filipinos that spoke a common language. The Unity Council therefore changed its name to the Spanish Speaking Unity Council in 1967 in order to portray its solidarity with other Spanish-speaking groups and to significantly expand its constituency. However, this language-based identifier did not adequately portray the racial/ethnic experiences of discrimination and inequality particular to Mexican Americans. Like African Americans, Mexican American leaders also understood the War on Poverty to be a form of compensation for racial injustices of the past. The term *Mexican American community* solidified their position as a group that shared experiences of racialized oppression and inequality.

Mexican American organizations took seriously their role as mediators between the Mexican American population and different state agencies. In their exchanges with state agencies such as the California Department of Employment, the City of Oakland, and federal antipoverty offices, Mexican

American leaders requested that these agencies be sensitive to the needs of a rising Mexican American population but also informed them that they were prepared to guide the community to vote in a particular fashion and to empower Mexican Americans as citizens for full civic participation. Newly created nonprofit organizations, as embodied by groups like the Unity Council, emerged as the principal stewards of the Mexican American community. Furthermore, these institutions became concentrated in the Fruitvale neighborhood—a place that was quickly becoming Mexican American and predominantly working-class.

Conclusion

Though War on Poverty programs had many limitations from the onset, they constituted unique political and institutional openings for local-based organizations and political action groups. As a devolutionary governmental program, the War on Poverty set up the architecture for the inclusion of nonstate entities—community-based nonprofit organizations—into a new schema of welfare provision. This served to transform grassroots movements into institutionalized federally recognized tax-exempt nonprofit agencies. This process shifted organizational goals from leadership development and advocacy to the proper management of programs and community development projects and aided in subduing the urgency and rising militancy of grassroots protest.

Robert O. Self's *American Babylon* (2003, 200) argues that for African Americans in Oakland, War on Poverty efforts "constituted a discrete phase in the evolution of black political capacity" and transformed Oakland's political culture. The War on Poverty equally catapulted Mexican Americans into political action. Not unlike their African American allies, Mexican Americans also deployed the War on Poverty agenda of empowerment to build leadership capacity and to consolidate disparate Spanish-speaking organizations into a united Mexican American movement. The War on Poverty did not initiate Mexican American activism; rather, it served to consolidate already active political organizations that together transformed themselves into institutionalized entities that guided the Spanish-speaking population and leveraged their pastoral technologies of government to represent, care for, and constitute the Mexican American community.

Through different culture-based projects of empowerment, Mexican American community-based organizations set in place specific power relationships. As Barbara Cruikshank (1999, 69) reminds us: "Whether inspired by the market or by the promise of self-government and autonomy, the object of empowerment is to act upon another's interests and desires in order to conduct their actions toward an appropriate end." Bestowed with responsibilities of care that included bridging relations between the state and the Mexican American population, organizations enacted governmental technologies of their own. These political techniques deployed the language of "empowerment" prioritized by federal antipoverty programs but rendered it Mexican American by suturing it with a project of cultural revitalization.

Enacting diverse culture-mediated technologies of citizenship, community-based political organizations sought to educate Mexican Americans about their shared interests, many of which parroted the state's integrationist agenda of democratic civic engagement. However, whereas War on Poverty programs focused on individual attainment, whether through job training, educational advancement, or self-development programs, Mexican American groups insisted on achieving collective improvement. These organizations thus enacted relations of government that both constituted and fundamentally transformed not a universal citizen-subject but a collective of Mexican American subjects. This collective of Mexican American subjects as well as their demands, organizational tactics, and relationship to the state emerged through a carefully crafted relationship with the civil rights movement and Black radicalism of the time.

Mexican American political mobilizations of this period unsettled the geography of both race and poverty in Oakland. Through their activism and institution-building endeavors, they also consolidated Fruitvale as a Mexican American community, with Mexican American organizations as its principle stewards. They challenged the automatic conflation of poverty with blackness and began to articulate their own unique experience of racial inequality and poverty that differentiated Mexican Americans from Blacks. By stressing the importance of issues of language and culture discrimination as well as experiences of international migration, Mexican American leaders cultivated their own organizing agendas and programmatic efforts. This historical account of the political formation of the Mexican American community offers a window into the study of changing racial/ethnic dynamics in post–World War II Oakland beyond the Black and white binary. The War on Poverty was thus an important period for the consolidation of Mexican American institutions such as the Unity Council and other community-based organizations that continue to provide services and guide Mexican American and other Latino constituents in Oakland.

REVOLUTION INTERRUPTED

The revolution will not be televised
Will not be televised
Will not be televised
Will not be televised
The revolution will be no re-run, brothers
The revolution will be live

Gil Scott-Heron, "The Revolution Will Not Be Televised"

Fruitvale, like any landscape, reflects a particular sedimentation of power relations. The entire neighborhood is significantly marked by one organization—the Unity Council. From the community's most prominent architectural symbol, Fruitvale Transit Village, to the Fruitvale Public Market, the annual Día de los Muertos Festival that attracts more than 100,000 people, and the street signage that signals community institutions, these representations of the neighborhood emanate from the same institution. Some of this tentacular reach also takes shape in the form of policy briefs, newspaper reporting, and lobbying on the neighborhood's behalf. There is no doubt that the Unity Council powerfully represents itself as the neighborhood's principal steward.

The neighborhood overflows with Unity Council spatial productions largely as a result of social movement institutionalization. The Unity Council began as a grassroots attempt to create a united voice for Mexican Americans in Oakland. In the late 1960s, it joined a sea of other minority groups that utilized newly formed community-based organizations to advance their cause. In this process, many formerly grassroots minority organizations quickly became professionalized and corporatized institutions. Institutionalization is often thought of in broad terms—as a process by which organizations become formalized, consolidate leadership, create a governance structure, enact programing, and so forth. In sum, this is largely understood as an aspatial process. However, Fruitvale reveals that institutionalization impacts the production of space. Furthermore, it also entails geographic connections forged through policy interventions, funding streams, and regulatory mechanisms often imposed from afar.

Institutionalization is also a contested process rife with contradictions and conflicts. At the start, minority organizations were armed with a revolutionary spirit of grassroots organizing. These institutions promoted a self-help mandate that prioritized neighborhood autonomy. Services and organizations would be designed by and for the community and not directed by outside forces. Even the social service approach contained a more transformative potential that was fervently political.[1] However, as projects developed and community demand for programming also grew, activists encountered a new dilemma—how would they attain economic resources to grow and maintain the services? And subsequently, how could organizations preserve the grassroots call for autonomy?

Activists wrestled with the inherent paradoxes of procuring funding from private foundations and confronted a new set of uneven power relationships. In these early stages of Chicano institution-building, philanthropic funding seemed like a panacea that could ensure the longevity and growth of institutions (see Gallegos 1989; Kohl-Arenas 2015). The most important player quickly became the Ford Foundation, which funded desegregation battles in schools, supported numerous Black service organizations, and financed the development of Black arts institutions (see K. Ferguson 2013). Through its funding, it strove to convince racial minorities that electoral politics could be an effective nonviolent terrain of struggle. The foundation believed that with the 1965 passage of the Voting Rights Act an unprecedented expansion of the minority electorate could be achieved.[2] It therefore made minority voter registration one of its top priorities.

Despite initial optimism, activists' relationships with private foundations were tempered with uncertainty. Chicano activists were not blind to the potential limitations of philanthropic funding. Well versed in Marxism, many activists were openly suspicious of money derived from capitalist exploitation, or what Erica Kohl-Arenas (2016) calls "twice stolen money" (see also Gilmore 2017).[3] They proceeded with caution and actively negotiated with philanthropic agencies, trying ever so carefully to hustle foundation money without losing sight of the social justice mission they envisioned.[4]

The federal government was also an important player in contouring the terrain of 1960s contentious politics. Most scholarship on this era has focused on the policing of radicalism, calling attention to how the federal government feared the rise of militancy among race-based social movements. The FBI's Counterintelligence Program, popularly known in activist circles as COINTELPRO, for example, surveilled and infiltrated many social movement organizations deemed radical or subversive. However, even the most moderate African American and Mexican American organizations were targeted. This happened both through FBI surveillance and indirectly via congressional scrutiny of the agency that funded these projects—the Ford Foundation. More specifically, federal agencies raised caution regarding the Ford Foundation's funding of minority voter registration projects.[5]

To demonstrate the impacts of federal and philanthropic regulation, I chronicle the formation of the Southwest Council of La Raza (SCLR), one of the first 501(c)(3) Mexican American nonprofit organizations in the nation.[6] Created to provide fiscal and administrative support for organizations throughout the Southwest, SCLR channeled Ford Foundation funds to Mexican American grassroots groups, including Oakland's Unity Council, with the goal of improving Mexican American neighborhoods through nonviolent advocacy and leadership development projects. Despite its relatively "safe" and power-evasive operations, within a year of its inception, SCLR came under close watch from the Ford Foundation.

Federal scrutiny came in the form of tax congressional reform in 1969 that increased federal oversight of private philanthropy and forcefully prohibited nonprofit organizations from engaging in political processes. Congress was concerned with the role of private philanthropy in both funding and organizing minority projects. Once imposed, the tax reform stymied the political fervor of 1960s social movements. This was a historical turning point in the incorporation of racialized movements into what were deemed more appropriate and moderate modes of mobilizing. Federal policing of Ford Foundation projects resulted in new philanthropic programmatic limitations on the foundation's nonprofit grantees. Although the federal government strictly linked "politics" with electoral processes, in practice the antipolitical mandate de-radicalized nonprofit projects because leaders feared that their actions would be prohibited.

Community development corporations (CDCs) were born at the intersection of these intense political debates, offering a new place-based, public-private model for economic and social development of the nonwhite poor (K. Ferguson 2013, 211). Coordinating social movement leadership, private philanthropy, and private industry, the CDC aimed to uplift minority neighborhoods by privileging capitalist economic development and other entrepreneurial projects. This new nonprofit entity sought to redirect activist energy from challenging institutional inequalities (including upsetting electoral politics) to productions of space. Because the Unity Council was intimately linked to Ford Foundation funding through SCLR, it quickly transformed itself into one of the nation's first Chicano CDCs.

The Ford Foundation model of economic development erased the plurality and local specificity of community approaches to care. Put differently, it privileged a singular approach to community improvement (economic development) in a context in which activists favored multiple methods of securing the well-being of the racialized poor. Most radicalized projects in Fruitvale, for example, focused on unhinging power relations and challenging US imperialism, capitalist inequality, and racism. The CDC model—although fortified with a mandate of transforming impoverished areas into respectable, upwardly mobile Chicano spaces—paled in comparison to the revolutionary visions of change that emblematized the 1960s. This model of community-based development, which also privileged the depoliticized delivery of services, however, quickly became the most respected and financially supported nationally. State officials, private corporations, and philanthropic agencies continue to support these kinds of projects with measurable "deliverables."

These social-political processes did not happen abstractly—the power relations became sedimented in specific places and subsequently contoured dynamics in neighborhoods like Fruitvale. Federal regulation, like philanthropic funding, limited the political fervor of 1960s social movements by constricting dynamic and manifold approaches to neighborhood improvement. The congressional move to regulate Mexican American Ford Foundation grantees exposes the limitations of philanthropic funding and its ability to effect social change.

Philanthropy and 1960s Social Movements

In her pathbreaking book *The Self-Help Myth*, Erica Kohl-Arenas examines how private foundations transformed US social movements and grassroots institutions in the decades following the 1960s. Her work demonstrates that "from the establishment of the Rockefeller, Carnegie, and Ford Foundations to the multiple general-purpose foundations making grants to nonprofit organizations today, philanthropic giving has clearly defined boundaries" (Kohl-Arenas 2016, 35). Benjamin Marquez (2003, 330) has also argued that foundation money began to transform Mexican American political mobilizations beginning in the 1950s, revealing that by funding social movements, Anglo-administered institutions had a profound influence on the contours of Mexican American political activity. Historian Karen Ferguson (2013, 11) reaches a similar conclusion regarding the Ford Foundation's relationship with Black organizations, suggesting that the "asymmetry of power relationships between the Ford Foundation and its Black grantees meant that the Foundation's social vision prevailed." As a result, projects designed to ameliorate inequality in fact privileged the prerogatives of powerful white interests and their deep investments in the status quo.

Partnerships between private philanthropy and social movements began with lofty goals that were ultimately hampered by ambivalence regarding the transformational potential of philanthropic funding. In the 1960s, both state and philanthropic agencies agreed that community action among the poor should be encouraged (Kohl-Arenas 2016). Yet it was unclear whether community action would maintain the status quo or instead encourage consciousness-raising and revolutionary action. However, a common thread in philanthropic funding was its consistent programmatic effort to draw attention away from critiques of structural inequality and antagonism (Kohl-Arenas 2015, 799). To this day, philanthropic funding frameworks exclude questions that challenge relationships of power and systems of inequality that contribute to enduring poverty and disempowerment. Instead, as described in chapter 2, foundation-funded projects consistently focused on the behaviors of the poor and shifted attention away from relationships of power that produce and maintain poverty and inequality.

As Kohl-Arenas explains, this is not a straightforward story of private philanthropy imposing its own agenda on Chicano social movement actors. The process was much more nuanced, involving compromises among differently positioned stakeholders. In fact, activists were the first to court foundations in order to make Mexican Americans legible to philanthropic agencies. Furthermore, nonprofit institutionalization and professionalization were pivotal to many leaders' goals and organizational methods. They understood that building institutions required access to state funding and heavy investments from private foundations. However, as late as the 1950s, Mexican American organizations were completely off the radar of private foundations and the bulk of federal poverty alleviation programs. As members of SCLR soon realized, the central racial issue of the time involved the alleviation of African American disadvantage: "Every time we would have a legitimate set of complaints to present to city hall, Watts was burning or Rochester was burning and the federal money was going to the black programs. This was also a source of frustration to la Raza."[7]

Foundations viewed Mexican Americans as "the other minority" and modeled their programmatic funding agendas on a longer history of working with African American institutions.[8] Like their funding strategies for African Americans, philanthropic foundations funded Mexican American organizations to "help" this minority group appropriately incorporate into American society. As Marquez (2003, 333) writes, foundations encouraged Mexican American leaders to create large bureaucratic organizations modeled after already existing African American institutions such as the Urban League and the National Association for the Advancement of Colored People (NAACP). The Mexican American Legal Defense and Education Fund (MALDEF), for example, was incorporated in 1968 with a five-year, $2.2 million start-up grant from the Ford Foundation (Acuña 2004, 316; Marquez 2003, 333; Tijerina 1968).

The Ford Foundation and the Midcentury "Urban Problem"

The Ford Foundation saw itself as a pioneer in the quest to find peaceful solutions to 1960s inner-city unrest. From 1965 to 1969, the foundation, under the presidency of McGeorge Bundy, granted more than $100 million in the area of "rights for minorities" (K. Ferguson 2013, 1). By 1970, spending for this purpose reached 40 percent of the foundation's budget for domestic programs. This funding was intended to "cool inner cities" in a context of massive urban unrest throughout the United States. At the height of civil rights struggles, minority communities protested overpolicing and government disinvestment in the inner city. Popularly understood as "riots," these forms of urban unrest brought national attention to racial segregation and economic inequality—a set of conditions that became euphemistically referred to as the midcentury urban problem. In this context of violence tied with the rising militancy of Black Power, the Ford Foundation hoped to educate minority groups about the importance of voting as an alternative to violence. It therefore worked with minority-run social movements to promote its program of democratic integration.

In order to bring a more diverse set of social movement organizations into the foundation's fold, its funding went from a strict integrationist approach (which funded primarily civil rights groups) to one that tolerated and at times even advocated the development of separatists movements (K. Ferguson 2007). The foundation therefore included militant groups within its grantees to educate them on more reformist methods of mobilizing. Furthermore, the Ford Foundation encouraged minority groups to develop their own separatist agendas during a period of transition, but without losing sight of the ultimate step of full integration. The foundation focused on programs that stressed "economic and educational advancement of disadvantaged minority groups" even within segregated settings, with the understanding that these programs would "in time normalize social integration" (quoted in K. Ferguson 2007, 85). By 1968, the Ford Foundation's new Division of National Affairs was explicit in its promotion of this model. In defending grant proposals directed at increasing the group identity and power of minorities, the Ford Foundation insisted that "in black identity (at least those manifestations free of reverse racism and destructive apartheidism) may lie the social strength that played so critical a part in the rise of other urban ethnic groups to political and economic status" (K. Ferguson 2007, 85). The foundation strategically selected radical and even Black nationalist organizations in order to promote their incorporation into a more integrationist agenda.

The Ford Foundation's attempts to steward African American projects is best exemplified by its surprising relationship with the Congress of Racial Equality (CORE). By the mid-1960s, CORE had shed its integrationist civil rights agenda and had become more Black nationalist and militant. As historian Karen Ferguson (2013) reveals, Ford Foundation funding of CORE was intended to steer the organization into what were deemed safer and more moderate projects. The foundation was strategic in establishing its relationship to CORE and took great care to direct its programmatic projects. On July 14, 1967, it awarded CORE a $175,000 grant to establish a Target City voter registration and leadership training project for inner-city African Americans in Cleveland (K. Ferguson 2007, 67). The Target City project in Cleveland, according to the Ford Foundation, strove to attain "the development of full, effective and responsible citizenship (as the alternative to civil disorder)."[9] The foundation continued to fund CORE activities after the Target City project through what it called Special Purpose Funds, which CORE utilized to develop programs in voter registration, youth leadership development, community relations, and economic development. Its most successful projects were voter registration and youth leadership development as it enlisted a broad base of support among community members. In

July 1969, for example, Mitchell "Mike" Sviridoff sent a letter to McGeorge Bundy, president of the Ford Foundation, applauding CORE for its work at preventing further violent unrest in Cleveland.[10] As Sviridoff wrote: "[CORE's] voter registration efforts have been important.... [CORE] also helped Mayor Stokes cool the ghetto after the assassination of Martin Luther King; and it has contributed to the feeling that positive things are on the way in Cleveland—a sharp contrast from last year's sentiment. It has served as a link between militant black groups, more moderate Negro groups, City Hall and business groups.... And—it has kept out of trouble."[11] Ford Foundation funds to CORE operated on multiple fronts to advance the foundation's approach to race-based organizations. First, the Ford Foundation created new and more expansive monitoring processes to assess neighborhood-level dynamics. The foundation was cautious in its affiliation with CORE and maintained oversight of activities through reports and site visits from program officers, ensuring that the organization was keeping out of trouble. As a Ford Foundation report of CORE activities stressed, "The Voter Education and Registration Program seeks to demonstrate that the political process is a realistic alternative to violence."[12] In a similar fashion, youth projects were aimed at channeling leadership into more moderate approaches. The 1967–68 program, for example, was expanded in order to concentrate on "youth who are presently occupying positions of leadership in anti-social gangs and who would provide different leadership in activities that were less destructive if they understood how to affect the establishment within the system."[13] Ultimately, the Ford grant strengthened those within CORE who had been moving that organization toward translating the slogan "Black Power" into a program of economic development. Therefore, the evaluation of the success of CORE's activities was based on its ability to broker interactions between different constituents and its efforts to pacify both urban unrest and Black militancy.

The Southwest Council of La Raza

Unlike African Americans, Mexican Americans were not on the radar of the foundation world. In 1963, Herman Gallegos, one of the most prominent Bay Area Mexican American leaders, met the vice president of the Ford Foundation while working in Hunters Point, a predominantly Black neighborhood in San Francisco. Gallegos recounts people's confusion when they saw him, a Mexican American, serving as an executive director of a Black youth project. He was asked: "'What is a Mexican American doing working in a black neighborhood?' I said, 'Well, it doesn't appear that [the

Ford Foundation] funds Mexican American projects, and so I have no other place to go to do what I like to do'" (Gallegos 1989, 36).

Through its affiliations with Bay Area leaders such as Herman Gallegos and Dr. Ernesto Galarza, the Ford Foundation began to align itself with Mexican American activists and organizations throughout the Southwest.[14] On June 10, 1968, the Ford Foundation awarded the SCLR a grant of $630,000 to become a 501(c)(3) tax-exempt organization. Funds were issued to Dr. Julian Samora, Dr. Ernesto Galarza, and Herman Gallegos, who then enlisted a diverse group of organizers and leaders of the Mexican American community to serve as SCLR's governing board. These participants represented a broad spectrum of organizations with both moderate and radical tendencies. The invited participants included self-described Chicano activists such as Maclovio Barrazo, an organizer with the AFL-CIO; Bert Corona, president of the Community Service Organization; and Alex Mercure, then a teacher in New Mexico alongside more reformist members like Albert Peña, an elected official from Texas.[15]

The SCLR organizers had ambitious plans to establish a set of community-driven barrio projects inspired by the farmworkers movement (Gallegos 1989, 68; Garcia 1994, 228; Mora 2009, 68). From the outset they did not want to create a centralized institutionalized organization like the NAACP or MALDEF. The initial organizers believed that the issues confronting Mexican Americans were far too diverse and spread out geographically for a centralized organization to adequately address all their needs. Instead, the organizers endeavored to channel funds directly to the grass roots, with a fundamental goal of social change—a vision that included immediate economic and leadership development projects, in addition to advocacy for the transformation of various institutions. This social change ideology was based on the ideas of liberation theology and Paulo Freire. As activist Bert Corona detailed in his memoir, leaders believed they needed participation of the people to achieve real political power: "[We were] impressed with what the farmworkers and César Chávez were doing, and we looked to the farmworkers' union as a model. ... In the barrios, it would involve a strong barrio organization. It would have to be an organization that would go into every nook and cranny of the barrios. The idea was to establish *concilios*, or councils, everywhere. ... These *concilios* would meet regularly to discuss common problems and to plan strategy for combatting the establishment" (Garcia 1994, 228). This mandate to support grassroots community efforts fit nicely within the Ford Foundation's goal of fostering minority-based organizations and leadership. It differed, however, from the foundation's emphasis on funding institutions and not grassroots struggles. It also differed in terms of the organization's goals. Whereas SCLR hoped to develop grassroots projects that would collectively combat the establishment, the Ford Foundation represented the very establishment that activists sought to dismantle, meaning its money stemmed from capitalists and the foundation was run overwhelmingly by elite white men.

In order to channel funding to community-based projects, SCLR pushed the Ford Foundation to allow it to become a subgrantee organization. SCLR opted to give local groups full responsibility and substantial freedom to operate. However, it closely aligned with the different community groups and quickly established methods by which it could monitor its subgrantees. The SCLR board members were concerned with assuring that the funds were used properly and that proposals were translated into actual programming and successful projects. One board member, Mario Vasquez, expressed fears about "falling flat on our faces" and questioned the level of responsibility SCLR would have over the actions of its subgrantees.[16]

SCLR worked closely with local groups in San Antonio, Los Angeles, and the San Francisco Bay Area to help them articulate clear goals and objectives. Each local organization was presented with a supplementary terms document outlining guidelines governing SCLR's relationship to local councils and neighborhood groups. Like CORE's projects in Cleveland, SCLR's board of directors wanted local groups to actively target youths. For example, SCLR recommended that Oakland's Unity Council develop greater student representation. Furthermore, it requested that students be part of the Unity Council's board of directors and also urged the local groups to have greater barrio community representation. Toward these ends, SCLR granted $2,500 to Oakland's La Causa Inc. to organize a student conference that brought together fifty to eighty student leaders from throughout the Southwest. Furthermore, SCLR scheduled meetings between student groups and its board of directors in order to "iron out ideological differences." The SCLR board understood its role as helping to stimulate, revitalize, and maintain intergroup and intragroup communication of Mexican American student and youth groups, and link them with resources.[17]

The arrival of Ford Foundation money fortified Mexican American translocal organizing and networking. Money for travel and meetings facilitated communication among different factions of Mexican American activists. According to Gallegos (1989, 64): "At that time, many Hispanics knew about each other but had never really met.[18] There were people like Reies Lopez Tijerina whom I had read about and heard about. I had never met him until the Ford grant. People—like Corkie Gonzales, Grace Olivarez—we were known to each other but had never met because we had no resources. So when [the Ford Foundation] asked us to go out, we began to sit down, and I talked to Reies Tijerina about the whole land grant issue and spent time with him." These interactions convened both radical and reformist Mexican American leaders and were instrumental in improving their organizational and collaborative potential. They united Mexican Americans as a group whose members shared conditions of inequality across the entire Southwest. Such encounters funded by the Ford Foundation, however, also sought to bring more radical groups into the foundation's goal of democratic integration.

SCLR funding transformed its subgrantees into 501(c)(3) nonprofit organizations. Prior to receiving Ford Foundation money, barrio organizations had been supported through membership dues as well as volunteer and other support services. They were true grassroots political organizations that met in members' homes; they were not directly in the business of service provision but instead coordinated services by referring clients to existing city and county services. Getting access to SCLR funding was their first formalized form of monetary aid and their first contact with the bureaucratic machinery of both private foundations and federal agencies that recognized them as tax-exempt organizations. Some of these leaders did not even know what a 501(c)(3) organization was or truly understand how to run a privately funded organization (Gallegos 1989, 69). One SCLR member recalled a community activist who "thought the Ford Foundation was a garment that women wear."[19] Furthermore, SCLR staff worried about community distrust: "The Chicano community was so fed up with brokers and so suspicious of people who came in carrying briefcases."[20]

Oakland's Unity Council utilized Ford Foundation money to fund small projects that engaged in community advocacy and leadership training. It issued mini-grants of approximately $1,000 each to a collection of small organizations in Oakland (Orozco, Austin, and Beale 2008, 21). The Unity Council hoped to develop and train smaller organizations with the aim of fulfilling the SCLR mission of promoting leadership development in communities. The mini-grant recipients included a Mexican American newspaper; the paper of the Oakland Brown Berets, a Chicano youth organization that mobilized in a militant fashion akin to the Black Panthers; the Filipino American Political Association; and Frente, a UC Berkeley Mexican American student organization. This group of organizations was varied not only in their purpose but also in their organizational tendencies. Some groups, like the Brown Berets, were much more radical than the others and could easily raise concern among conservative and moderate constituents. The Unity Council decided to fund these organizations because it deemed them to be most in need of leadership development. It also believed that these organizations were at the forefront of community needs and desires. It helped to train these membership-based organizations to apply for Unity Council mini-grants and gave them their first experience with a formal application process. Through these funding processes, the Unity Council established relationships of mutual support among existing community-based organizations.

The 1969 Tax Reform Act

Mexican Americans' initial engagement with private foundations proved to be productive of political and economic openings. Additionally, Ford Foundation funding legitimized them as institutions that could be trusted. Federal authorities were not blind to the triangulations of nonprofit organizations, social movement actors, and philanthropic foundations. Responding to media and lobbying from conservatives, Congress became vigilant of race-based organizations' escalating authority within communities of color. Lawmakers were especially concerned with the success of voter registration projects headed by both CORE and SCLR. By proxy, they also kept a close watch on the philanthropic organizations that funded them. In what follows I analyze key Mexican American and African American mobilizations that accelerated congressional moves to establish new limitations on private philanthropy, which culminated in the Tax Reform Act of 1969. This congressional regulation policed foundations' funding practices, which subsequently delimited their grantees' programmatic efforts. The tax reform was therefore part of a constellation of responses to race-based organizations that limited the expansion of their political movements.

The Ford Foundation envisioned itself as a philanthropic institution empowered to guide minority groups into appropriate forms of mobilizing. It worked hard to bring more militant Mexican American organizations into its purview. SCLR leaders understood that philanthropic funding was aimed at preventing further militancy among Mexican American organizations, and many of these leaders themselves firmly advocated nonviolence. According to Gallego's (1989) oral history, the Ford Foundation funded SCLR to broker relationships with groups that it deemed militant and potentially violent. Gallegos (1989, 65) specifically recounts fear of the rising militancy spearheaded by Reies López Tijerina and the land-grant issues occurring in New Mexico, which he reported to Ford officials could "erupt in violence unless something is done to resolve the claims that Reies is presenting."

Ford Foundation oversight of SCLR-funded activities and its subgrantee organizations, however, was never panoptic. In fact, because of the diversity of programmatic efforts that Mexican American communities needed, the foundation granted much more autonomy to SCLR than it normally did to its grantees. This relative autonomy allowed SCLR to fund some of what it deemed as more "protest"-based activities, which included voter registration programs designed to raise consciousness about electoral processes and several demonstrations and marches (Mora 2009, 72). SCLR also equipped community affiliates with resources to organize conferences and rallies. One of these community affiliates in San Antonio, for example, funded the Mexican American Youth Organization (MAYO) student conferences that protested racial discrimination in public schooling. MAYO, which was made up of second-, third-, and fourth-generation students, organized against what it deemed rampant discrimination and enforced social constraints in the Texas educational system (Acuña 2004, 316). Its membership was key to the establishment of the Raza Unida Party, an alternative third party that began in Texas and eventually spread throughout the Southwest. Chicana/o leaders formed the Raza Unida Party because they believed that a third party was necessary, since neither the Democratic Party nor the Republican Party truly represented their issues. These supporters of the Raza Unida Party were frustrated that although they routinely supported Democratic Party candidates, the party failed to honor some of their basic demands as Chicana/o constituents (see J. A. Gutierrez 1999; Pulido 2006, 114).

Mexican American Youth Organization Conflict

Chicano movement activism entailed multiple fronts. As Chicano activists advanced their own electoral campaigns and voter registration drives, they infused them with a sense of urgency and militancy. Young leaders envisioned electoral gains as far more than merely entering US mainstream politics. They viewed electoral advances as a major means of challenging white dominance in political and economic processes. The Ford Foundation, under pressure from Congress, became concerned that SCLR subgrantees, like the Mexican American Youth Organization, were endorsing violence. On April 8, 1969, a public speech by Jose Angel Gutierrez, a prominent MAYO leader, gained national attention because he was accused of endorsing antiwhite hatred.[21] Gutierrez's statement negatively impacted public and congressional perception of SCLR-funded projects. As Gallegos (1989) recounts:

> Jose was appearing to advocate violence. He made some comments about "getting rid of the Anglos." [People wondered,] "You mean, kill them?" He said, "Well, you can take it any way you want." Well, that's all that Congress wanted to hear because the next thing you know, the accusation was that Ford was funding programs to foment violent behavior. What Jose Angel Gutierrez was saying was, "Look, we are 90 percent of the population in city after city, but we don't control any of the bread or the beer delivery franchises, we have no economic control of those towns." His idea was to get rid of the Anglos and let Mexicans own a piece of the pie. (70)

As evidenced by Gallegos's recounting of the incident, Gutierrez's statement was not militant per se. Instead, congressional and public response to his statement raised another key issue: white political and economic elites' fear regarding increased Mexican American electoral gains and growing economic clout. Chicano historians differ on the intent of Gutierrez's words. Lorena Oropeza (2005, 77–78) argues that as an organization was unapologetically anti-gringo and viewed Anglos as the "enemy": "Although members sometimes drew finer distinctions between sympathetic and racist Anglo Americans, the organization's aim was to present a clear choice to Mexican Americans in South Texas: Did they stand with MAYO or with the enemy?" Rodolfo Acuña (2004, 323) downplays MAYO's militant stance and argues that Gutierrez was simply advocating ending white control over Mexicans. Regardless of the intentionality of violence, the congressional "fear" of Mexican American political activity included both violence and growing Mexican American electoral and economic clout and its impact on existing white social structures.

Critiques of this new cadre of Chicano leadership were also fueled by disputes among Mexican American leadership. MAYO's most vocal critic was actually a Mexican American congressman from Texas, Henry B. Gonzalez, who questioned the new kinds of leadership funded by the Ford Foundation. Gonzalez raised concerns over some of the barrio-driven projects that he believed were advocating hatred against whites and militancy among his constituency. Speaking before Congress, he accused the Ford Foundation of creating disunity in the Mexican American community: "As deeply as I must respect the intentions of the foundation, I must at the same time say that where it aimed to produce unity it has so far created disunity; and where it aimed to coordinate it has only further unloosed the conflicting aims and desires of various groups and individuals; and where it aimed to help it has hurt."[22] Gonzalez, who described MAYO as a militant group that distributed hate speech, alleged that the Ford Foundation sidestepped his authority in his congressional district. Gonzalez also critiqued the Ford Foundation's attempts to create new forms of leadership where there was already an existing leadership, as well as the foundation's lack of responsibility over the actions of its grantees.[23] Gonzalez communicated his concerns with representatives of the Ford Foundation in multiple letters, such as this one from November 1969: "My concern has been that grantees in San Antonio are not all that had been expected, or as they represented themselves. The best designed of grants may well be meaningless if the grantees have no judgment, dedication, skill or energy. SCLR operations in San Antonio have been haphazard, and the council does not operate as it would have you believe, or affectively as it believes."[24] Gonzalez's criticism was also linked with spatial distance between SCLR and the projects that it funded throughout the Southwest. He questioned the ability of a youthful (and allegedly militant) group of leaders to appropriately administer new programming and services.

In addition to critiques from elected officials such as Gonzalez, newspaper coverage of the MAYO conflict blamed the Ford Foundation, with headlines such as "Do Ford Grants Breed Hate?," "Foundation Cited in Hate Crime," and "MAYO Warns It Might Start Killing Gringos." This national newspaper coverage produced a flood of letters deploring the foundation's funding of violent behavior.[25] Numerous owners of Ford vehicles condemned the foundation's actions and wrote the Ford Motor Company, the Ford Foundation, and even CEO Henry Ford II. One loyal Ford car owner, for example, wrote the following: "For years Fords served my family well.... When I bought my first automobile, I chose a new 1960 Ford.... However, because of the recent activities of your Ford Foundation in South Texas, I have decided I will never again buy a Ford automobile or any other Ford product. You are using the vast sum of money at your disposal to divide one American against another and to foment distrust and class hatred among Americans of different ethnic origin."[26] Although the Ford Foundation is entirely separate from the Ford Motor Company, consumers did not differentiate between the two. In May 1969, the Ford Community Affairs Committee of San Antonio, Texas, wrote McGeorge Bundy, president of the Ford Foundation, asking for it to disassociate itself from Mexican American "hate groups." The letter alleged: "The widespread adverse publicity which is being directed at the

Foundation is also being directed to the Ford Motor Company, its products and dealers. Our business is definitely suffering because of this situation."[27]

Ford Foundation officials did not stand idle. The foundation defended its position in funding SCLR and MAYO's work in San Antonio, especially regarding public education. Siobhan Oppenheimer, program officer for the Ford Foundation in charge of the SCLR fund, for example, wrote the following: "Mr. Gutierrez of MAYO tried to make it clear that the MAYO aim was not the elimination of the white man but the elimination of the racist attitudes held by some white men so that the Mexican American could be free to fulfill his potential as a citizen with dignity and security. In this connection, our Program Officer was informed that there was no intention on the part of Mr. Gutierrez to be critical of all whites, but only those with racist attitudes."[28] In a defense of MAYO's activities, Oppenheimer further asserted that the organization had received a subgrant from the Mexican American Unity Council to work on educational programs to ameliorate the educational situation for Chicano students in San Antonio. She applauded MAYO's efforts in education and its work with youths. In this way, Oppenheimer presented a fuller picture of MAYO's activities by detailing its many accomplishments in San Antonio.

This more generous response, however, was not expressed by all at the Ford Foundation. Recall that for the foundation, electoral processes were supposed to be the alternative to violence, not a conduit for greater conflict. In a letter dated April 30, 1969, a Ford Foundation director critiqued SCLR's funding of MAYO activities. Mitchell Sviridoff, vice president of the Ford Foundation, wrote to Herman Gallegos, then executive director of SCLR: "As I stated in our various telephone conversations, the Ford Foundation is concerned about press reports relating to public statements made by leaders of the Mexican-American Youth Organization.... The Ford Foundation cannot condone the advocacy of violence or racial hatred by its grantees. Forceful advocacy of legitimate objectives is understandable, but the apparent advocacy of violence is not."[29] In his oral history. Herman Gallegos recalls receiving an angry call from a Ford Foundation officer saying. "What the hell are you funding? I want you to get rid of those guys and not give them any more money" (Gallegos 1989, 71). The following day, the Ford Foundation released a press release announcing that the grant to MAYO was being cut off.

Congressional moves to delimit philanthropic power were also a response to increasing private foundation support of Mexican American voter registration. The 1960s were a period of great electoral gains for Mexican

Americans. In 1963, a slate of Mexican American candidates won control of the city council in the small South Texas town of Crystal City (Oropeza 2005, 47). By 1965, three Mexican Americans—Henry Gonzalez, Edward Roybal, and Eligio de La Garza—were elected to the US House of Representatives (Mora 2009, 66). At the same time, the United Farm Workers, under the leadership of Cesar Chavez, Dolores Huerta, and Larry Itliong, led successful marches and boycotts, all of which garnered national attention and linked thousands of Mexican Americans throughout the Southwest. Politicization among the newer generations promised further electoral gains by the late 1960s.

SCLR quickly became a major motor in voter registration projects for Mexican Americans. From its inception, SCLR formed the Political Research Education Project (PREP) and voter registration project, which had gained tremendous traction in urban barrios.[30] According to Herman Gallegos (1989, 70): "To make matters worse, a young man by the name of Mario Compean, just a street kid, ran for mayor against Mayor McAllister and scared the hell out of him because the population of San Antonio is very heavily Mexican. A Hispanic surname running could attract a sizable vote. All of a sudden it looked like here was a mammoth revolution coming with violent behavior in the wings." White elites at the time viewed Mexican American political gains as a threat, especially given shifting demographics in major Southwest cities like San Antonio. They also questioned Mexican American candidates' affiliation with Ford Foundation–supported organizations and charged that philanthropic organizations were interfering in areas like electoral politics that were strictly the domain of the federal government. This concern spurred subsequent congressional moves to limit the political projects of race-based nonprofit organizations.

Although cloaked as anxiety over militancy, the desire to curb nonprofit organizations' political culture reflected a fear of the growing efficacy of Ford Foundation–funded voter registration campaigns. As described earlier, the Ford Foundation channeled funds to CORE's voter registration projects in Cleveland, Ohio, a city undergoing massive racial transformations contoured by white out-migration and Black in-migration, which resulted in a rising significance of the African American electorate. CORE understood this demographic transition and acted to increase the number African American voters, which analysts speculated had led to the election of Carl Stokes as Cleveland's first African American mayor (K. Ferguson 2007). Elected on November 7, 1967, Stokes was the first African American mayor of a major US city. This successful Black mobilization, coupled with the fear of Mexican

American political organizations emulating these gains, further propelled Congress into action to curb philanthropic funding of voter registration campaigns and other "political" projects.

In this tense context of national racial movements demanding greater equality through both the ballot box and the streets, the 1969 Tax Reform Act can be read as linked to these contentious processes. One of the most direct limitations concerned the funding of voter registration projects. As SCLR soon realized, because of provisions of expenditure responsibility specified by the new tax reform, voter registration became extremely difficult to fund. SCLR history papers make this clear: "In order to receive money from foundations for voter registration, you had to be incorporated in five of our states. You had to get help concurrently from five or more foundations, and no more than 25 percent from any one foundation. It was hard enough to get support from 1 foundation, let alone 5."[31] SCLR continued to push for the PREP voter registration project but encountered obstacles within the conservative Nixon administration.

The 1969 Tax Reform Act not only led to more regulatory scrutiny through the Internal Revenue Service (IRS) but also increased fear of policing from other federal agencies. The federal government reserved the right to step in should tax-exempt organizations engage in any type of prohibited activity. This, in turn, influenced the behavior of major philanthropic organizations like Ford. Program officer Siobhan Oppenheimer, for example, explained the foundation's changing relationship to MAYO in the following fashion:

> The Ford Foundation did not withdraw funds from MAYO. They rejected a proposal for refunding when careful investigation showed that the organization had openly supported specific candidates in a city election.... The Foundation believes that Mexican Americans should be politically involved and exercise the right and responsibility to vote. However, the Internal Revenue Service does not permit 501 (c) 3 Tax Exempt organizations such as Foundations and their grantees to be involved in partisan politics. Therefore, we cannot continue supporting any organization undertaking partisan political activity without jeopardizing our tax-exempt status.[32]

Whereas Ford initially raised caution regarding the alleged militancy of MAYO's leadership, by the end of 1969 it utilized a new language to explain its changing relationship to MAYO. Under the stipulations of the tax reform, it could no longer support organizations that were actively engaged in partisan political activity, which threatened its own tax-exempt status.

New tax reform regulations increasingly made the Ford Foundation more cautious toward all its grantees, including Oakland's Spanish Speaking Unity Council. On September 21, 1970, for example, the foundation received an anonymous call alleging that the Unity Council had funded a Mr. Richard Amador, who was also running for a local government position. The caller claimed that Mr. Amador had used a portion of the Unity Council funds for his political campaign. Oppenheimer cautioned Arabella Martinez of the Unity Council: "Under this new tax legislation, you must exercise expenditure responsibility."[33] Martinez explained to Ford Foundation officials that the Unity Council paid Richard Amador of the Los Angeles–based Community and Human Resources Agency a total of $14,000 for leadership development workshops. In an interoffice memorandum, Oppenheimer wrote to another Ford Foundation officer asking for guidance regarding the documentation that would be needed to prove that no Ford Foundation money was used to fund Amador's political campaign. Oppenheimer wrote that the foundation should focus on "protecting them [the Spanish Speaking Unity Council] from themselves."[34] Although the Unity Council quickly provided documentation that proved that it paid Amador's organization for leadership development workshops, it questioned the Ford Foundation's response to an anonymous call. Arabella Martinez and James Delgadillo wrote:

> Needless to say our Council is extremely disturbed by the allegation and more so by the anonymity of the telephone call. From our experience in the past we have found that anonymous allegations usually have no basis in facts but are used to divert attention away from program tasks. As a result, the Council adopted a policy of not dignifying anonymous letters or telephone calls. Therefore, we would appreciate your notifying us in writing of the recent and any future charges as well as actions required to clear such charges.[35]

This exchange shows that this was not a straightforward story of the Ford Foundation imposing its authority on its grantees. These were complex relationships whereby Martinez, Delgadillo, and Oppenheimer actively communicated and negotiated the frameworks by which they would respond to potential IRS scrutiny of nonprofit activities. As a subgrantee agency, SCLR also had to initiate its own monitoring services whereby it would send affiliates to oversee the actions of local regional offices.[36] Federal regulation therefore operated at a distance, pushing philanthropic foundations to redesign their programmatic efforts for nonprofit agencies. As funders and nonprofit stewards, private foundations were expected to have greater oversight over the actions of their grantees.

The Ford Foundation also progressively influenced the composition of the board of directors of its minority grantees. It recommended, for example, that SCLR welcome a number of new members onto its board of directors. The SCLR leadership emphatically but respectfully opposed the Ford Foundation's request, responding: "It is our position that the question may be examined, when and if, in the judgement of the Board, expansion of the Board is germane to the strengthening of the program of the Southwest Council of La Raza."[37] As Herman Gallegos recalled: "This is where we definitely drew the line and said 'no way.' ... They were looking at the board and they were probably recognizing that we were too militant and they were nervous about it."[38] The Ford Foundation also requested that other grantees shift the composition of their boards of directors. The Center for Community Change, for example, was told that it had too many leftist "Bobby Kennedy" types on the board and it had to get more moderate "Hubert Humphrey" types.[39]

The Ford Foundation's Shift to Community Development Corporations

The Ford Foundation also responded programmatically by prioritizing funding for what became known as minority "hard programs." It accelerated plans to establish the CDC as a new nonprofit entity intent on producing the measurable development of impoverished minority communities (see Ford Foundation 1973). These local nonprofit organizations would "undertake broad social and economic problems—to improve the quality of life and strengthen the economic base of their communities."[40] The central idea behind "hard programing" was for minority CDCs to serve as catalysts for economic development in their own communities. The bulk of the energy was dedicated to the consolidation of CDCs in African American neighborhoods, the largest being Brooklyn's Bedford-Stuyvesant Restoration Corporation.

The Ford Foundation envisioned that the CDC model would channel nonprofits away from direct public actions or protest activities. The transition into solely funding minority CDCs crystallized the Ford Foundation's new programmatic focus on "product rather than on process" (Magat 1979, 123). As the foundation deemed it, "a couple of hundred housing units is worth more than 'telling whitey off'" (123). It understood that a transition into "measurable results" would direct less energy into minority protest movements. Instead of fomenting protest, nonprofits were encouraged to focus their efforts on the redevelopment of space. As the foundation explained in 1974, "Although support will continue for organizations that protect the legal rights and interests of Blacks, Mexican Americans, American Indians, and Puerto Ricans, they will be urged to seek a broader base of financial support."[41]

Historian Karen Ferguson reveals that community development was instrumental in 1960s social movement calls for self-determination. However, her study demonstrates that the CDC model materialized from top-down initiatives mandated from outside the community. The CDCs therefore consolidated the visions of white elites in US government and private philanthropy and supported their goal of managing minority leadership. She shows how Democrats and Republicans flocked to these projects, as did philanthropic and government funders, all based on community development's promise to solve racial problems without any fundamental social, economic, or political disruption (K. Ferguson 2013, 213).

Like previous Ford Foundation projects for minority grantees, the concept of community-led development began with grand dreams that did not fully materialize. The ambitious goal that a community agency could successfully muster the support of government grants, private industry, and philanthropic agencies to single-handedly redevelop impoverished inner cities was a mammoth and untenable expectation for these newly developed organizations. In addition, it was a tremendous shift in the responsibility for alleviating impoverishment. Instead of the state initiating projects of urban development and eradicating social inequalities, individual communities were expected to pull themselves up by their own bootstraps, a model of urban redevelopment that was consistent with the "self-help" myth exposed by Erica Kohl-Arenas.

Ford Foundation monitoring reports of SCLR's grantees reveal the challenges groups encountered in setting up economic development projects. First of all, few staff members had specific expertise in housing development. The Unity Council, for example, sent its staff members to Washington, DC, to receive training to become housing specialists. It also forged new relationships with private industry, including Kaiser Industries, Crocker Citizens National Bank, the *Oakland Tribune*, Safeway, and the Pacific Telephone and Telegraph Company. Additionally, Arabella Martinez joined the board of directors of the Oakland Economic Development Council Inc. to advocate for more projects for the Chicano community. Monitoring reports routinely applauded the Unity Council's gains in its educational programing and its manpower projects geared at skills training for community members. However, these reports also questioned the council's ability to expedite community development projects:

> As I mentioned in my previous reports, Marty [Arabella Martinez] and all of the other Council directors always seem to be on much surer ground when they are talking about education and community action projects; but they become semantically fuzzy when they wander into the field of economic development. I wish someday that I could hear one of them talk about something as practical as a day-care center—but none of them have. Once again, I was left with the feeling that these gentlemen are struggling to accomplish something in the field that is totally alien to them, but they have simply acquired a new set of business phrases.[42]

The Unity Council was not the only SCLR subgrantee encountering difficulty in transitioning to a CDC. These new minority CDCs were confronted by tense development politics that requires proximity to power, social and hard capital/wealth, a deft political hand, and privilege. The Ford Foundation expected these newly formed organizations to acquire these skills and assets from one day to the next. It is therefore not surprising that numerous reports detailed how Henry Santiestevan, SCLR's president, acknowledged the difficulty many organizations were confronting with economic development projects. Like the Unity Council, Santiestevan reported that other CDCs experienced challenges in recruiting staff and setting up a viable technical assistance capability in housing and economic development areas.[43]

Additionally, the tax reform and the Ford Foundation's restructuring of its grantee program exacerbated already tense divisions within SCLR's diverse membership. According to Gallegos (1989), the 1969 Tax Reform Act brought about a curtailment of the advocacy agenda so integral to the activist fervor of these organizations. Other board members alleged that the foundation's new focus on "hard" programs aimed to produce "safe" programs that did not challenge power structures. In the end, SCLR leadership agreed to the new agenda of hard programs and prioritized education and economic and housing development. Firm in its commitment to continue to serve as a subgranting agency, SCLR steadfastly affirmed, however, that there would "be no change in the relationship between the Southwest Council of La Raza and the local councils and the Southwest Council of La Raza should continue to serve as a funnel."[44]

SCLR underwent major transitions that were influenced by its shifting relationship with the Ford Foundation as a result of the tax reform. By 1973, SCLR changed its name to the National Council of La Raza (NCLR) and relocated its headquarters from the Southwest to Washington, DC. G. Cristina Mora (2014) argues that this transition brought the organization into closer relationships with the federal government. Its funding went from primarily Ford Foundation grants to mainly federal grants and a more diverse set of private foundation funding. At this point, NCLR became a more pan-ethnic Latino organization that included Puerto Rican and Cuban groups (Mora 2014). It also became more focused on research and advocacy through the federal government. In short, NCLR became detached from the grassroots community struggles in the Southwest that had propelled Mexican American leaders to form SCLR.

Conclusion: The People Are Our Business

By 1980, the Unity Council had become an organization that prided itself for its business approach to community improvement. This was a completely different organization from its initial focus on community enhancement through leadership development and organizing constituents to demand changes in state institutions. The Unity Council now measured its organizational goals as well as its outcomes in business terms: "While historical conditions have modified the applications, the original goal has never been lost—to improve the social and economic health of the community. The *People are Our Business*. The Unity Council knows that the business of the community and the people of the community are one and the same."[45] As the preceding quote demonstrates, the organization now understood its work as an investment in the community, and it quantified its outcomes as profits. The Unity Council also framed its target population as a type of business, and improvements in the community's social and economic health as a business transaction. This degree of institutionalization and professionalization meant increasing ties with major corporations. I view this change as part of the Unity Council's navigation of a shifting terrain of funding. It also shows how the organization engineered strategies to legitimize itself in a new landscape of constricted public funding for social services. There is no doubt that the organization continued to be invested in providing services for the community and in expanding opportunities for Mexican Americans and other Latinos in Oakland. These were the organization's initial goals at its foundation in 1964.

The Unity Council responded to state and private foundation regulatory mandates that channeled it into this particular route. Yet the organization also found strategic political and economic openings in these new routes of service provision and urban development. The organization's aggressive business approach was contoured by the Ford Foundation's requirement to produce "measurable" results. The Ford Foundation has been a key player in contentious negotiations over the proper comportment of racialized minorities, especially African Americans and Mexican Americans. It viewed these groups relationally and funded organizations that channeled minority leadership into what it deemed safer modes of organizing. The Ford Foundation, along with state officials of the time, therefore attempted to craft specific kinds of Mexican American and African American subjects. In these negotiations, nonprofit leaders enacted their own politicized maneuvers to work around philanthropic and federal regulations. This triangulation of state agencies, nonprofit organizations, and private foundations plays a powerful role in contemporary projects of racial formation and development in many Black and Chicano neighborhoods.

A central concern of geographers is to better understand how spaces are produced within an ever-evolving geometry of power (Massey 2007). Furthermore, geographic analysis emphasizes a socio-spatial ontology that conceptualizes "space itself as constituted through relations that extend beyond a singular place" (Elwood, Lawson, and Sheppard 2016, 746). Keeping with this spatial register, this chapter has focused on events in San Antonio, Texas, and Washington, DC, in order to explain how congressional tax reforms impacted Oakland-based Chicano nonprofits. These flows and connections between places allow us to see the complexities in the mutual constitution of race and space. Thinking about history and memory in a cartographic fashion allows us to see how the organizations and political-economic processes that shaped social relations in Fruitvale were not bounded to the geographic confines of the neighborhood. They were connected to faraway centers of power, influenced by policy pathways and innovations shaped elsewhere, and linked to how other racial groups were treated. For example, programmatic innovations developed to ameliorate poverty in Black communities were applied to Chicano barrios. Similarly, if the actions of social movement actors in one neighborhood were seen as suspect, the activities in other geographies would be subsequently affected. This also entailed a global understanding of inequality, whereby both social movement actors and private philanthropy linked the ghetto to conditions of underdevelopment found in the third world.[46] Viewing the past in a cartographic way, or as a methodology for understanding the history of place-making, also allowed me to further understand how some organizations became institutionalized and more prominently anchored in specific places. These processes converged in a place called Fruitvale to shape the conditions of possibility of social movement organizations; they offer us a glimpse of how power relations become sedimented through place, privileging some modalities of neighborhood improvement over others. Oakland's Spanish Speaking Unity Council has used its role as a CDC to develop Fruitvale, therefore showing how negotiations between private philanthropy, state officials, and nonprofit leaders continue to impact the production of space (see chapter 4).

Through the 1969 Tax Reform Act, the federal government created a strict register of what constituted appropriate nonprofit political projects and prohibited tax-exempt organizations from engaging in any kind of voter registration campaigns or advocacy that would impact electoral processes. As Susan A. Ostrander (2005, 38) argues, this antipolitical prohibition "to this day discourages funding for social justice work for fear of overstepping these bounds."[47] Congressional debates that led to the 1969 Tax Reform Act saw both Mexican American militant protest and moderate electoral campaigns as threats to the white-controlled institutions of the time. Radical and moderate activists occupied a singular register of threat to existing social-spatial conditions at the time.

The intense debates between the federal government, nonprofit organizations, and private foundations were competing claims to authority in urban racialized neighborhoods. They also spatialized the self-help ideal— the idea that impoverished communities could pull themselves up by their bootstraps by adequately managing their own economic development and forging their own forms of capitalist growth. At the heart of these debates were questions surrounding the political possibilities of Mexican Americans. This preoccupation with politics linked with economic growth and control over resources was also relationally linked with African American struggles in Oakland and beyond. Therefore, Mexican American nonprofit forms of race-making were relational to the racialization of African Americans. These nonprofit-mediated forms of racializing Mexican Americans and other Latinos were also fundamentally spatial.

DEVELOPMENT FOR THE PEOPLE!

The pastor must really take charge of and observe daily life in order to form a never-ending knowledge of the behavior and conduct of the members of the flock he supervises.

Michel Foucault, *Security, Territory, Population*

What stands out are the ways we can trace the past to the present and the present to the past through geography.

Katherine McKittrick, "Plantation Futures"

On July 9, 1999, an unusually large crowd assembled near the Bay Area Rapid Transit (BART) station in Oakland's Fruitvale district. The multitude included state officials, residents, and representatives from Oakland's largest Latino nonprofit, the Unity Council. Attendees gathered to celebrate the groundbreaking of the Unity Council's biggest development project to date—Fruitvale Transit Village—a 100-million-dollar state-of-the-art apartment, community resource center, and retail complex that would become the new face of the Fruitvale BART Station. Typically, either city officials or private developers orchestrate large-scale projects such as this. However, the Unity Council, a community development corporation (CDC), was the project's principal driving force. Rodney E. Slater, at the time the US secretary of transportation, delivered a speech in which he praised the new ensemble of transit, housing, and revitalization of urban space.

4.1 Mural dedicated to Oscar Grant III to commemorate his murder at Fruitvale BART Station. Photograph by Graciela "Chela" Rios Muñoz.

Transportation, remarked Slater, "should be about more than concrete and steel. It should be about building communities and we are all looking to Fruitvale as an example of how that can happen" (Wadhwani 1999). A cheerful crowd applauded, and with the cutting of a ribbon, Fruitvale Village became a national symbol of the power of community-led redevelopment.

Fruitvale emerges on the Bay Area map principally because of its BART station.[1] Descending from BART, one enters a quaint plaza reminiscent of small towns throughout Latin America. Fruitvale Station stands apart from others because of its unique architectural aesthetic and its complex and contentious history. The station looms large in the minds of most Bay Area residents as the site of the fatal shooting of Oscar Grant III in 2009.[2] It is at once ground zero for a large movement against police brutality and anti-Black violence and—contradictorily—also a symbol of the vibrancy of Oakland's Latino community. Black death, resistance, and Latino vitality are all embodied within a singular architectural edifice.

Completed in 2003, Fruitvale Village instantly became a kind of architectural messiah for the neighborhood: residents, activists, and merchants alike hoped the new development would literally "save" Fruitvale and launch it into a new era of safety and progress. As the owner of Casablanca Bridal and Tuxedo, Jimmy Grogg told the *Tri-Valley Herald*: "Like everybody else in the neighborhood, we have big hopes about the Transit Village, and hope it will help change the whole area" (Counts 2004). A proud Arabella Martinez, then executive director of the Unity Council, told the press: "It's beautiful. I think that beyond anything else this is really transforming the community. Ten years ago this was dirt, filth, and bars" (Counts 2004).

Fruitvale Village is a real estate development project enveloped by a mandate of community empowerment and service delivery. As the project manager, Manny Silva, observed, Fruitvale Village is a "social services center wrapped within a real estate project" (Scully 2005). It includes, for example, thirty-seven market-rate apartments along with ten affordable units, office space, and more than twenty retail stores. Paradoxically, however, this real estate project is anchored by social services whereby its major tenants are publicly funded agencies. They include a new City of Oakland senior center, a Head Start child development facility, the César E. Chávez Branch of the Oakland Public Library, and a brand-new home for the neighborhood's major health care provider, Clínica de la Raza (Kirkpatrick 2007; Scully 2005).

Fruitvale Village represents the continued traction of 1960s Chicano movement activism in the neighborhood. In this chapter, I examine how the Unity Council advanced a social movement mandate of community improvement to solidify its claims to power, but what does Fruitvale Village have to do with social movements? To understand these connections, it is important to historicize the social movement milieu from which the Unity Council arose (see chapter 2; see also Sandoval 2021). As it explains on its website: "The Unity Council was established in 1964, during the civil rights movement, by a group of community members who wanted to ensure the political representation of the Latino community." Its first programs focused on the immediate needs of the neighborhood: childcare and job training. In its fifty-plus years of existence, it has constructed its pastoral power by routing resources to the neighborhood and representing the needs and desires of its residents.[3] As it further explains on its website: "Officially named The Spanish-Speaking Unity Council of Alameda County, our geographically based community development strategy now focuses on building an economically vibrant, physically attractive, and a livable neighborhood regardless of ethnic affiliation or national origin. The Unity Council identified the need to invest in long-term neighborhood assets and began purchasing and renovating properties and public spaces to create more livable and affordable neighborhoods" (Unity Council 2018). The

4.2 Fruitvale Village as passengers descend from BART. Photograph by Graciela "Chela" Rios Muñoz.

organization is charged with a mission to develop and improve the neighborhood. This history serves as a legitimizing force and a political tool to expedite its projects.

In order to erect Fruitvale Village, the Unity Council politicized its historical care of the neighborhood that hinged on its social movement origins. Caring practices entailed linking residents to social services as well as defending the community from private investors and city government–planned projects deemed foreign to Fruitvale. A central component of the Unity Council's improvement project included marketing the neighborhood as a vital Latino community ripe with potential. Planners deployed Latinidad as a homogenizing planning issue and a tool to attract new, more affluent residents and capital investments (Sandoval 2021). They rendered the neighborhood's geography, architecture, and culture as Latino and constructed this Latinidad as Fruitvale's distinctive feature vis-à-vis other Oakland districts.

The Unity Council positioned itself as an efficient community steward by challenging state-organized policies that ignored the welfare of Fruitvale's residents. In this chapter, I analyze three key practices by which it marketed itself as the neighborhood's rightful guardian: (1) the Unity Council's assertions of its expertise in routing resources to the community in opposition to a disinterested state and private sector investors; (2) the Unity Council's portrayal of itself as the voice of the community; and (3) planning strategies to market ethnic culture, whereby the Unity Council functioned as custodian of the region's culture, celebrating and marketing its Latinidad.

4.3 Fruitvale Village as passengers descend from BART. Photograph by Graciela "Chela" Rios Muñoz.

Opposing Indifferent Bureaucracies

In 1991, BART officials unveiled plans to build a colossal five-story parking structure adjacent to Fruitvale Station. The transit agency alleged that the station was losing ridership due to its lack of parking. Marshaling its power to represent and protect the neighborhood, the Unity Council organized against what it deemed to be a violation of Fruitvale's ability to decide how and when to change its public space. Utilizing language of community control emblematic of movements of the late 1960s, it built an entire mobilization against the proposed parking structure. In so doing, it constructed a history of state disengagement and bureaucratic mismanagement of community resources as proof of the need for it to enact its own more appropriate projects of urban renewal. The central culprit of this mismanagement became the authoritarian Bay Area Rapid Transit agency, which the Unity Council alleged ignored the Fruitvale community. The Unity Council enacted its own technologies of community mothering in order to protect the neighborhood from what it deemed as "greedy outsiders."

The Unity Council and other community-based organizations opposed the new parking structure because they argued it would further isolate the neighborhood. They also alleged that Fruitvale was never the intended beneficiary of BART redevelopment plans. Instead, the proposed towering parking structure would stand between Fruitvale's commercial hub and the station. The Unity Council and its activist allies blamed patronizing bureaucrats for attempting to compartmentalize space and further isolate Fruitvale from neighboring geographies of affluence. As Frantz Fanon ([1963] 2004) argued, spatial compartmentalization is a process of imposing power through the policing of space and unequal allocation of resources. Fanon contended that compartmentalization served to maintain conditions of subordination and thus reinforced unequal power relations. Fruitvale activists drew on a past history of government disengagement in the district and argued that BART had a long history of compartmentalizing Fruitvale's space to serve the needs of affluent riders.

Historical Formation of Fruitvale Station

The Fruitvale Station was completed in 1972 as part of the newly established service connecting Fremont to Oakland. The station was planned as a "collector" of ridership from outside the neighborhood and not a "destination." This image of Fruitvale as a collector station was confirmed in a 1973 study that analyzed the impacts of BART on Bay Area neighborhoods. The transit agency's research team found that most riders utilized Fruitvale Station only to reach other destinations such as downtown Oakland or San Francisco. The urban planners of Gruen and Gruen and Associates of San Francisco wrote: "By 1975, Fruitvale Station is expected to have one of the heaviest patronages of all of the stations in the East Bay, totaling 16,674 trips on an average day. The great majority of all trips, or approximately 85 percent, are expected to be trip productions. Thus, Fruitvale is conceived primarily a collector station, with its use as a destination playing a relatively minor role" (Gruen, Gruen & Associates 1973, 191). In this study, Fruitvale's poverty and crime became predictors for neighborhood ridership trends and also shaped how BART planned the station and its surroundings. Unlike more affluent neighborhoods like Oakland's Rockridge, Fruitvale Station would not jump-start developments in the area. Gruen and Gruen and Associates assured BART that new residents and business would not move to the Fruitvale solely because of the station. The study concluded that the region's poverty, as evidenced by its low rents and declining housing values, would deter future residents and investors. Similarly, researchers argued that Fruitvale residents, due to their "poverty and economic and social isolation," would not use BART to any significant degree (192).

Gruen and Gruen and Associates recommended that the BART station should shield passengers from Fruitvale's poverty and crime. Planners perceived the neighborhood and its people as economically insignificant. To justify their recommendations, they stressed concerns about Fruitvale's decaying built environment and the fear of public safety. Planners advised BART that its top priority was to guarantee riders' safety. Unlike other areas where improvements in the neighborhood accompanied BART developments, little attention was paid to creating a more attractive and usable space for Fruitvale's residents.

Unity Council representatives argued that Fruitvale Station had long been forgotten. It became a magnet for crime and what urban planner Mario X. Turner-Lloveras (1997) described as "social disorder." By the 1990s, Fruitvale Station had the second-highest crime rate among BART stations. Its descent into a space of crime and violence was emblematic of the entire neighborhood's downward spiral. Residents and researchers from UC Berkeley agreed that, like its BART station, Fruitvale had gone into decline in the 1980s and early 1990s, and the area's economic decline was understood in race-neutral terms. The neighborhood's deterioration was attributed to vague causes such as economic restructuring, suburbanization, or the descaling of the welfare state. In these accounts, the neighborhood had deteriorated due to a natural process of blight. Researchers never identified the people or agencies responsible for blight but instead liberally blamed an abstract blighted environment for the region's underdevelopment. Turner-Lloveras (1997, 62), for example, noted: "The district is blighted by several vacant properties, poorly maintained storefronts, and streets filled with litter, trash and overflowing trash receptacles. The area is rarely used by shoppers and pedestrians and has become a haven for dunks and disorderly behavior." He further highlighted that blight was accompanied by homelessness, degenerate activities such as public drunkenness, and what he described as other "disorderly behavior."

Neighborhood stakeholders blamed state policies that did not prioritize impoverished postindustrial neighborhoods like Fruitvale. Gilda Gonzales, the CEO of the Unity Council from 2004 to 2013, told me in an interview that Fruitvale was "like other urban communities through the eighties that really took a hit with the crack epidemic, and the urban flight that was taking place along with disengagement by government. Those were the Reagan years and Republicans were winding down social services, and so you had a real decline in urban America, and Oakland was really symptomatic of that situation."[4] Government disinterest left Fruitvale with countless unmet needs, and these were coupled with the ravages of the crack epidemic that Gonzales further credits for devastating Oakland. Again, the blame for Fruitvale's decline was placed on abstract Republican-led government policies and drugs. As urban planner Alberto V. Lopez (1996, 1) revealed, a growing concern among residents and nonprofits was that Fruitvale was being overlooked by both city hall and outside private development interests.

Centering Community Improvement

In direct opposition to this history of neglect, the Unity Council projected itself as the competent caretaker of the region's development. It argued that BART's vision of Fruitvale solely as a collector station signified how this region and its people had been overlooked by municipal bureaucrats, planners, and private developers. Additionally, it argued that BART's proposed high-rise parking structure would further isolate the Fruitvale district and its people. The Unity Council harnessed its power in the neighborhood by employing a gendered vision of care that positioned the organization as the principal agent in the proper rearing of the community. This entailed "fostering people's relationships and social connections," a form of labor that has been referred to as "kin work" or as "community mothering" (Glenn 2010, 5; see also Hondagneu-Sotelo 1994). Coupled with the Unity Council's practices of caring, its mobilizations sought to produce a triumphant milieu to shape a new meaning of Latinidad in Oakland.[5]

Development for the People!

The Unity Council's role as a community steward stems from its origins as a social movement organization. The movements of the 1960s were anchored by the goal of transforming racialized communities into vibrant and self-sufficient places. These mobilizations sprung up in response to a long history of segregation in the United States and challenged spatial inequalities. As historian Brian D. Goldstein (2017, 19) argues for Black Power mobilizations in Harlem, "The right to shape the built environment represented a civil rights issue equally to the right to decent education, public accommodations, or employment." This was as much an ideological as a practical matter. In many impoverished communities, the existing buildings were deteriorating as a result of segregation and the abandonment of the urban core. Therefore, the creation of social movement services such as health clinics, childcare services, and cultural and arts organizations required improvements in the urban form.

Chicano movement activists prioritized the development of impoverished barrios as vital to the task of liberating the Chicano people. Like most contentious processes involving a community with manifold stakeholders, activists took varying approaches to accomplish these ends. For some more radical activists, development meant finding alternatives to an exploitative capitalist system built on inequality. Others, however, found minimal contradictions in utilizing capitalist forms of development to shape their own spatial projects. Despite internal differences, activists agreed on the ultimate goal of improving conditions for Chicano communities throughout the United States.

The Unity Council emerged from this movement to develop Mexican American communities. As the first Latino nonprofit organization in Oakland, it received a grant from the newly formed Southwest Council of La Raza (SCLR) in 1969. The mission of the SCLR was to create a framework for the development of Chicano community-based groups that would help to improve barrios through the provision of resources and infrastructure improvements. Most important, SCLR mobilized to ensure that resources intended for minority communities in the aftermath of civil rights gains reached Chicano communities. The organization received a multiyear grant from the Ford Foundation, which it subsequently used to fund smaller grass-roots organizations, including the Unity Council (see chapter 3). Through its relationship with SCLR, the Unity Council went on to receive continued support from the Ford Foundation for a series of community development projects. In 1969, the Ford Foundation channeled the Unity Council to become a CDC, a new nonprofit entity intent on developing impoverished neighborhoods. Instead of funding politicizing projects, the Unity Council now had to produce what were dubbed "measurable" results, which included services such as Head Start or educational or job placement opportunities for residents. However, the core of these measurable results was the actual production of brick-and-mortar buildings—such as senior housing, apartments, and other community improvement projects.

Community development corporations emerged across the United States in the late 1960s, including in places like Harlem, Brooklyn, Cleveland, and Philadelphia (Goldstein 2017, 119). By 1971, approximately seventy-five urban CDCs were operating across the United States. These new organizations relied on a series of state and philanthropic funding streams made available for community-based organizations. [6] As place-based organizations, CDCs varied dramatically based on the specific needs of local communities. However, as entities emerging from incredibly well-networked social movements, they also shared programming and funding sources. Some invested in local businesses and sought to develop neighborhood entrepreneurs and artists. Others, like the Unity Council, went on to primarily provide social services, loans, and technical assistance. These CDCs were charged with an excruciatingly difficult task—to create infrastructural and economic developments in communities that had long been forgotten and that had few economic resources. Furthermore, because of their origins in 1960s social movements, they were also committed to the philosophical ideals of community control. One of the central contradictions became how to route bureaucratic and financial resources into the community without losing sight of the strong social movement mandate of self-determination (see Goldstein 2017).

Most funding for CDCs went to African American institutions and their respective communities. Only a handful of Mexican American CDCs existed in cities such as Phoenix, San Antonio, and Los Angeles. These Chicano CDCs emerged from the networks of community organizations developed by SCLR that built on a long tradition of Mexican American organizing throughout the Southwest. These CDCs worked to prove that Chicanos were also a minority group that lived in specific geographies in desperate need of development.

As a CDC, the Unity Council was empowered to make physical changes in urban space. The organization and its leaders viewed their development projects as political because they served to fashion a new image of Mexican Americans through productions of space. As Henri Lefebvre argued, the production of space enacts a "logic of homogeneity and a strategy of the repetitive" with the ultimate goal of reproducing the social relations of production (Lefebvre 2009, 189). Unity Council development projects disrupted this homogeneity by branding their projects as Mexican American. This production of Mexican American space was a highly political act. As Doreen Massey (1994, 5) argues, "The identities of place are always unfixed, contested and multiple," which therefore means that any attempts to stabilize the meaning of a particular place involves "a social contest, battles over the power to label space-time, to impose the meaning to be attributed to a space."

The Unity Council's development projects consolidated its authority as an efficient community steward. In 1973 the Unity Council completed its first development project—sixty-one units of family housing called Las Casitas. This was the first time the Unity Council was able to prove itself as a CDC. As Arabella Martinez (1991, 36) recalls: "When we had our open house for Casitas there were a lot of people and the community was excited because I mean ... Mexicans built this." This was not just any kind of development; it was an entirely Chicano project that proved that Mexican Americans could engineer large-scale developments. It was also a testament to the Unity Council's savvy fundraising capabilities, leveraging federal redevelopment funds, private loans, and important development loans from the Ford Foundation (Martinez 1976).

Community development did not come without complications. Fruitvale community-based planners, for example, waged a political battle to be recognized as legitimate developers. Initially, the organization was not taken seriously because it lacked experience. Many city officials and other institutions also questioned its affiliations with protest movements. As one of the first Unity Council planners, Ramon Rodriguez, recalled, "It was an uphill battle to be taken seriously for obvious reasons: we were new in the business and we were young, and I guess we talked like radicals ... [and I] still had long hair!" As a recent college graduate, Rodriguez quickly understood that development projects were not devoid of politics. Development projects, especially for this new organization, required a deft political hand.

As Rodriguez described it, most white-owned establishments distrusted a long-haired Mexican American. Although Rodriguez was in no way a militant, as a recent college graduate in the 1960s, he was perceived as radical. He admits that he had to learn new ways of comportment. He learned from watching Arabella Martinez in action. As he described: "Arabella was never perceived as radical; she was a little bit more state savvy, a little bit more conservative. All of her stuff was Cal [UC Berkeley] stuff. We learned that there was the code for dealing with people." As Rodriguez's comments reveal, this "code" entailed differentiating the Unity Council from more militant sectors of the Mexican American community by leveraging contacts and connections with state and university officials.[7]

Community development also revealed the core contradictions of the institutionalization of 1960s grassroots struggles. Many of the activists involved with the formation of organizations like the Unity Council critiqued the corporate style it quickly adopted when it became a CDC. In fact, radical activists claimed that by the mid-1970s, the Unity Council had been taken over by the "suits," a moniker for the new professionalized nature of the organization. For these more radical activists, nonprofit organizations were to become the administrative and bureaucratic arm of La Causa, or the cause to liberate and empower the Chicano community. The construction of multimillion-dollar development projects represented just the opposite. Despite these critiques, an equally vociferous group of community stakeholders applauded the Unity Council's enduring dedication to improving Fruitvale.

The Unity Council prided itself on how the economic development programs made improvements in the physical environment of the community. Its crowning glory was the construction in 1971 of the agency's headquarters, which it marketed as a community resource center. Arabella Martinez saw this architectural site as proof of the Unity Council's financial dexterity and its ability to deploy its affiliations with both state agencies and philanthropic institutions. As Martinez (1976, 201) described, the Unity Council harnessed a grant of $406,200 from the US Department of Commerce's Economic Development Administration to build the community resource center. Furthermore, through her contacts, the Unity Council secured a $325,000 loan from the Ford Foundation. This financial deftness required the skillful management of institutional relationships. The Unity Council deemed this work as a means to direct capital for the benefit of the community. Moreover, it saw its various construction projects as directly impacting how Mexican Americans were perceived as a group. By 1976 the

4.4 First Unity Council Community Resource Center located at 1900 Fruitvale Avenue. Photograph by Graciela "Chela" Rios Muñoz.

Unity Council had three housing projects, two completed and one in progress. As Ramon Gutierrez recalled: "We were in our own sweet brand-new building that everybody knew as the Spanish Speaking Unity Council building. We learned to develop, at least to do some commercial development. Though the Unity Council headquarters is only three stories high and not huge. It was built from the ground up. And in those days everything had to be Mexican! You had to hire a Mexican architect! A Mexican planner!"[8] The new Unity Council building was seen not just as any kind of redevelopment project; it was understood as a Mexican American accomplishment and an architectural symbol of the group's ability to succeed.

It was precisely this selective history of the Unity Council's development projects that it utilized to maintain its prized position in the neighborhood. This history of development, however, was anything but perfect. Like most other CDCs, the Unity Council wrestled with shifting leadership, limited resources, and difficulties in planning for a volatile market.[9] Needless to say, some of the Unity Council projects did not go as smoothly as planned. Among these projects was a car rental service at the Oakland International Airport and other enterprises that sunk the organization into massive debt by the 1980s. In the early 1990s, the Unity Council faced bankruptcy, a reality that launched a vocal campaign to save the beloved Latino institution. Arabella Martinez returned as the executive director and led a massive fundraising scheme that brought the organization back to financial solvency.[10]

Fiscal Expedience

Despite its imperfect record in community development, the Ford Foundation's long-term support allowed the Unity Council to prove its financial accountability as well as its pragmatism as an incubator of diverse forms of funds. Furthermore, Ford Foundation funding buttressed the organization with prestige and respect. In the late 1990s, the foundation granted the Unity Council a large infusion of funds, about $1.8 million, which allowed it to pay off all its debts and to invest $500,000 in the Fruitvale Transit Village development (Orozco, Austin, and Beale 2008, 51).

The Unity Council demonstrated and celebrated its entrepreneurial prowess during the opening ceremonies of Fruitvale Village in 2003. It commemorated the completion of the project with a press tour, a reception, and a gala dinner, titled "Realizing the Dream." The keynote speaker was Susan Beresford, president of the Ford Foundation, and guests included Oakland mayor Jerry Brown; Ajay Banga, president of Citigroup's North American retail banking unit; state senator Don Perata; and Raul Yzaguirre, president and CEO of the National Council of La Raza (NCLR) (Orozco, Austin, and Beale 2008, 85).[11] This tightly woven group of both public and private representatives, as well as long-term national Latino organizations such as NCLR, were all commemorated for their fiscal and bureaucratic contributions to the construction of Fruitvale Village. The attendees were not bureaucratic disembodied state and private foundation employees—they were personal and long-term friends of the Unity Council and its leadership.

The Unity Council attracted different fiscal patrons through a translocal process that activated networks from outside the neighborhood, especially long-term connections with federal agencies in Washington, DC. Arabella Martinez, for example, drew heavily from her work as assistant secretary of health, education, and welfare for the Jimmy Carter administration (Martinez 1991, 39). While in Washington she gained important training and courted prominent allies in different federal agencies as well as with organizations like NCLR. These Washington allies provided critical financial and bureaucratic assistance for the initial Fruitvale Transit Village planning and feasibility studies. Federico Peña, then secretary of the Federal Transit Administration, for example, first heard about the project in 1992 through his personal connection with Arabella Martinez. After only a couple of meetings, he personally presented the Unity Council with a check for $463,000 to be used for predevelopment planning, which included economic, traffic, and engineering studies of the area (Orozco, Austin, and

4.5 Plaque at Fruitvale Village honoring Arabella Martinez for her work with the Unity Council and the redevelopment project. Photograph by Graciela "Chela" Rios Muñoz.

Beale 2008, 80). As a former Unity Council board member, Alex Zermeño, recalled: "We took a picture with [Federico Peña] with a big enlarged check to start [planning] when we hadn't even submitted our proposal, because we knew each other.... Arabella knew him from the National Council of La Raza."[12] He continued: "Arabella collected every ally that you could think of and created new ones.... [Through these connections] we started working with City Bank and other big institutions."[13] Validation and trust from long-term patrons such as the Ford Foundation and federal agencies such as the Department of Transportation opened doors to more complex fundraising schemes. Through this deft management of resources, the Unity Council projected itself as a more efficient community steward, capable of leveraging multiple sources of funding and support.

A Space of Circulation

Community opposition to BART's proposed parking was principally a fight to secure the proper circulation of people and resources that would best benefit the Fruitvale neighborhood. According to the Unity Council and community stakeholders, Fruitvale's future depended on the ability to channel new resources and capital investments into the community.[14] The proposed parking structure became the villainous impediment to this idealized flow of resources. The CEO of the Unity Council, Gilda Gonzales, described this in the following fashion: "[Before Fruitvale Village was built,] the neighborhood had its back to the world. By the world, I mean a regional transportation hub where people are coming from different cities of the Bay Area and [Fruitvale] had its back to them. The parking structure ... [would create] a physical barrier between access to the world and the natural corridor of International Boulevard. The parking structure would forever seal the fate of the neighborhood that is already isolated."[15] Gonzales's statements demonstrate the high stakes of opposing BART's proposed parking structure. First, she situates Fruitvale in a position of disadvantage vis-à-vis other richer Bay Area regions such as the neighboring city of Alameda and Oakland Hills—zones from which many BART riders come to board trains at Fruitvale Station. Second, she positions Fruitvale as a victim of unfair planning strategies from "outsiders"—the BART agency—that planned to build the parking structure that would partition Fruitvale from the "world." Third, Gonzales's comments propel Fruitvale into a strategic position to attract riders from the more affluent Bay Area cities, which she claims would push Fruitvale to develop as an equal partner in the region. Collectively, all these positions are concerned with achieving proper circulation of people, goods, and capital through Fruitvale, with a telos of harnessing some of this flow to thrust Fruitvale (and its residents) onto a productive path of economic development. The struggle to build Fruitvale Village was not just a fight against unjust planning practices; it was fundamentally a battle to situate Fruitvale's "vibrant Latino community" within what Foucault (2007, 13) called a "space of circulation." The Unity Council therefore organized to prevent the construction of what Arabella Martínez called the "neo-fascist parking structure" that would further compartmentalize Fruitvale (quoted in Orozco, Austin, and Beale 2008, 79).

Fruitvale's entry into a space of circulation was essentially framed as a project of efficient community care and improvement. Although planners sought more efficient capitalist development, they also planned for the expansion of existing nonprofit services. The César E. Chávez Branch Library and Clínica de la Raza, for example, both developed as grassroots volunteer-run organizations in the late 1960s. Their new offices, which are bright and beautifully designed, emblematize a new level of institutionalization. For planners, Fruitvale's entry into a space of circulation was not just concerned with the efficient flow of goods and capital but also was heavily invested in providing services to Fruitvale's residents. Fruitvale Village would project a new image of this neighborhood, which committed itself to the proper care and guidance of its residents. Speaking to the press about the opening of Fruitvale Village, Arabella Martínez proudly stated: "My vision was to transform the Fruitvale district by creating a more vibrant and livable community. Further, in the wake of negative publicity about Oakland, we want people to know there are organizations like the Unity Council that care about the community we serve. By enriching the quality of life of families in the Fruitvale District we're creating a healthier and safer community for everyone" (quoted in Paoli 2003). The Unity Council's entrepreneurial and bureaucratic expediency was transformed into a benevolent process of "community mothering" that positioned it as Fruitvale's sole guardian.

The Unity Council demonstrated its care of Fruitvale's residents by incorporating an entire social services unit in the complex. "This is not a shopping center," Gilda Gonzales clarified. "This is a community resource center." As she described it, planners organized Fruitvale Village as a "one-stop community center where people could come and avail themselves of different social services, that being a health clinic, Head Start services, the city library, an official city senior center, and a multitude of different kinds of services."[16] Fruitvale's path toward development, and its entry into a proper space of circulation, depended on providing for its residents, and Fruitvale Village would be the new epicenter of resources.

A Voice for the Community

The Unity Council strategically deployed community participation as a way to secure its authority as neighborhood steward. Although the Unity Council was indeed concerned with the welfare of Fruitvale's residents, community became abstracted as a marketable commodity. In most accounts of the project, community participation was central to constructing the project's novelty and importance. It was essential to branding the project as a local production and not imposed by outside developers. Unity Council planners asserted that Fruitvale Village represented the authentic needs and demands of *all* Fruitvale residents. As Arabella Martínez proudly proclaimed: "This is not the usual planning process. It came from the community and the people that live here" (quoted in Orozco, Austin, and Beale 2008, 82). Left in abstract terms, *community* came to symbolize everything but specified very little.

Fruitvale Village planners often extolled the degree of community participation. What planners deemed as "community participation" accurately described the desires of a small but active cadre of residents who formed part of the Fruitvale Community Collaborative. This collaborative cultivated a group of grassroots community leaders consisting mainly of mothers. It also built patron-client relations between residents, the Unity Council, and Fruitvale's city council member at the time, Ignacio de la Fuente. For residents engaged in these grassroots beautification and neighborhood rehabilitation projects, the Unity Council and de la Fuente became Fruitvale's institutional and bureaucratic guardians.

In 1995, the Unity Council established the Fruitvale Community Collaborative to cultivate participation in Fruitvale's redevelopment. The collaborative built on longer-term grassroots engagement initiated by other organizations such as Clínica de la Raza. Maria Sanchez, for example, began her activism at Centro Infantil, an alternative elementary school that emerged out of Chicano movement mobilizations. She also volunteered at Clínica de la Raza, where she participated in courses on diabetes and nutrition. As she recalls: "When I arrived in Fruitvale [from Mexico] I didn't know anyone. I really enjoyed volunteering because I had people to talk to. I was a volunteer for many years and then one day at La Clínica they told me that the Unity Council was looking for a community member who spoke Spanish and could help bring in more Spanish-speaking people."[17] Today, Maria Sanchez is perhaps the most highly regarded Unity Council representative in the community. A humble, kindhearted woman, she exudes pride in the neighborhood and the collaborative work she has helped to foster.

Maria Sanchez organized a series of grassroots community beautification projects to encourage resident participation. She told me how before these projects were implemented, neighborhood residents had little pride in their community: "It was really interesting back in those days at Christmastime no one would decorate their homes. Fruitvale residents felt like they were in prisons. They were afraid of signing petitions. They would open their doors with a lot of fear."[18] Maria Sanchez and other Unity Council organizers were confronted with fearful residents who had no pride in their neighborhood and little trust in institutions. To nurture people's trust, the Fruitvale Community Collaborative organized residents block by block. As Sanchez recalls, the group would knock on doors and slowly established rapport with residents.

This grassroots mobilizing strategy gave residents a sense of neighborhood identity and taught them to act as a collective. The Fruitvale Community Collaborative assembled more than fifteen neighborhood block associations. As Sanchez modestly recounted, each group created a name for themselves, such as Neighbors of 38th Avenue and the Defenders of Fruitvale Avenue. Members of these block associations learned how to work with state institutions. They were especially instructed in how to report crimes to the police, how to report broken streetlights, and how to arrange for trash cleanups. As such, they were inducted into the process of being engaged citizen-subjects who could make demands for protection and care of their neighborhood.

Victoria Pequeño was one of the activists involved in the mobilizations. As an immigrant from Peru, she has lived in Fruitvale for more than thirty years and has been invested in several organizations. Instead of starting a conversation about her work in Fruitvale, she simply handed me a binder she brought with her. She immediately opened it to show me a remarkable collection of certificates. She had a certificate of participation or recognition from almost every major nonprofit organization in Fruitvale, yet the most prominent were the countless awards and recognitions Pequeño had received from the Unity Council.

Despite her fuzzy memory of the particulars of each award, Pequeño's extensive collection of awards, recognitions, and training certificates told a story about her long-term participation in Fruitvale improvement projects. It also chronicled the important role of nonprofits like Clínica de la Raza and the Unity Council in creating that connection to the neighborhood. In fact, her entire binder was an archive of this past involvement in Fruitvale, which she fondly recalled as her most valued "memories." The binder was not a particularly well-cataloged archive of her activism—it was not arranged by date or by organization. Nevertheless, it showed the organic nature of her community activism that did not revolve around a radical transformation of Fruitvale but rather was a gradual, sometimes incoherent, but always active, way of bringing about neighborhood change. Furthermore, Pequeño's activist binder, and narration of it in the form of cartographic memory, revealed how her experiences were foundational to the formation of a Fruitvale "community" that cohered through the active work of different nonprofit organizations.

Coupled with their devotion to the Unity Council, other neighborhood activists also praised Ignacio de la Fuente for his commitment to Fruitvale's improvement. Agnes Ramirez, for example, told me how de la Fuente was the central municipal representative who supported the creation of Fruitvale Village: "Ignacio de la Fuente did a lot to push the Fruitvale Village forward. We decided to commemorate this by naming the entryway De La Fuente Avenue.... He has worked hard for this community and everybody knows him."[19] Though she admits she could not keep up with all the planning meetings, Ramirez was fully cognizant of de la Fuente's commitment to the project. As she described: "Committees would change and others would come . . . but Ignacio really worked hard on getting the money."[20]

The Fruitvale Village planning process rendered technical this history of community-based activism, transforming the heartfelt experiences and attachments to their work of neighborhood activists into a university-created and university-tested "model for citizenship participation." In May 1993, the Unity Council partnered with the UC Berkeley's National Transit Access Center to sponsor a community design symposium at which architects translated participants' ideas into a plan for the station area (Blish-Hughes 2004). For example, Alberto V. Lopez, a UC Berkeley urban planner, wrote a report about the use of three-dimensional modeling techniques in community participation forums in the pursuit of involving a diverse community in the design process. He hoped that his report and three-dimensional model and citizenship participation program would give "an equal voice to various cultural, economic and social groups who because of the technical and professional nature of Urban Design and Planning, may feel they have no voice in the process" (Lopez 1996, 18). Reports like these and a series of citizenship-participation workshops gave voice to the Fruitvale community and translated years of Unity Council community engagement into an enumerative process that objectively measured residents' needs and desires.

Years of community activism also became translated into residents' signatures in support of Fruitvale Village. As Guillermina Jimenez recounted: "Back when the Transit Village project was happening, and I say this with a lot of pride, we [the community members helping the Unity Council] proposed that every person would get at least five hundred signatures. I was able to collect more than two thousand. I did it because I wanted to show that we were in need and invited others to support us."[21] These acts of enumerating support for the project, and subsequently statistically representing the entire community's support of the project, reveal how the Unity Council utilized the technoscientific approaches of its university allies along with the devotion of long-term-community activists to prove that it represented the united demands of the entire neighborhood. As mentioned earlier, this included enumerating community participation and rendering it technical via three-dimensional modeling techniques utilized during community participation forums. These practices homogenized the Fruitvale community and solidified the Unity Council's commitment to neighborhood care. This commitment to citizenship participation also became the cornerstone of how the Unity Council presented itself as the defender of the community against processes of urban blight and the opposite—neoliberal gentrification.

Merchants and the Latino Fruitvale District

Fruitvale Village planners routinely emphasized how the new structure respected community needs and desires. The Unity Council interpreted community as representing both residents and merchants and thus targeted these two groups in its organizing schemes. Planners and Unity Council representatives understood the important role merchants played in shaping the neighborhood's commercial infrastructure, and they organized to harness the potential of this sector by bringing disparate and often competing merchants together within a unified plan of neighborhood improvement. Unity Council efforts to conscript merchants' support were also intended to calm their fears that Fruitvale Village would bring unfair competition to their ethnic businesses.

Planners understood that the Fruitvale neighborhood symbolized Latinidad because of the important work of small merchants who constructed it as a Latino space. In my interview with Jose Dorado, owner of Dorado Tax Services, for example, he recounted the history of the development of a Fruitvale district by telling me the story of the neighborhood's changing merchant landscape. In his narrative, Italian stores and shops run by the Portuguese immigrants were gradually replaced by new Latino stores run by Mexicans. As the owner of a tax preparation and bookkeeping business, Dorado understood that merchants had transformed the neighborhood and, in so doing, attracted more Latino residents.

I met Dorado at his office after having heard much about him from other residents. Aside from being a merchant, he has a long history of political engagement in the region and in 2011 ran for a city council position for Oakland's Sixth District, which includes Fruitvale. Such were his political connections and interest in the history of Latinos in Fruitvale that he personally had invited Claudia Burgos from Ignacio de la Fuente's office to sit in on our meeting. Burgos was then council member de la Fuente's liaison to Fruitvale's nonprofits. Dorado could not tell the history of the Fruitvale district without referencing the neighborhood's merchants who, as Dorado described them, were a prominent force in the transformation of this neighborhood. As he recalled, "Chuy Campos started where Guarache Azteca [now] is, that's where Otaez Restaurant was. Where the *taqueria* is now that used to be a Portuguese bar and right next to that there was an Italian grocery store."[22] According to Dorado, these small merchants were critical to the economic growth of this region. The merchants saw themselves as powerful actors in the neighborhood and marshaled their history of contributing to its economic and social development to command more political authority.

Hugo Guerrero of Hugo's Travel and Tours was perhaps the most boisterous of the merchants. I met Guerrero in his travel agency, where the furniture and the tourism advertisements that adorn the walls exuded the aesthetics and fashions of times past—specifically, the late 1970s, when he first came to Fruitvale. As a self-described leader of the merchant community, Guerrero was always professionally dressed. Unlike other merchants who dressed in a more relaxed style and were less outspoken, Guerrero would never be seen without his sports jacket, and he spoke with a manner and proper diction that commanded attention. Guerrero's retelling of Fruitvale's history emphasized the strong role Latino merchants played in transforming the community into a respectable and economically solvent place. As he detailed:

> My assistant and I arrived in the area [in the 1970s] and the whole avenue was empty. International Boulevard was a prostitution runway and there were drugs. The only types of businesses left were bars. Prostitution, drugs, and assaults became the norm. You had to be careful if it was dark outside, otherwise you'd get mugged. A lot of people thought that the pioneer business owners were stupid [for coming into this neighborhood]. But we came here to service the needs of Hispanic clients. By then Hispanic customers had needs such as a travel agency, Hispanic food, and other services.[23]

Portraying himself and fellow merchants as pioneers, Guerrero retold a story of the pastoral role these merchants played in charting new economic territory. They risked thousands of dollars investing in an impoverished area solely to provide services for a growing Latino population. They not only were savvy entrepreneurial subjects but also were intent on securing residents' well-being and providing services. Their entrepreneurial projects were fundamental to the transformation of this region. As Guerrero described the results of these pioneering efforts: "Then this district began getting better. Once people noticed we were doing well, others came. More Latinos began buying property. In ten years Fruitvale was booming. By 1992 you couldn't find an empty space to rent."[24] Given their pioneering role in setting up the Latino infrastructure in the neighborhood, they joined forces to argue that, as merchants, they were paying higher taxes and, as a result, their political and economic clout should also increase. They also did this to fortify their position as Latino merchants in the area who had led the way in the neighborhood's ascendance after decades of economic decline.

In order to encourage merchants to support the Fruitvale Village, the Unity Council worked closely to bring them into its fold. Maria Sanchez of the Unity Council began to offer an institutional space in which the merchants could gain greater access to city programs. The Unity Council attained grants from the City of Oakland to create greater cohesion among the various stores. The consolidation of the merchants as a united entity was also visually incorporated into the architectural redevelopment plans. As one planner argued: "The Unity Council hopes to build on the existing cultural and ethnic diversity of businesses in the Fruitvale District, and will market/promote the area around a Latino theme because of the high concentration of Latinos in the community" (Turner-Lloveras 1997, 10). The homogeneity of the merchant corridor pivoted on the valorization of its Latino culture.

Marketing Latinidad

In addition to serving as a voice for the community, the Unity Council strategically marshaled Latino culture as a marketable commodity to brand the neighborhood and its residents (Sandoval 2021). Latinidad became detached from the heterogeneity of country of origin, class, as well as immigrant and native-born distinctions that crosscut this community. Latinidad also became intimately tied to a social movement past, a history that cloaked the project with a sense of security and care. The Unity Council marketed this ethnic culture and branded itself as the custodian and ambassador of the region's vibrant Latino culture.

By infusing Fruitvale Village with a Latino aesthetic, the Unity Council advanced architecture and urban planning toward political ends.[25] Architecture, as Eyal Weizman (2007, 6) defines it, is a "conceptual way of understanding political issues as constructed realities." Principally, the Unity Council and other Fruitvale community members utilized architecture to create a sense of belonging and political claims to a spatial terrain. As Gilda Gonzales, the Unity Council's CEO recalled, the alternative to the BART parking structure was "to build a beautiful pedestrian plaza that reflects the cultural experience of this neighborhood which has become very Latino.... We had to be mindful of what this neighborhood had become, and so when you think about the plaza, if you stand over at the

4.6 Fruitvale Village plazas. Photograph by Graciela "Chela" Rios Muñoz.

furthest end of the plaza, you see the church, St. Elizabeth's, and so it mirrors centers in Spain and Mexico. It just made a lot of sense for what we were trying to create here."[26] According to Gonzales, Fruitvale Village accurately represents the racial and cultural image of the neighborhood—or what anthropologist Jaqueline Nassy Brown (2005) calls a suturing of race and place. Fruitvale Village solidified a triumphant image of Latinidad that positioned the neighborhood within a path of development—yet with a selective attachment to key anchors of tradition such as the church and a longing for a kind of pastoral, family-oriented village. So important was the preservation of the church as a key community institution that residents did not want the project to obscure views of nearby St. Elizabeth's Church. According to urban planner Jason Scully (2005), Fruitvale Village was limited to only four stories by design, even though zoning would have allowed newer building structures to go higher. This limitation was upheld to ensure that St. Elizabeth's Church was visible from Fruitvale Village. The church, family, and nonprofit practices of community mothering proved how this Latino neighborhood was able to care for itself.

4.7 Fruitvale Village plazas. Photograph by Graciela "Chela" Rios Muñoz.

The design aesthetic represented the neighborhood's historical foundation as part of the Spanish mission system. As described by Scully (2005, 5), "The project evokes the California Mission style, while other parts are more influenced by local reinterpretations of Mediterranean and Mexican styles. Chosen with the intention of creating a festive atmosphere, the color palette also reflects the aesthetics of the region." The design became a linking of past and present architectural and cultural styles that solidified itself as Latino through its "festive" atmosphere and color palette. It also emphasized the historical importance of the Latino aesthetic in the region—a legacy of California's history as a former Mexican and Spanish territory.

Fruitvale Village's Latino branding radiates outward to other sectors of the neighborhood, especially the merchant sector along International Boulevard. The Unity Council worked with city council member Ignacio de la Fuente to obtain $185,000 in Community Development Block Grant funds for an ambitious program of store facade improvements, park and playground upgrading, graffiti removal, street lighting, and tree planting.

Businesses along International Boulevard were transformed beginning in 1996 from run-down cookie-cutter storefronts to lively, colorful, and quaint "Latino" stores replete with murals and designs. The design aesthetic is characterized by a mélange of Mexican- and Spanish-influenced stucco facades colored at key places by Aztec hieroglyphics, vibrant murals imbued with Indigenous and Mexican symbols, and colorful signage to welcome customers.

Planners standardized storefronts to create harmony along Fruitvale's commercial district. One of the critical design goals was to create homogeneity in signage and to enhance the existing architectural styles. As early as 1996, for example, the Unity Council partnered with the Main Street Program, a national organization that redesigns decaying commercial sectors. The Main Street Program organizes communities to establish "consensus and cooperation by building partnerships" among various groups—for example, merchants, property owners, and individual citizens—that have a stake in commercial districts (Turner-Lloveras 1997, 15). As Turner-Lloveras has detailed, the program was designed for small towns with a homogeneous white population and had never been implemented in racially and ethnically mixed inner cities. Fruitvale's participation in the program became a testament to the Unity Council's ability to harness different kinds of experts to expedite its development projects and to conscript diverse stakeholders into a coherent plan.

Fruitvale's unambiguous branding as a Latino space was a strategy to attract a unique market niche. The planning approach was precisely to distinguish Fruitvale from the rest of Oakland (Chew 1991; Lopez 1996; Montaña 1981). As urban planner Alberto V. Lopez (1996, 5) described: "The project is proposed to give the Fruitvale area a more regional appeal with a distinct cultural identity within a new development setting. The neighborhood has a distinct Mexican/Latino flavor within a larger diverse populous." Planers fashioned Fruitvale as an "authentic Latino community" whose residents shared immutable cultural backgrounds. The underlying goal was to transform Fruitvale into a retail and service destination rather than an automotive thoroughfare and transfer point (Chew 1991, 11). This representation of Fruitvale as an ethnic enclave was produced through these different projects rather than being a naturally existing phenomenon. Furthermore, Fruitvale's distinct regional identity was produced through mobilizing people and experts from "outside" the neighborhood.

Since the 1980s, studies sponsored by the Unity Council and UC Berkeley's Department of City and Regional Planning encouraged Fruitvale to harness its Latino culture to attract more investment in the neighborhood. Susana Montaña's (1981, 27) study, for example, recommended that the city condemn and acquire property near the Fruitvale Station and sell it to a local CDC for development of a commercial market and cultural center. As Montaña suggested: "The project should feature a Latino theme and identity and should encourage weekend and fiesta cultural events serving the Latino community" (27). The proposed cultural center and market were intended to cater to the neighborhood's Latino residents but, more important, to "stimulate increased patronage and further private sector investments" (25). The Unity Council organized studies such as this to convince its supporters that Latino culture could indeed be used as a marketable tool to channel resources into the neighborhood. In this way, Fruitvale's Latino culture could be viewed as what anthropologist Arlene Dávila (2004, 10) calls "an instrument of entrepreneurship" that is used as "a medium to sell, frame, structure, claim, and reclaim space." The Unity Council branded Fruitvale Village as a successful project to reclaim Fruitvale's space and its ability to decide its future development. By celebrating its social movement origins and its commitment to care for and protect the neighborhood, the Unity Council secured its role as community steward and the premier Latino organization in the Bay Area.

The Politics of Development

On October 6, 2016, the tech giant Google opened an office in Fruitvale Village. The topic of multiple rumors, community members and nonprofit stakeholders had long waited formal confirmation of this development. In many neighborhoods across the Bay Area, the sheer mention of Google raises numerous red flags. Community stakeholders braced themselves as they asked, would Fruitvale be the next site of a Google office park? Would the neighborhood become the next Mission District filled with white hipsters on every block?

The following day, the Unity Council published news of the new Google offices in Fruitvale Village. "First, let me say that Google is not re-locating its offices to Fruitvale. Their lease in the Fruitvale Village is for an afterschool program, not for their newest office park," wrote Chris Iglesias, current CEO of the Unity Council. Named Code Next, Google's after-school program endeavors to train youths in coding skills and cultivate the next generation of Black and Latino computer scientists. The program will work with neighborhood schools to train sixty-five eighth graders each school year.

"This program is very much in alignment with the overall mission of The Unity Council, to help individuals and families build wealth and assets, and this is an initiative that our own organization would otherwise be unable to take on," assured Iglesias (quoted in Unity Council 2016).

The Unity Council welcomed the new program into its property despite a public uproar on social media and angry reactions from social justice organizations. "Building up the work of local community development corporations like The Unity Council is the best way to preserve and celebrate Fruitvale's history and local culture," wrote Iglesias. For the Unity Council, the establishment of programs like Code Next was precisely the kind of development that it sought to harness through the construction of Fruitvale Village. Unlike critics who feared that Code Next was just an example of Google's ability to freely colonize Bay Area space, the Unity Council assured that the tech giant was simply investing in Fruitvale's development: "This is about investing in place. Private investment will always catalyze change, but by running private investment through a CDC, it is more likely that the investments will promote community development and help grow local assets." As a CDC, the Unity Council stressed its commitment to development and indicated that it would appropriately vet any kind of corporate presence in the neighborhood and assure residents' safety and prosperity. As a product of 1960s social movement struggles, the Unity Council once again utilized the language of community improvement to harness new resources for the neighborhood. This, however, was not without inherent contradictions.

Social movements come into existence through spatialized practices. They not only take shape in actually existing places but also fundamentally produce space. This relates to the built environment but also to place-specific social relations, impacting which social relations are privileged and which ones are foreclosed. Chicano movement social relations, for example, helped to build organizations like the Unity Council. These organizations became rooted in the neighborhood and helped to route resources, linking Fruitvale to broader networks of both activism and state resources. Through these spatialized practices, they help to cohere communities and create a sense of belonging that has long-lasting effects. The social movement production of space that emerged from 1960s Chicano movement activism arose out of an entire cultural, political, and intellectual movement that sought to celebrate Mexican American and Latino culture. Fruitvale Village sutured Latinidad with place and positioned it within a propitious path of development. Subsequently, the neighborhood's Latinidad became enmeshed with a modern progress-oriented ethos that certified that Fruit-vale residents not only were deserving of state money but also were model citizens of consumption and respectability. Yet as with any representation, these representations of what Dávila (2008) would call "marketable" Latinos can help to consolidate polarities between Latinos and other minorities—most specifically Blacks, who are the unnamed reference against which these representations are made. Furthermore, by advancing and marketing these success stories, the US media and other projects that advance notions of multiculturalism enable the formation of permissible forms of being Latino—further fragmenting Latinos along the lines of citizenship, race, and class (Dávila 2008, 8).

In this chapter, I have analyzed how a particular space called Fruitvale became represented by social movement organizations. Furthermore, I revealed how organizations like the Unity Council advance the mission of community improvement to push forth development projects. Some readers will question my choice of the Unity Council. In fact, most radical activists would not characterize the Unity Council as a social movement organization. For these activists, the Unity Council and its leadership "sold out" by colluding with state and philanthropic agents and essentially abandoned the social movement from which it emerged. My purpose in selecting the Unity Council is to reveal that social movements take mul-tiple forms and indeed change over time and place. Furthermore, social movements are a product of complex political processes that include federal and philanthropic regulation. Fruitvale Village shows the contradictions of the institutionalization of grassroots activism. In fact, diverse activists produced an impressive number of different social movement organizations and community-based projects, which also advanced alternative futures for Fruitvale. What if some of these other projects had gotten greater traction and more sustainable funding streams and had materialized different kinds of projects for Fruitvale today? Imagine, for example, if Fruitvale Gardens had expanded as a project so that the neighborhood would be known today as the epicenter of sustainability and food sovereignty projects in the en-tire Bay Area (see chapter 5). Or think how the neighborhood could have looked had other more radical activists' visions for development prevailed. As described in Laura Pulido's (2000) pathbreaking work on environmental justice, landscapes are artifacts of contests over power and embody gener-ations of sociospatial relations. Fruitvale Village and other Unity Council redevelopment projects can be read as the sedimentation of these battles over authority in urban neighborhoods.

We are intent on thinking of Chicano movement mobilizations as a thing of the past. However, when we view the spatialized effects of social movements, we can create a better register of the continued traction of civil rights and the Chicano movement in neighborhoods across the United States. Nonprofit organizations that hail from social movement activism view themselves as community stewards and continue to impact political and spatial formations. These organizations must also wrestle with debates about the nature of development.[27] Is the development appropriate? Is it the kind of development that is best for the community and for the social movement legacies that it embodies? The fact that there are competing perspectives is a testament to the very politics of the production of space, and the simultaneity and multiplicity of space.

MAPPING
INTERLINKAGES

Caminante, no hay puentes, se hace puentes al andar.
Voyager, there are no bridges, one builds them as one walks.
Gloria Anzaldúa, *This Bridge Called My Back*

On a busy and sunny September afternoon in 2018, I watched as a boisterous and excited group filled a meeting room at Fruitvale Village. My voice competed with the music playing in the background as I helped guide the crowd to colorfully decorated tables. Attendees wore their best clothing and represented the neighborhood's diversity in terms of nationality, class, immigration status, and length of residency. Children played between tables as families greeted one another.

Organized by the Fruitvale History Project, the event was held to commemorate the history of activism in Fruitvale. Given that historical accounts of Oakland-based activism have ignored Fruitvale's mobilizations, activists I worked with organized to recuperate this history. This was truly a momentous occasion as I was able to reconnect with many activists I hadn't seen in years, and meet others for the first time. The Unity Council graciously hosted us all and even provided food. Centro Legal de la Raza brought members of the Youth Law Academy, a program that educates high school youths about the law and encourages them to pursue careers in law. I was able to meet family members of many of the activists I interviewed. This was an emotional process as I heard from their children how they

5.1 Fruitvale History Project sign that welcomed visitors to the commemoration of activism in the Fruitvale district. Photograph by the author.

were involved in just about every program in Fruitvale—they attended the Escuelita, Centro Infantil, and the Youth Academy and participated in various arts organizations. It was through these programs that they became socially conscious and were also routed along particular trajectories that included attending college and pursuing better employment opportunities.

Regina Chavarín has always been a central character of this story. On the day of the event, she was one of the many activists who brought something to display. Chavarín constructed an elaborate folding poster that showed a timeline depicting major events that happened in Fruitvale alongside key events that defined the Chicano movement and Chavarín's personal history. She was worried that she might have omitted some of the key historical dates. She had organized the events by color, with each color representing a different historical scale: personal history, Fruitvale history, national events, and international events. I think she expected me, as a professor, to correct some of her representations of facts. But I didn't pay close attention to the dates on the timeline. Instead, I was most astonished by the story of space-time interconnections that the timeline told. Chavarín could not

5.2 Activist Regina Chavarín standing in front of her timeline of events. Photograph by the author.

chronicle Fruitvale's activism without connecting it to events that happened in other places. As much as an accounting of Fruitvale focused on the local specificity, the timeline encouraged us to think about spaces as interlinkages. Although the timeline emphasized time, it did so by situating history in place and intimately connected to the making of her political subjectivity. This personal, local, national, and international story was woven together by social movement activism.

This was not the first time that Regina Chavarín and other activists had schooled me about the geographic extent of their activism. When I first met her in 2012, I remember that she stopped me when I would bring her narrative back to events that took place in the confines of the neighborhood. "I wasn't just doing Fruitvale-oriented stuff," Chavarín boldly proclaimed. I think at this point she was annoyed that I once again had stubbornly prompted her to bring her recollections back to Fruitvale. Out of all the activist I interviewed, Chavarín was the only one born and raised in the neighborhood. She was perhaps the most "authentic" Fruitvale resident, which made it jarring to hear her say that her activism was not bound solely to the neighborhood. As she explained, "Over the years I came to understand I had to be county-wise, state-wise, and be astute regarding all the bigger stuff in order to get things done," she clarified. I remember at that time I simply acknowledged her remark and understood it as an example of the dexterity and breadth of her activism. It was only later that I thought seriously about the significance of her remarks.

All researchers, despite ideals of professed objectivity and impartiality, go into a project—and by extension into particular geographies—with a specific agenda. I began this work yoked to the idea that I was studying the making of an ethnic Latino community and therefore always sought to recenter conversations about activism and politics to focus on Fruitvale. Even though I was examining social movement activism (which by nature is about making connections), I was obsessed with spatially bounding activism to a specific geographic location, especially during interviews with activists like Chavarín. As much as I now write against this idea of a bounded, isolated, "marooned" ethnic enclave, I have to admit that when I began this project, I believed that closed-off ethnic enclaves existed. This is not surprising given the profound traction of this term in academic and popular understandings of urban spatial differences. Entire careers have been made by academics, journalists, filmmakers, and other cultural producers who portray ethnic "hoods" in a particular bounded fashion. Furthermore, I grew up in one of these kinds of places, where I knew only fellow Latinos and other people of color. I therefore went into Fruitvale precisely because I felt it cohered as a Latino barrio. In my mind, it was a barrio because of its insularity.

In addition to my coming to consciousness about the porosity of places I once considered insular, it was during conversations with activists like Chavarín that I realized I needed to better account for the porosity of all spaces, including supposedly disconnected—and bounded—ethnic enclaves. I realized that I was doing a disservice to the project by stubbornly bounding activists' memories to the neighborhood. I had to listen to activists' cartographic memories that mapped a different relationship between Fruitvale and other spatialities.

My meeting with two other activists, Tomas Acuña and Ana Rojas, clarified this facet of the social movement production of space. I was initially going to interview only Acuña, but when I showed up to our meeting, I saw that he was joined by Rojas. I could not have asked for a better duo to take me back to the lived experiences of Fruitvale's geographies of activism. Both

Rojas and Acuña were in their early twenties when they were introduced to Fruitvale. They are now in their midsixties, recently retired, and living life with gusto, surrounded by grandchildren.

Rojas and Acuña were excited to meet me as they had heard from other *veteranos* about my book. They smiled as I told them that the focus of my project was on social movement activism in Fruitvale. As soon as they began to tell me their stories, however, they immediately called upon faraway geographies and other social movements. To my surprise, their stories of activism did not begin in Fruitvale. They did not even start in Oakland. Instead of interrupting the conversation to bring the discussion back to Fruitvale, I encouraged them to continue. And, sure enough, their stories became routed through Fruitvale, yet not always spatialized in the neighborhood. Rojas and Acuña made interconnections a centerpiece of social movement activism. Principally, this had to do with how they described themselves as internationalists, in direct opposition to the nationalist tendencies that characterized the Chicano movement. This internationalist activist identity emphasized commitments to places beyond the United States and materialized into a monumental third world movement that shaped the formation of ethnic studies and people of color organizing in the Bay Area.

In this chapter, I highlight another dimension of the social movement production of space: the vast and robust connections that activists created beyond the specific geographic confines of the neighborhood. Activists' cartographic memories framed Fruitvale as an interlinkage of sorts. Fruitvale acquired an identity as a place through a recognition of the connections activists' made beyond the neighborhood, and activists' memories entailed a process of mapping the interlinkages to that "beyond." These connections were political claims to the powerful role the Fruitvale neighborhood played in the making of national and international struggles.

Empirically, this chapter follows multiple forms of activism that transcended, yet were routed through, Fruitvale. First, I define how activists linked Fruitvale activism to the formation of a national Chicano movement. Although the Bay Area rarely factors into the historiography of the Chicano movement, these activists detailed how the Fruitvale neighborhood was a fertile ground for both the theorization of Chicano thought and the production of the major founding documents. Next, I reveal how Merritt College, as an epicenter of Oakland's leftist thinking, helped to produce an internationalist and third world framework that animated activists' interracial and transnational forms of organizing. This included cross-pollination between the Chicano movement, the Black Power movement, and the American Indian Movement (AIM) and a redefinition of their respective spatialities of struggle. Tracing the formation of the Comité de México y Aztlán (COMEXAZ), I then return to Fruitvale in order to map the sites that the organization connected through its news monitoring projects. I conclude with a discussion of how international solidarity movements connected activists' political imaginaries to other countries such as Cuba, Argentina, and Nicaragua.

Interlinkage and Social Movement Activism

The sheer multiplicity of these stories of interconnections made me rethink how I had previously interpreted activists' memories and the mappings they set forth. Traditional mapping entails the demarcation and graphing of space. The word *geography*, derived from the Greek words *geo* and *graphein*, literally means "earth writing." Cartography is therefore a process of "earth writing" that entails bounding space within modular forms (i.e., independent and self-contained units), and therefore any graphing of the earth involves an abstraction and compartmentalization of space. As we have seen, activists' memories put forth a graphing of the neighborhood that could be read as insular, or bounded. Its product, Fruitvale, was a geography shaped by the Chicano movement.

Matthew Sparke (2005, xvi) further reveals that "every geography, whether assumed or explicitly elaborated as such, every mapping, picturing, visualization, landscaping, theorization, and metaphorization of space becomes re-readable ... not just for what it includes, but also for what it overwrites and covers up in the moment of representing spatially the always already unfinished historical-geographical process and power relations of its spatial production." Following Sparke's provocations about the power-laden and unfinished nature of spatial representations, I reconsidered how I can recenter interlinkages and translocal relationships in activists' mappings. I am not suggesting that earlier mappings of the neighborhood are incorrect. Fruitvale's identity did cohere as Chicano and Mexican American, and a geography shaped by the Chicano movement. However, as the late Chicana feminist theorist Gloria Anzaldúa (2015, 69) reminds us: "Identity is relational. Who and what we are depends on those surrounding us, a mix of our interactions with our *alrededores* (surroundings)/environments, with new and old narratives. Identity is multilayered, stretching in all directions, from past to present, vertically and horizontally, chronologically and spatially." The social movement production of space entailed both the creation and the bounding of a Chicano neighborhood. This, however, only occurred in relation to other places and through the actions and social movement solidarities that linked presumably isolated geographies.

Fruitvale, as a place of interrelationships, became much more expansive than a modular map could show. "Mapping begets further mappings," wrote the late geographer Denis Cosgrove (1999, 13). As Cosgrove clarifies: "This is true not only in the sense that all maps are based on prior records ... and are very often multi-authored productions, but also in the sense that a map, like any text or image, once completed and produced, escapes the contexts of its production and enters into new circuits of culture" (13–14). Indeed, as I pushed my thinking about cartographic memories and shared my ideas with activists and other interlopers, Fruitvale failed to cohere as simply a place one could find on a map.

During the 1960s and early 1970s, revolution was in the air, meaning that the entire world was in struggle. In historian Alan Eladio Gómez's (2016, 16) words, "The 1970s was a time when solidarity deeply influenced the political imaginary and social movement activity. Inspired by the Cuban Revolution, anticolonial struggles in Asia and Africa, and the momentum of Black Freedom struggles and the US Third World Left, Chicano/a left-ists expanded their political activity to engage with political movements in Mexico and Latin America" (see also McCaughan 2012; Pulido 2006). Therefore, social movement activism in Fruitvale belonged to a set of global antiestablishment and decolonial struggles. At a more localized scale, activists understood that Fruitvale belonged to a broader social-political space called Aztlán, rendered legible to most as the US Southwest. The space called Aztlán was then, and arguably still is, a powerful geography in the minds of Chicano movement activists. Aztlán is a geographic metaphor by which to lay claim to political, social, and cultural belonging in the territory now called the United States.[1] Sometimes dismissed as mere mythology, Aztlán, or the ancestral homeland robbed by the imperialist United States, vigorously connected Chicano movement geographies of struggle.[2]

I use the analytic of interlinkage to conceptualize how social movement activists forged relationships to disparate spaces and social movements, and most important, how those relationships helped to produce specific neighborhood dynamics. I use the term *interlinkage* because it implies a mutual constitution of spatialities linked together in some sense. An interlinkage is much more than a simple connection or network. It gestures toward specific acts or states of being in the world that necessitate that dynamic interrelationships between different spatialities. I am informed by the work of Walter Nicholls (2009) that shows the development of what he describes as "social movement space. "Nicholls explains how much recent research on social movements has revealed that networks play a pivotal role in coordinating principal activities and tasks (see also Gómez 2016; Johnson 2013; Pulido 2006; Ramirez 2007). He argues that geography and mobility generate particular social movement network structures. While networks are indeed important for social movements, the ways in which these networks are constituted geographically play a decisive role in shaping their specific functions within social movements and the relational dynamics that unfold in them.

Focusing on networks and transnational organizing, however, does not mean losing sight of local politics. In fact, it opens up the political space by which to critique what constitutes the local and the global and to blur the distinctions that are often ascribed to each category (Massey 2004, 2007). Doreen Massey (2004, 6) explains: "Thinking in terms of networks and flows, and living in an age of globalization, refashions, but does not deny, a politics of place." In a similar way, it is important to construct "a politics of place which does not deprive of meaning those lines of connections, relations and practices, that constitute place, but that also go beyond it" (9). By mapping Fruitvale through interlinkages, it is possible to more fully understand how local and intimate community spaces were influenced by global social movement activism and solidarity movements.

Given its positionality within a greater geography that many activists called Aztlán, Fruitvale was not simply a place on which social movement activism operated. One of the main arguments of activists' cartographic linkages was to show the powerhouse that Fruitvale represented in relation to the national Chicano movement. The San Francisco Bay Area was a major organizing hub for the Chicano movement, and in addition to the Mission District, Fruitvale was the neighborhood with the greatest concentration of community-level activity. In two significant ways, it was an agentic place in the development of the national Chicano movement. First, because of its proximity to rural areas, it was important for the United Farm Workers (UFW) and the struggle of farm labor. Second, neighborhood organizations created and distributed some of the first Chicano studies materials, making the neighborhood a place that vigorously animated the development and growth of the Chicano movement.

As discussed earlier, Regina Chavarín, like many of the activists I interacted with, was initially politicized through the United Farm Workers. As a student in high school she wrote a paper on the UFW that inspired her passion for assisting the movement. "We got to go to Coachella when Cesar Chavez asked all the colleges to send students," she told me, emphasizing that she clearly remembers how her roommate borrowed a car from her parents to drive there. Chavarín said, "I think we did the lettuce boycott" but assured me that this was just one of many actions. "Every Saturday we were picketing," she explained. "We normally picketed at two Safeways—either the one on North Berkeley or the one in Rockridge." For Chavarín, UFW activism showed how her activism transcended Fruitvale. When in these spaces, however, she represented a contingency from the neighborhood that demonstrated the community's solidarity with farmworkers.[3]

Alfredo Cruz was another proud supporter of the UFW. As a child, Cruz had been a farmworker who worked the fields just outside of Bakersfield. He therefore knew the difficult circumstances that farmworkers faced and was moved by the work Cesar Chavez was doing with the UFW. He recalled how during the grape strike he was part of a food caravan to the then rural city of Vallejo. Like other activists, Cruz argued that support of the UFW struggle was both a personal and a Fruitvale community-wide effort. "We went to Berkeley, to San Leandro, Hayward, and Alameda," he told me. "My wife was totally afraid because I took my kids, one in a stroller and the other one was barely walking."[4] Cruz and others protested not as individuals but as representatives of specific community organizations.

Activists like Cruz were deeply inspired by UFW modes of organizing and farmworkers' intimate connections to the land. As a result of his activism with the UFW, Cruz along with other community members got the idea of creating an urban farm in Fruitvale. They cleared the way for the establishment of what became known as Fruitvale Gardens. As Cruz, who was appointed president of Fruitvale Gardens, told me:

> It started about 1969 and went till about the mid-eighties. . . . It was about 50 feet wide and 150 feet long and located on Thirty-Ninth Avenue. A really positive thing that came out of this was an introduction to various plants new to the area like *chayote*, various types of corn and chilies. Fantastic stuff! One day one of the counselors from El Barrio Youth Center came and asked us if they could use a plot because it would be ideal to teach the kids how to grow food. We said, "Oh, yeah! This one is

not being used," and it was all weed infested. They came in and cleaned it all up and planted.[5]

Cruz and other community members imagined and constructed their own connections to land and agriculture, just like the farmworkers they supported in distant places. The formation of Fruitvale Gardens mapped this relationship to land that inspired an entire generation of Chicano activists. Long before urban farming became a trendy feature of cities throughout the United States, Fruitvale neighborhood residents used the urban farm to grow food and inspire a greater sense of community. In addition, urban farming served as a pedagogical tool to teach youths about the land and the farmworker struggle.

Another way in which UFW organizing was localized was through the intimate relations between neighborhood leaders and famous farmworker activists. Liz Meza remembered the intensity of UFW connections in the neighborhood in the following fashion: "One of our leaders, Carmen Flores, knew Dolores Huerta very well and she held many meetings at her house. And Dolores Huerta's daughter used to live in Fruitvale. So people knew her, and Carmen knew Dolores. Dolores would always send people to Carmen's house. Carmen would let them set up their headquarters for the week, while they were organizing."[6] It is not surprising that the neighborhood had an intimate connection to the UFW, one of the largest Chicano causes of the time. However, Meza's assertions about the almost familial relationships to the movement reveal intimate links, anchored by the very residence of Dolores Huerta's daughter in Fruitvale. UFW organizing in the neighborhood was explicitly mapped to key spaces: the homes of Dolores Huerta's daughter and Carmen Flores. As in other instances, activist memories conjured up specific landscapes to lay claim to how the Chicano movement was spatialized in the neighborhood. However, in these specific recollections, a new argument emerged: activists did not just attend UFW marches, boycotts, and demonstrations—they contributed to the making of a spatiality that helped the development and growth of the farmworker movement.

Development of Chicano Studies

In a similar vein, Roger Chavarín and Alfredo Cruz invoked another organization, La CAUSA, to demonstrate the neighborhood's role in the development of Chicano studies curriculum. Located near St. Elizabeth's Church and school on Thirty-Fourth Avenue, La CAUSA was organized by Armando Valdez, who was then completing his doctorate at Stanford University. After earning his degree, Valdez became associate director of Stanford's Center for Chicano Research and through this affiliation assured a connection to the newest publications about Chicanos. La CAUSA was therefore an organization strongly connected to university resources and itself became a scholarly place. "La CAUSA was a place for us Chicanos and an outlet for publications," Roger Chavarín affirmed. "They had real books on us, as few as there were at the time. I could read about me!"[7] As an intellectual center, La CAUSA played a major role in the printing of one of the foundational documents of the Chicano movement—El Plan de Santa Barbara. Furthermore, as I will detail, La CAUSA was also an important source for the circulation of Chicano studies textbooks.

Hailed as one of the most important documents of the Chicano movement, El Plan de Santa Barbara is an educational manifesto that calls for the formation of Chicano studies programs. It was developed and adopted in 1969 during a student conference at UC Santa Barbara. As an undergraduate major in Chicano studies, I studied this document and always assumed that it was produced solely in Santa Barbara, as its name suggests. In my interview with Cruz, however, he told me that he helped to print El Plan de Santa Barbara with a printing press donated to La CAUSA. According to Cruz, the manifesto's printing was a translocal process involving La CAUSA, a community resource center in the neighboring city of Hayward, the Graphics Arts Department at San Jose State, and Berkeley. "You see the plan was edited in UC Berkeley," Cruz recalled. Although the printing press was donated to La CAUSA, it was actually set up in a community organization in Hayward due to space constraints. Cruz emphasized that he taught the Hayward students how to use the printing press in exchange for printing El Plan de Santa Barbara. He further clarified that one of the Chicano students at the graphic arts department at San Jose State helped put together the printing press. "It was made and finished by Cinco de Mayo, and by September of the next year it was implemented in five Southwest states in the community and in the colleges," Cruz proudly recalled.[8]

Roger Chavarín offered another example of how La CAUSA helped the development of ethnic studies, mainly by supplying books for some of the recently created college classes in the early 1970s. "Funny thing about Raza studies [at San Francisco State]," Chavarín recollected, "they went through so much to start the program and somehow they forgot to put in the orders for books." Although students flocked to the new Raza studies classes, they soon found out that there were no books available in the bookstore. "So now you have the class, but there ain't no books! Books exist because we've seen them, but they were not in the bookstores," Chavarín proclaimed. As a student at San Francisco State, Chavarín knew that La CAUSA had an ample supply of Chicano books. Armando Valdez had alerted him about this demand, and so Chavarín prepared to come to the rescue (and make a profit). Chavarín enthusiastically told me: "I would take a backpack full of books, and I would stand in the hallway and sell the textbooks to the students who were going into La Raza studies." Chavarín made the trek from Fruitvale to San Francisco State with what he guessed was about 120 pounds of books in his backpack. Young and entrepreneurial, he continued this endeavor for more than three weeks. "It was already hard to find Chicano books in the bookstore, and that's where La CAUSA came in and saved the day," Chavarín told me with an animated smile. His retelling of course centered his youthful, almost superhero attempts to save Raza studies by being the sole and omnipotent purveyor of books. However, his memories of the events that transpired fundamentally highlighted the political and educational opportunities that La CAUSA enabled.[9]

Little is known about the operations that took place at La CAUSA. I learned about the organization through scattered memories, as I did about many of the organizations that existed for only a couple of years. Chavarín remembered that the book episode took place in early 1971. By 1973, according to Chavarín, the organization had closed its doors. La CAUSA's existence now lies almost exclusively in the memories of activists like Cruz and Chavarín and the fact that they are able to place it in Fruitvale and link it to a broader social movement struggle. As Chavarín recalled: "It was a house. So the meetings were held in the family room or in the dining room, or sometimes in the kitchen depending on the size. Sometimes we had two meetings going on."[10] Chavarín recalled that many of the meetings centered on the creation of a Chicano studies curriculum for high schools and newly created university programs. This was entirely new curriculum, and community members helped to construct the material.

Cruz's and Chavarín's memories summoned up La CAUSA to tell their heroic stories of how they saved the day. I did not verify the validity of these claims. Instead, I thought thoroughly about the implications of the assertions advanced by these activists. In other words, instead of questioning the truthfulness or authenticity of the claims, I chose to ask, why are these various people making these claims? I believe that part of the answer is that, as with other cartographic memories, these assertions centered their activism and their contributions to the making of a national movement. These claims at once pointed inward to Fruitvale but also essentially linked the neighborhood with a broader social movement geography of struggle. At their core, these arguments boldly proclaimed: we were there, we contributed to the formation of Chicano studies! And these activists were there not as individual subjects but as part of a broader collective of activists who belonged to specific organizations, such as La CAUSA, routed through Fruitvale.

Merritt College and the Spatiality of Social Movement Activism

Without fail, my conversations with activists regarding their politicization were linked to educational access. The University of California, Berkeley was an epicenter of student activism and politicization. Oakland's geography of student activism revolved around Merritt College, then located on Grove Street (now called Martin Luther King Jr. Way) in the flatlands of North Oakland. In spite of numerous protests by students and community members, Merritt College was relocated to the Oakland hills in 1971. For an entire generation of 1960s activist, the college was the site of mass mobilizations. It was at Merritt College that the seeds were sown for organizations like the Black Panthers and COMEXAZ. The college represented a confluence of many social movements that made the school both a ground for struggle and a launching pad for community-based mobilizations.

Activists' personal stories of politicization and their subsequent activism in Fruitvale, had important origins in Merritt College. Ana Rojas moved to Oakland from Los Angeles to follow her older brother, who lived just a few blocks from the college. "I got my GED and started taking college classes with some of the most incredible people," Rojas remembered. "We were at Merritt College with Angela Davis, with the Panthers, with the Brown Berets." Merritt College rapidly became a hub of organizing and internationalist thinking. As Rojas described: "There was all kind of thinking. There was the very far Maoist. One of my first classes was Racism in America, which starts at Merritt College with Froben Lozada. It was a movement to liberate our ways of thinking."[11]

Tomas Acuña came to the Bay Area in the late 1960s without knowing what steps his life would take next. He grew up in Arizona and relocated to Berkeley in 1967 to finish high school. His sister was a teacher and had been the first member of the family to go on to college. She encouraged him to enroll at Merritt College. As Acuña remembered: "So once I enrolled in school and all of a sudden I was being approached by other Chicanos and other people."[12] Being of both Native American and Mexican ancestry, Acuña admitted that he had affinities for organizing with both groups. However, he decided to work more closely with his Mexican American peers because he recalled that Chicanos were more organized.

Andres Cisneros Galindo arrived in Oakland right at the start of the social revolution happening throughout the Bay Area. Born in Tijuana, he came to the United States in 1961 as a farmworker. "I had done some studies back in Mexico, in art and a little bit of politics," he told me, "so I came in in '67 and I quickly enrolled at Merritt College." According to Cisneros Galindo, he was fortunate to land at Merritt College at the right time. As he told me: "In '68, students were forming the Chicano Student Union, as I remember the Third World Strike in UC Berkeley was happening, and so we went on strike to demand the Chicano Student Union and Chicano studies."[13] For all three of these activists, Merritt College represented the epicenter of their political awakening and the start of their socialization as activists.

The politicization of Chicano/Latino students did not happen in isolation. Instead, it occurred in a relational fashion and was linked to other social movements of the time, particularly Black and Native mobilizations. Unlike in Southern California, where groups were more isolated from one another, in the Bay Area people of color were in much closer proximity. This momentous meeting of Black, brown, and Native struggles had a great deal to do with geography and to the proximity of Merritt College to social movement spaces of struggle. As Ana Rojas detailed: "Merritt College was on Fifty-Second and Dover. It was by the Children's Hospital, on the borderline of Berkeley and Oakland. You see around the corner there was the [Black Panther] children's breakfast program, we were focused on educating everybody."[14] By mapping her connection to Merritt College, Rojas opened up the space to talk about its proximity to Black Panther Party programs and how the campus helped to mobilize all kinds of social movement activism. "The Black Panther headquarters was just a few blocks away from Merritt College," Acuña told me.[15] Ana Rojas interjected: "It was right around the corner. And the breakfast program. I worked at that breakfast program."[16] Despite the fact that the Black Panther Party is often framed as an exclusively Black organization, Rojas's assertions that she and other Chicanos/Latinos helped with the breakfast program reveal the tremendous cross-pollination between different social movements. Activists belonged to multiple groups and shared solidarities around the basic human need for housing, food security, and health care and the politicization of the community.

Students of color at Merritt College experimented with social movement activism to make greater demands. This was best exemplified through the example of the lettuce boycott that the UFW initiated on August 24, 1970. Students of color at Merritt College supported the boycott and used it to expand their demands on campus for the establishment of free and reduced-priced food for students. "I think it was one of the first colleges to not get lettuce because we picketed, I think we locked the faculty in the room," Rojas recalled.[17] Tomas Acuña added: "We locked them in and they could not leave. They couldn't call the police or anything. We forced them to make a decision."[18] In addition to compelling the college to support the UFW lettuce boycott, Rojas and Acuña were incredibly proud of how they had mobilized to ensure student food security on campus. Rojas recalled: "We established a free food program in the cafeteria.... If you didn't have money you were eligible to eat free in the cafeteria. We issued food tickets. And everybody benefited from that, it wasn't just Chicano, it was Blacks, anybody. Everybody working together. It was a unified thing."[19] In these instances of campus mobilizing, we can see the convergence of different social movement demands. The first gain signaled solidarity with the UFW and support of farmworker struggles. Students of color also mobilized around the basic Black Panther demand of services and basic human rights for communities (Nelson 2011). This included the right to food, medical care, and other essential human needs that were not being delivered by state social welfare programs.

Through their campus and collaborative work with Black and Native organizers, Merritt College students developed a uniquely translocal and multiracial mobilizing framework. Activists developed what became known as a third world movement that required an ideological and material inter-linkage of places. One of the most transformative experiences for Native and Latino activists like Rojas and Acuña was their participation in the occupation of Alcatraz, spearheaded by AIM.[20] "We went on Alcatraz," Acuña recalled, "we stayed and helped them pick up the school, they were making the school, and we distributed food and so forth."[21] Acuña further recalled how everyone slept on Alcatraz and how influential that sense of solidarity was for an entire generation of Chicano activists. As he detailed, many of the Chicano activists were proud of their Mexican and Indian blood.

Chicano activists' interactions with other third world social movements in Oakland made them rethink some of the nationalist tendencies that pervaded the Chicano movement. "We developed an international perspective," Acuña proclaimed. "It was not a nationalistic perspective meaning we are Mexican, and we cared only about our group," he added.[22] Even within Chicano activism, they incorporated non-Mexicans whether they came from

Guatemala, Venezuela, Arizona, or Denver. The ethos of collaboration and internationalism, according to Acuña and Rojas, reduced the amount of separatism and divisiveness. As Rojas told me: "Even among the Chicanos, myself being Venezolana [Venezuelan] not being a Chicana, I did encounter those very nationalistic people, but we had a dialogue. Yes, we had bickering, but we always wanted to educate ourselves and go above that quarrel. We always fought things that kept us down. That is exactly what we learned at Merritt College."[23] The bulk of the activists who formed Fruitvale organizations like COMEXAZ came from very different Latin American countries, and some were even of mixed heritage. As Acuña told me: "In COMEXAZ, for example, you had Ana who is from Venezuela, I am originally from Arizona, and then there was George Singh, whose father is East Indian and mother is Mexicana from here, a farmworker."[24] This kind of group synergy helped activists to think broadly about their organizing and the kind of political projects they took on.

The centerpiece of activism for Chicano- and Latino-identified students was the establishment of the Department of Latin American and Chicano Studies, which was the first of its kind at a junior college and became a model for other departments in community colleges and universities. The merging of Latin American studies and Chicano studies in a singular analytical framework and department was instrumental to the creation of an internationalist political framework. As Acuña told me: "It was like rewriting history and writing the correct history of what really happened, basically what we never learned in American schools."[25] This relearning of their own history had direct impacts on their political outlook. More specifically, the curriculum pushed students to engage in neighborhood-level projects. It was within this educational and political milieu that Chicano/Latino students from Merritt College formed organizations such as COMEXAZ in Fruitvale.

COMEXAZ and the Making of Translocal Projects

The connection between Merritt College and communities like Fruitvale reflected both social movement forces and political economic factors. "The whole Fruitvale area was a newly formed Chicano community," remarked Andres Cisneros Galindo, "and well of course the rents were cheaper so all of us students flocked there."[26] As more and more politicized students relocated to Fruitvale in search of cheaper housing and a Chicano community they could call home, they realized that the people living in the area were in dire need of services. I met Cisneros Galindo in his home in Richmond,

5.3 Activist Andres Cisneros Galindo at his home, showing his archive of artwork, newspaper articles, and posters. Photograph by the author.

California, where I was immediately introduced to his own archive of social movement activism. He was trained as an artist and throughout the years had amassed an extensive collection of poster art that he designed or helped to produce. He had a poster for just about every organization he had been involved with, and many had been produced in Fruitvale. Cisneros Galindo's experience with the establishment of COMEXAZ was the starting point for other projects in the neighborhood.

COMEXAZ was created as a news service agency that would provide a single source of information about Mexican Americans and Chicanos in the US Southwest and Mexico. The agency first started as the Instituto de Investigaciones de México y Aztlán (IIMA), as an attempt to collect information about the issues affecting the Chicano community. Although COMEXAZ operated as a coherent organization with a politicized mission of informing the Chicano community, it was not immune to intragroup disputes. One of the most serious disputes, which actually broke the organization in two, was the major split between the nationalist and internationalist tendencies of the early membership. Cisneros Galindo detailed: "IIMA became COMEXAZ at one point precisely because of that split . . . it was more a conflict of ideology. I don't remember all the details, it was like one of those things that happened that involved divisions between Stalinists, Maoists, pro-Soviets and the communist party from here."[27] He admitted that he remembered very little about the split. What he did recall was that despite taking different paths, members of the two groups continued to be friends. According to Cisneros Galindo, COMEXAZ "became more internationalists than anything else, with some tinge of nationalism. Of course, I mean you're Mexican, and nationalism makes sense."

Modeled after the North American Congress on Latin America (NACLA), COMEXAZ put the Mexican American community at the center. Based out of New York City, NACLA had a more international political outlook that mainly covered events in Latin America. COMEXAZ, as a Fruitvale-based organization, stood front and center in the circulation of knowledge for and by Chicanos. The newspaper service not only routed Fruitvale to other places but also joined the US Southwest as a united geography committed to the liberation of the Chicano community. The sense of "community" that Fruitvale activists mobilized to protect was therefore not limited to the geographic confines of the neighborhood.

Most members of COMEXAZ met as college students and realized that the Chicano community needed a better way to stay abreast of the issues affecting it. In this spirit, COMEXAZ envisioned how these kinds of interconnections could be materialized. The answer was a news service agency that monitored the major newspapers throughout the US Southwest. As Cisneros Galindo recalled: "We started with seven newspapers of the Southwest plus a few from New York. There was the *LA Times*, *San Francisco Chronicle*, *Arizona Republic*, the *Albuquerque Journal*, *El Paso Times*, *San Antonio Express*, and the *Denver Post*."[28] Ana Rojas recounted how extensive the entire process became: "We would take all of the Southwest newspapers and get articles about Mexicanos and Chicanos, Mexican Americans so that it could be cataloged, and then it went to UC Berkeley and other universities, then to the Library of Congress, and finally to individual subscribers."[29] This was the time before newspapers were easily found online, and COMEXAZ was the first to archive news coverage about Chicanos throughout the Southwest.

The news monitoring service was especially useful for college students, given the lack of available material regarding Mexican Americans. Tomas Acuña described the kind of institutions that subscribed to the news monitoring services: "Those that subscribed were basically the other Latin American

5.4 Photograph of image created by *El Mundo* newspaper to show how COMEXAZ news monitoring services connected the United States to broader struggles in Mexico and beyond. Photograph by the author of newspaper article in Lenor de Cruz's personal archive.

and ethnic studies departments so they could use it for the curriculum. And then there were individuals, people that just wanted it. Even a mayor from Arizona, who at that time was Latino and was very interested in the Chicano struggle, got the subscription."[30] The COMEXAZ news monitoring endeavor built an early archive for the emergence of ethnic studies and Latin American studies. It also fueled social movement connections. Activists could connect with each other based on particular causes covered in the news monitoring service: police brutality, immigration, cultural events, legislation impacting Mexican Americans, and so on.

Producing the catalog was a complex process and reveals how Fruitvale was linked to other geographies. Reading the different newspapers was just the start. More significantly, the process entailed following the events that occurred in other places and coming to know them intimately in order to account for the development of particular stories. As with any archive, members of the COMEXAZ team edited the content that was subsequently presented to subscribers. Acuña recounted: "So what we did is we subscribed, and then the newspaper was sent in the mail, and that's how we got the information."[31] Rojas interjected: "And we just went through them! And we would cut and paste." After this, the pertinent articles were cataloged and indexed, which facilitated the way people searched the contents, as in an encyclopedia. As Ana Rojas told me: "So if somebody used it, say, in a class to find something about Chicanos, and Mexican immigrants and voting, for example."[32] Acuña detailed how involved the process of putting together the catalog was:

> So if a killing occurred, say, in Santa Fe, New Mexico. Let's say a police officer there killed a Mexican in the community, and so we would follow that story. We would clip the article and then we would follow the sequence of events. A week later we would continue that article till the end, and so we could get the full story of what was taking place. There could be another issue taking place that came out of the Bay Area, out of Oakland where there was a political issue over voting that had to do with a Mexican or Chicano/Latino, we would follow that story, and the election.[33]

The breadth and scope of the newspaper editing were tremendous. It required the labor of an entire team of activists who did this work for little pay. The editing process was admittedly extremely political. COMEXAZ was a more militant and radical organization, so the coverage reflected that. As Acuña added: "Obviously, there was a lot of articles that we politically disagreed with, so we would eliminate those. We didn't pay too much attention to sports, for example."[34]

The COMEXAZ membership diligently followed the newspapers and went out of their way to stay abreast of the latest news. For example, when the *Arizona Republic* no longer mailed the paper to the COMEXAZ offices in Fruitvale, Tomas Acuña came up with an innovative way to continue to monitor news from Arizona: Acuña recruited one of his friends to monitor the *Arizona Republic*. As he recounted: "I had a personal high school friend in Arizona who agreed to get the daily paper there, and he and his wife for three years took articles and sent them to us. They identified with the struggles and were not being paid. They did it on their own, after work and on weekends."[35] The COMEXAZ membership was composed of an international and translocal set of activists who had political affinities that bridged distant geographies. This example also demonstrates the intimate sense of connections that shaped activism of the time. Activists networked not just because of political affinities but because geographies were connected by a shared experience of racism that included police brutality, housing discrimination, and issues pertaining to lack of access to educational and other services. In addition to being concerned about the issues affecting the Fruitvale neighborhood, activists were also concerned with demonstrating its connections to other spaces and struggles.

Solidarity Movements and Transnational Connections

The kinds of local, national, and global interconnections that developed through Fruitvale-based activism extended beyond the COMEXAZ news monitoring service. Throughout all my interviews, activists repeatedly reminded me that they wore multiple hats, a notion that is common in social movement activism and has been well documented. Among the COMEXAZ members, for example, in addition to running the news monitoring agency, they all helped with other community projects (see chapter 1). Less appreciated, however, is how these practices of wearing multiple hats entailed translocal engagements that linked not just activists but also disparate places. Just about every activist I met, for example, was involved in a number of international solidarity movements. As Andres Cisneros Galindo told me: "So we [at COMEXAZ] became informed because we had to read the newspapers, which meant that we had to keep abreast both of US and international issues."[36] Activists belonged to an expansive social movement milieu that was connected to global movements, especially those taking place in Latin America. To be an activist in this period required an understanding that activism took shape along multiple scales. "The solidarity movements were part of the time," recalled Annette Oropeza. "There were so much overlap in movements going on."[37] Chicano/Latino liberation would not happen in isolation. It was necessarily linked to local and global struggles against imperialism, social injustices, and racism.

Doctor Beatriz Pesquera came to the Bay Area from Los Angeles and grew up in a family household with a strong tradition of pride in their Mexican heritage.[38] In retelling me her background, she admitted that it was not difficult to become politicized. As she remembered: "As a Mexican young child, coming into the US was very traumatic."[39] She recalled that she was called a dirty Mexican and people would commonly treat her as if she was dumb. Given her light skin, some people told her she could easily pass as Italian. She, however, vehemently refused. In addition to these experiences, she credits Black radical thinkers for truly awakening her politicization. As she told me: "The first way I think I became politicized was reading the autobiography of Malcom X and a book by Claude Brown, *Manchild in the Promised Land*. I made the connection between African American experience and oppression and struggle and my own."[40] For Dr. Pesquera, her own politicization relied on a relational analysis of the effects of racism in the United States. This politicization emerged from seeing the shared experiences of racism experienced by Mexican Americans and Black populations in the United States. Activists also traveled extensively to support various international causes, especially the Cuban revolution. For Dr. Pesquera one of the most transformative and politicizing experiences was going on the Venceremos Brigade to Cuba. As Dr. Pesquera told me:

> In that I got to see a society that functioned at a very different level. You can read all you want about this, that, and the other right. But when you're there on the ground experiencing the kind of solidarity, the kind of discipline, the kind of passion, that and they were building a new society. There's a lot of problems with Cuba, there were problems then, it wasn't all rosy, I didn't think everything was wonderful and everything. But it was such an amazing experience to see something different, and you felt it, you heard it, you lived it.[41]

Dr. Pesquera's intrigue with her experience in Cuba was not just about supporting the Cuban Revolution. It entailed imagining and experiencing alternative frameworks for social relations and seeing the ability to construct new forms of relating to one another as humans. As another activist and educator, Connie Jubb, added: "You just got this perspective on being outside of your country and in a situation where there's so many other models. It doesn't have to be that way, it doesn't have to be the way that we do things in the United States, there's other ways of organizing a school or a group, there's other ways of human relations."[42]

The Venceremos Brigade was a wave of people from the United States who went to Cuba to learn about the revolution. Liz Meza elaborated: "They would go to Cuba and work for a while, get to know people, get to know what society was like and then they would come back and introduce the idea of Cuba to people in the United States."[43] Fruitvale activists who participated in the Brigade furthermore interacted with other activists from all over the United States. Tomas Acuña and Andres Cisneros Galindo went on their first trip to Cuba in 1970 with the Venceremos Brigade. Cisneros Galindo told me: "There were seven hundred people, easily about two hundred from the Bay Area alone. This was around 1970, and we spent two months in the island. We were very impressed. I was born in Mexico, and I knew what poverty looked like there. Cuba was supposedly a poorer country than Mexico, but you didn't see beggars on the streets, everybody went to school and young people went to the university. There was health care for everybody. It was a shock, to say the least."[44] The Venceremos Brigade was a prominent fixture in the social movement production of space. For an entire generation of Chicano and Latino activists, Cuba symbolized the possibility of an alternative to capitalism. Well versed in Marxism and socialist struggles throughout the world, activists went to Cuba not only to support the revolution but also to learn from the Cuban people and to borrow mobilizing strategies. The idea of free education and health care, for example, can be seen in many of the projects that activists put forth in Fruitvale. Unlike the socialist state in Cuba, the capitalist state in the United States did not guarantee those services for all. Chicano activists marshaled the educational, health, and other social service models they saw in Cuba to critique the failures of the capitalist state. In the absence of state services such as those they saw in Cuba, activists created their own. Annette Oropeza told me the following: "Everyone was going to Cuba for the Venceremos Brigade year after year and we all knew the major organizers of the Bay Area chapter."[45] Naturally, because she belonged to COMEXAZ and the Comité del Barrio, Oropeza went to Cuba for the first time in 1976.

Meza was not personally connected with the Venceremos Brigade. She was much more active in the Olga Talamante Defense Committee (OTDC). A California native, Olga Talamante was imprisoned and tortured by the right-wing government of Argentina in 1974. Talamante was a student at the University of California, Santa Cruz, where she majored in Latin American studies. She was active in the anti–Vietnam War movement and the Chicano movement and was involved in the struggle for justice for farmworkers. In 1963 she went to Argentina to learn about the social revolution happening in the country. Soon after that, the right-wing government took control and issued punitive restrictions on demonstrations and other forms of organizing. In response to Talamante's imprisonment and torture, thousands of people were propelled into action and formed an Oakland-based international movement to free her.

The international OTDC was localized in Fruitvale as it easily resonated with the multiplicity of social causes that shaped the neighborhood's social movement milieu. In addition, OTDC activism helped route new activists to Fruitvale. Annette Oropeza, for example, told me how her work on OTDC connected her with the neighborhood and its activists. "I was not born in the Bay Area. I am from East LA," Oropeza told me at the start of our conversation. "I was just a crazy Chicana and left and just decided I was going to something else and I came up here to Oakland." Her brother worked in San Francisco, and one day he asked her to join the OTDC. This forever changed her life. As she described: "So I joined the Olga Talamante Defense Committee in 1975 and from there I started meeting other people; they were people from Fruitvale who were involved in helping the committee.

People like Gilbert Gonzales, Liz Meza, and Leonor de Cruz, who were all involved with COMEXAZ." From that initial engagement came an entire life's work in Fruitvale.[46]

These solidarity movements were not just excursions abroad that ended once people returned to the United States. These acts and movements of solidarity were part of the creation of collective consciousness that subsequently impacted community-based projects. As historian Alan Eladio Gómez (2008) argues, Talamante's story "forms part of a broader history of how Chicana/os and other Latinas/os—along with African Americans, Asian Americans, American Indians, and radical whites—engaged in a multiracial and transnational politics of solidarity" (163). These engagements in turn led to future forms of solidarity with other countries and with transnational migrants. In addition to her work with the OTDC, for example, Oropeza told me about how she was actively involved in the Nicaraguan Solidarity Committee in the early 1980s: "I belonged to an organization that was supporting the Sandinistas, but we were a cultural group too. We were a group of artists and musicians in solidarity with the Nicaraguan revolution. So we went down there in 1985 ... it was just so wonderful. Then coming back with those ideas and ideals that were all about solidarity."[47] I asked how impactful these experiences had been to events that took place in Fruitvale. Like all humble activists at the time, Oropeza replied: "I am not quite sure if I would have been sophisticated enough to recognize that then, but I am sure of it because again that [internationalism] was part of the time." Despite not being fully cognizant of the far-reaching impact of their activism, Oropeza and others were involved in mobilizations that linked the local to the global to create a social movement spatiality that spanned multiple geographies and scales. Furthermore, internationalist organizing linked multiple approaches to mobilizing and formed an entire generation of activists throughout the world borrowing from one another and building communities of resistance.

Conclusion

In the spring of 2017, I had one of many emotional days while working on this project. After years of learning about COMEXAZ, I was finally able to track down a collection of its news monitoring series. It had been under my nose all the time, located at the Ethnic Studies Library at UC Berkeley. Sometimes, although you think you know a particular place, there are surprises right around the corner. "I am so happy that this collection is going to be used

5.5 Detail of
COMEXAZ news mon-
itoring service collec-
tion at UC Berkeley's
Ethnic Studies
Library. Photograph
by the author.

again because it is truly remarkable," remarked Lilian Castillo-Speed, the
Chicano studies librarian. The collection had been held in the library since
the early 1970s, and it was rarely used. I opened up two of the books and
felt chills running through my body. I shed a tear as I browsed through the
contents and finally came to understand the complexity of COMEXAZ and
the translocal work the organization dedicated itself to. As I glanced at the
various places and events covered, I came to better understand Fruitvale's
expansive spatiality of activism. As Denis Cosgrove (1999, 15) so poignantly
argued: "All utopias require mapping, their social order depends upon and
generates a spatial order which reorganizes and improves upon existing
models." The COMEXAZ news monitoring collection represented just that—a
utopic mapping. It reorganized discrete and isolated geographies into one
coherent register. Despite the particularities of different places, they were
united not just by a mutual experience of discrimination and racism. They
also cohered as a result of social movement activism that connected these
places to a mission of revolution and social transformation.

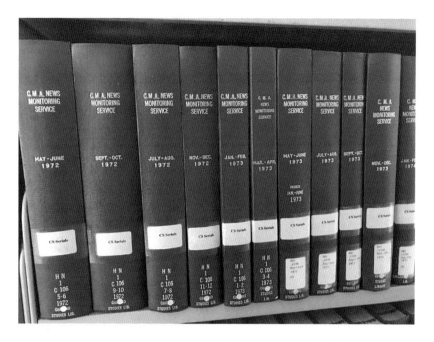

5.6 COMEXAZ news monitoring service collection at UC Berkeley's Ethnic Studies Library. Photograph by the author.

In this chapter, I have offered a different mapping of Fruitvale that centers the interlinkages social movement actors forged through their activism. Activists' cartographic recollections branded activism as processual—involving networking and brokering between spaces. In their recollections of movement activism, activists highlighted these links to emphasize how they mobilized as a collective. These connections to other spaces of activism revealed the porosity of the neighborhood and recentered Oakland as a key geographic and cultural milieu that had an impact on the national Chicano movement and other international social movement projects. This participation also helped to shape Fruitvale and the social movement activism that took place there. In these memories, Fruitvale came to represent an interlinking of distant geographies that came together due to social movement organizing. Furthermore, neighborhood projects were not an isolated phenomenon—they were part of the larger national and international challenge to white supremacy, US exceptionalism, and capitalist oppression.

The social movement production of space is a process that points outward as much as it is inward-looking. This kind of conceptualization of Fruitvale's identity as one of connections beyond challenges popular conceptions of urban Latino barrios as always already insular, forever marooned as ethnic enclaves disconnected from an allegedly non-ethnic "mainstream." It also challenges the assumptions that we as researchers bring to analyses of neighborhood-level activism. By already thinking of "neighborhood" as a scale stuck in the local, we don't fully come to comprehend the way in which the local and the global are entwined. Only by mapping interlinkages are we able to appreciate the multiscalar process embedded in the social movement production of space. As Doreen Massey (1994, 5) reminds us, "The particularity of any place is . . . constructed not by placing boundaries around it and defining its identity through counter-position to the other which lies beyond it, but precisely (in part) through the specificity of the mix of links and interconnections *to* that 'beyond.'"

CONCLUSION
ACTIVISM
IN SPACE-TIME

Unfortunately, too often our standards for evaluating social movements pivot around whether or not they "succeeded" in realizing their visions rather than on the merits or power of the visions themselves. By such a measure, virtually every radical movement failed because the basic power relations they sought to change remain pretty much intact. And yet it is precisely these alternative visions and dreams that inspire new generations to continue to struggle for change.
Robin D. G. Kelley, *Freedom Dreams*

Space can never be that completed simultaneity in which all interconnections have been established, and in which everywhere is already linked with everywhere else. A space, then, which is neither a container for always-already constituted identities nor a completed closure or holism. This is a space of loose ends and missing links. For the future to be open, space must be open too.
Doreen Massey, *For Space*

The Bay Area will be forever graphed onto my psyche and just about every cell of my body, helping to create what the late Chicana theorist Gloria Anzaldúa describes as a unique geography of the self. I long for the bay breeze, the proximity of everything, the hum of BART trains, the food I grew to love, and the social relations I built there. I spent some of my most formative years in Oakland and Berkeley attending graduate school and conducting research for this book. I left the Bay Area in 2013, and every time I go back, I am astounded by changes. Friends have finished graduate school and gone to other places. New buildings and services now contour a distinct campus feel at UC Berkeley. The surrounding community is also quickly changing as San Francisco–style mega-development is increasingly enveloping so much of the East Bay. Encampments of unhoused people are now peppered more prominently throughout. Homes that were once used as student housing and truly makeshift dwellings are now newly flipped million-dollar listings.

My feeling of loss and nostalgia regarding these transformations truly struck a chord on August 23, 2019, the day I arrived on my most recent trip to the Bay Area. I quickly set out to explore my old stomping grounds. Naturally, the first places I sought out were restaurants—I am a proud *gordito* (let's just say that is the Spanish translation of "foodie"). I sped across the Bay Bridge imagining the Indian buffet I would eat once I arrived in Berkeley, but my favorite Indian restaurant was nowhere to be found. As I approached the intersection of University Avenue and Sixth Street, all I could see was a brand-new high-rise development. I don't remember the name of the restaurant that once stood there; I just remember it served amazing food. Feeling lost and still hungry, I then sought out a pizza joint that I loved near the UC Berkeley campus.[1] I drove around downtown Berkeley for nearly twenty minutes to find parking because, well, the pizza is that good. I finally found a spot, parked my rental car, and dashed to the famed place where I knew delicious pizza would await. I walked up and down the street but could not find the restaurant, which also had closed down. I couldn't even identify what stood in its place. Frustrated and now ravenous, I found something to eat close by and devoured my lunch. I then drove straight to my favorite café in North Berkeley's Gourmet Ghetto to get some writing done. That of course was Philz Coffee, where I wrote most of my dissertation and where I did some of my best thinking. I parked and went to that location only to find in its place a new, bland, hipster coffee shop. I paused, looked up in disbelief, and angrily dashed back to my rental car. The Bay Area that I had once experienced and loved was no longer there. I lamented the changes because I hardly recognized the place I once knew so well. I felt angry and sad.

We as human beings are obsessed with wanting to arrest space, to sequester it and expect it to remain unchanged, especially as we grow older. We long for the spaces we once traversed, where we built our lives, constructed friendships and community, and where we envisioned futures. We expect or hope for these spaces to stay put. Who wouldn't want their favorite Indian restaurant and pizza joint to be a permanent fixture in space? To be forever graphed onto the earth? And can you imagine the disappointment of having a favorite café close down?

Space, however, is always in production, continuously changing and open. Geography is constantly being graphed in new ways as new borders are drawn on planet earth and new political divisions redesign continents that are actually continuous landmasses. As I grow older, I realize that spaces rarely stay put. My old hometown of Santa Barbara, Guatemala, has changed tremendously since I left (yes, not *all* Latinos are Mexican in California). When I returned to Los Angeles after completing graduate school, I realized that the City of Angels had also changed tremendously. My parents, family, and friends had also changed. Some had new children, others had moved to different residences. They, like their attending spatialities, had moved on.

Like other places so intimately tied to my sense of self, the entire Bay Area is experiencing massive transformations due to real estate speculation and gentrification. Entire communities and families are being displaced and forcibly relocated to the fringes. This same phenomenon is happening in Fruitvale, where rents continue to increase and landlords push to evict long-term tenants in order to rent at market rate. Businesses and nonprofits also have to relocate because they cannot afford exorbitant leases. Because of these experiences encountering spaces that fail to remain put and static, I became intrigued by the political forces that are required to keep a specific spatial conjuncture alive or ongoing. I realized that it takes tremendous amount of work, dedication, and struggle to maintain certain spatial formations.

Despite the rapid changes happening throughout the Bay Area, nearly fifty years since the heyday of the Chicano movement, many of the institutions created out of social movement struggle are still providing services in Fruitvale. I am not saying that the institutions have not changed, but rather they are constantly remade. Yet they survived multiple recessions and the conservatism of the Nixon, Reagan, *and* Trump administrations, and they currently are combating displacement caused by gentrification. Furthermore, other organizations have developed to meet new and pressing needs. How do we understand this continuity in projects of care for disenfranchised people, and the fight for social justice rooted in Fruitvale, despite the continual production and changing nature of space?

In order to "see" the sustained traction of social movement activism in Fruitvale, we must reassess how we measure social movements and their impacts. Most social movement scholars seem obsessed with analyzing social movement life cycles, drawing attention to the birth, rise, and fall of mobilizations. But if we assume that social movements die once they reach the supposed end of their life cycle, we also ignore the openness of space. Throughout this book, I have argued that many social movements that we view as having occurred "in the past" have an afterlife that most scholars have missed. For example, institutions and spaces produced out of social movement struggle are still in formation and embedded in urban landscapes. If space, as Doreen Massey (2005) tells us, is a set of "loose ends and missing links," then it presents us with the traces—both materially and ethereally—of multiple, dynamic, and competing processes of human-environment relations or "stories-so-far." Fruitvale is an example of that multiplicity and simultaneity of ongoing stories. In this conclusion, I think seriously about what it means to study the social movement production of space while accounting for the openness of space. I first situate the multiple competing "stories-so-far" that Fruitvale represents in order to ask how and why it is that Mexican American and Chicano movement activism still has traction in the neighborhood. I argue that present-day and historical activists perform the important work of maintaining and reinterpreting this social movement mandate of neighborhood improvement—showing us that the Chicano movement and prior forms of mobilization never fully died but are ongoing. How else would we explain the movement's continued effects in a place called Fruitvale? Furthermore, activists I interviewed are organizing to preserve the history of their Fruitvale-based activism. In this way, 1960s and 1970s activism continues to shape neighborhood politics, resources, and conditions of possibility for activism today.

Social Movement Place-Making

Fruitvale is home to numerous sites that signify historical processes of spatial formation. The very name—Fruitvale—stands in for the fact that the region used to be one of the biggest farmlands of the East Bay, dotted with fruit orchards and other bucolic environments. Today one can visit, for example, the Peralta Hacienda Historical Park, a site that reminds us that Fruitvale sits on stolen Indigenous land. Indigenous people were killed or forcibly relocated to missions and other settler formations like the Peralta Hacienda. The neighborhood is also contemporaneously home to the Native American Health Center, located just three blocks from the famed intersection of Fruitvale Avenue and International Boulevard. The health center, which was created in the late 1960s to provide medical services for American Indians who call Oakland home, is a symbol of Indigenous survival and resistance against elimination. There is also Fruitvale Station, a strip mall that sits on the site of a former railroad station that connected Fruitvale to other commercial regions. The railroad carried products from canneries and other industries that peppered the area. The region near Fruitvale Station is popularly called Jingle Town, a name left over from when it was a Portuguese working-class community. At the height of the Portuguese presence in Jingle Town, the neighborhood got its name from of the sound of coins jingling in the pockets of workers who had just gotten paid. The site of the Cesar E. Chavez Education Center on the corner of Twenty-Third and International Avenue was previously Fruitvale's impressive Montgomery Ward store. In the 1920s and 1930s, the neighborhood was a rival of downtown development, with a vibrant commercial hub connected by streetcar to downtown Oakland. Today, the presence of Central American, Indigenous Mayas, queer and gender nonconforming activists, and hipster gentrifiers reminds us that the neighborhood space is still open and is primed for the creation of new, differential, and intersecting "stories-so-far."

In her now-classic book *For Space*, Doreen Massey once again urged us to think of space and time in relation to one another, and as mutually constituted and produced through social relations. "Perhaps we could imagine space as a simultaneity of stories-so-far," asserted Massey (2005, 9). Despite representing a multiplicity of "stories-so-far," the neighborhood is understood as a "Latino barrio" and, in my reading, also a "geography of activism," precisely because of the gravitational force of the Chicano movement and a longue durée of Mexican American activism. This activism set in motion a major "story-so-far" that forever changed the neighborhood. It has also made the neighborhood a prime receiving community for newer waves of migrants, including Indigenous Guatemalan Mayas and other Central American migrants. I propose that this particular "story-so-far" has such salience because it represents the continuation, in our current space-time conjuncture, of inequalities shaped by settler colonialism. Our modern world continues to be divided up by race and other forms of human differentiation normalized by settler colonial logics anchored in white supremacy. This form of racial capitalism naturalizes multiple forms of suffering and dispossession (Cacho 2012; McKittrick 2013) and engenders pernicious forms of georacial management (McKittrick 2006). It also sets the conditions for the emergence of spatialized forms of resistance such as Fruitvale.

Another important reason that Fruitvale's Chicano movement "story-so-far" is prominent relates to the institutionalization of grassroots activism. Many of the institutions built through social movement struggle are still in operation, and new ones have emerged, inspired by previous generations. Additionally, countless activists remain active in the neighborhood. Some organizations no longer exist materially, although they remain alive in activists' cartographic memories.

Cartographic memories about activism in Fruitvale are alive and robust, and they continue to be reproduced by neighborhood-level social relations. As this book has shown, cartographic memory brings attention to the fact that experiences are overwhelmingly remembered through invocations of place. Activists dearly remembered how they experienced their activism by graphing neighborhood spaces and highlighting the social relations they built there. By mapping their activism, activists demonstrated how social movement activism focused on improving neighborhood resources and producing material changes. In these instances, neighborhood spaces became a kind of archive of social movement activism. Like all modalities of remembering, cartographic memory is also a situated form of knowledge that demonstrates selective retellings of activism. The more memories that are available, the greater detail we get about the complexity of social movement activism. On March 8, 2018, for example, I cruised Fruitvale with two *veteranas*, Annette Oropeza and Betsy Schultz. Like Oropeza, Schultz was involved with founding the Street Academy, an alternative social justice school rooted in Chicano politics. After an obligatory lunch of good food and conversation, we drove along International Boulevard toward Fruitvale Avenue, the locus of so much of the neighborhood's activism. As we approached Fruitvale Avenue, Schultz pointed to a Wendy's fast-food restaurant on the northwest corner of the avenue's intersection with International Boulevard and told me: "That was the first site of the Street Academy. It was an old warehouse, and we converted it into a school." After the Street Academy relocated to another site, the building became a swap meet where all kinds of small vendors sold their goods. That structure was demolished to build the Wendy's that now stands in its place. We continued up International Boulevard to the second site of the Street Academy, at 1449 Miller Avenue, in a building that the school leased from the City of Oakland. A handsome building that previously was a city library, much of its original structure still stands despite having recently suffered a fire that left it condemned. As we sat in the car looking at the building, Schultz began to choke up: "Oh, I am going to cry. This place brings back so many memories. We did so much here." After the Street Academy moved closer to downtown Oakland, the building was rented by another nonprofit and finally was abandoned after it was structurally damaged by the Loma Prieta earthquake in 1989. As we drove to Oropeza's home, Oropeza and Schultz kept on pointing to the buildings where other nonprofits once stood. We passed by the Unity Council's first senior housing project, which Oropeza pointed to as she remarked: "The Unity Council ... they did well back in the day. They got lots of money from the federal government and the Ford Foundation. That's why everyone resented them."

This casual drive through the neighborhood demonstrates the long-lasting effects of social movement activism on this community. We can see that certain organizations continue to stand, while others were forced to close down. We can also see internal geometries of power: the Unity Council is an institutional giant that has adeptly regenerated and expanded. Fruitvale also represents the effects of federal and philanthropic support and regulation, showing how funding favored certain organizations and spatial formations over others (see chapters 2 and 3). It also reveals that more radicalized organizations such as COMEXAZ (see chapters 1 and 5) overwhelmingly did not survive. Establishments such as the Street Academy relocated to other areas and became formally included within Oakland's Unified School District. We must therefore understand space as "the sphere of the possibility of the existence of multiplicity in the sense of contemporaneous plurality; as the sphere in which distinct trajectories coexist; as the sphere therefore of coexisting heterogeneity" (Massey 2005, 9). No space can ever be a bounded homogeneity (or enclave), forcibly disconnected and therefore forever distinct from other spaces.

Remembering the Past (in Space) Matters

In March 2018, I was made an honorary member of the Fruitvale History Project. The activists I interviewed organized themselves to preserve Fruitvale's history of activism. Many of these activists have recently retired and are building new spaces to organize. Annette Oropeza was at the centerpiece of the mobilizing, along with Regina Chavarín, Liz Meza, and other activists featured in the previous chapters. "You know, the way you describe our activism and Fruitvale, that's the way that it was," a nostalgic Oropeza told me. "We had been thinking of collecting our stories for a long time, and then you came along, and your analysis and work of compiling all of our stories made us think that we could do our own historical project," she explained. She was specifically intrigued by the way I had characterized the cartographic power in their memories, asking me: "What is that kind of memory I have, carto what?" "Cartographic memory," I reminded her. "Yes, I love how it really captures the work that we did. And I love that I have cartographic memory," she added. Acknowledging themselves as agents and bearers of history, other activists quickly joined the project to preserve the legacy of their activism.

These veteran activists began to organize once again around their identities as social movement actors. They reconnected to collect video-recorded oral histories that preserve the legacy of their work. As a brochure about the Fruitvale History Project explains:

> The 1960s brought the civil rights movement, the anti-war movement, and the beginnings of many struggles for economic and social justice to the nation, to Oakland, and to the Fruitvale community. It was during this period that many social service agencies were created in Fruitvale such as Centro Legal de la Raza and La Clínica de la Raza, in order to fill the legal and health needs that were lacking. The Spanish Speaking Unity Council had been created to address economic development in the area; the Narcotics Education League made drug abuse an issue that could be treated rather than hidden; Centro Infantil and La Escuelita were formed by parents who wanted to see a more culturally relevant approach to education. These are but a few organizations that still exist today because of the struggles by the people of that era to bring much needed services to the community.[2]

This historical project is not devoid of politics. First, the narration of the project links Fruitvale to a national and even worldwide movement against injustice. Second, it presents Fruitvale activists as agents of change, involved in more than mere episodic and ephemeral street protests. Activists view their efforts as part of a wider movement to obtain neighborhood resources. As the brochure details, little historical memory exists of this longue durée of mobilization. However, some organizations that activists created are still in existence. As in other cartographic memories, here too urban space serves as an archive of social movement struggle. Space is therefore intricately tied to a politics of recovering memory and historicizing activists' contributions to the neighborhood. Space also presents us with an argument about the longevity of social movement struggles. The Fruitvale History Project argues that it is essential to situate social movements in place. When you emphasize the geographic or spatial nature of history (history being the record of human actions, social relations that occur on space *and* create space), it is easier to see not only historical ruptures but also continuations, longevity, and social movement legacies that too often are missed by episodic analyses of oppositional politics. If movements allegedly die at some point, it would require the spaces and humans that animated those movements to equally disappear.

The Fruitvale History Project argues just the opposite. Activists boldly proclaim, "We are still here." We can more comprehensively appreciate the openness of space: there are numerous historical and present-day stories that give meaning to the space called Fruitvale. However, these social movement actors are making a concerted effort to preserve the memory of their particular "story-so-far": "The Fruitvale History Project was formed to preserve the memory and legacy of these decades.... Our intent is to bring these stories to the public so that the present and future generations may continue to preserve them and most importantly, can learn from them." According to activists who form part of the Fruitvale History Project, the story of 1960s and 1970s activism has important lessons for the present, a current space-time conjuncture in which many inequalities that activists fought in past decades continue to exist. As the brochure concludes: "This is a project that has no end ... as long as there are stories, and people to tell them."[3] Activists contend that this history of the Chicano movement needs to be told not just because they helped to shape it but because it is an essential part of San Francisco Bay Area organizing. And a history that they lament has been overwhelmingly left out of commemorations and historical accounts of activism in the region.

Raising awareness of this activism entails bringing the community together for collective remembering. The Fruitvale History Project's first public event, named "Legacy of Organizing in the Fruitvale," was held on September 12, 2018. I was invited as one of the guest speakers, and Joel Garcia, who was one of the founders of Clínica de la Raza and Tiburcio Vazquez Health Center in Hayward, was honored for his work. For months I saw how the *veteranos* planned the event, and I realized that their activist skills, like many of the institutions they built, are still remarkably powerful. I also realized how intimately tied they still were to the neighborhood: they knew exactly which community members and organizations they needed to contact. My friends who worked for Centro Legal de la Raza contacted me weeks in advance, excited that I would be speaking at the event. I had not given them notice, but they learned about the event from the advertising facilitated by the Fruitvale History Project. The *veteranos* had adapted their organizing repertoires to the present time. Although in the past they had spread news through their contacts and by physically going to different institutions, they now cast a wider net through email and listservs. At the event, a room full of more than 120 guests offered validation of their successful promotion of the event.

It was fascinating to see the group in action. It was organized to a T, with everyone having a task as they planned for the event. One thing was clear: once an organizer, always an organizer and activist. Someone took care of the signup sheet; another person made the arrangements for the space. On the day of the event, different people brought specific side dishes. We all worked together to set up the room, arranging circular tables covered with vibrant tablecloths and transforming a stale meeting room into an organic, homelike Chicano space. Someone even brought flowers to place at the center of each table. On one side of the room, activists displayed photographs and movement ephemera. Many of the activists, especially the women, remarked on how youthful they all looked in the photos. The room buzzed with the sound of different community stakeholders coming together. Old, young, Latino, Black, and white, this was a multiracial and intergenerational gathering. Activists like Regina Chavarín, Betsy Schultz, Joel Garcia, and Annette Oropeza glowed with enthusiasm as they reconnected with fellow activists and community members. Additionally, there were representatives from just about every organization in the room: new generations of leaders who worked at Centro Legal de la Raza, as well as elected officials, teachers, and other community stakeholders.

At the event I was reminded that these activists also have a remarkably broad understanding of what constitutes a social movement. In the flyer for the event, for example, they specified what they defined as "organizing": nonprofit agencies, solidarity committees, anti-police crime coalitions, parent-teacher bilingual groups, community/grassroots organizations. In sum, there was no emphasis on what organizations were considered "conservative," "radical," "better," or more "effective." Activists emphasized the entire breadth of organizing and focused especially on the effects of organizing: providing resources, creating consciousness, politicizing people—in sum, caring for the community. As Joel Garcia would later describe: "The essence of activism is taking action."

Putting forth Fruitvale's history of activism is linked to passing down this information to the next generation. The activists did this with their own children who grew up in the movement and understand the importance of mobilizing for social change. But they also want to impact other youths. They want the new generations to understand that Fruitvale is still primed as a space for activism. And they want Fruitvale as a whole, including most of the new residents who are recently arrived immigrants, to know that there is a legacy in the neighborhood.

These activists' memorialization of their activism is also linked to a broader attempt to highlight the role of Chicanos and Latinos in reshaping Oakland's cultural, social, and arts landscape. By centering Fruitvale through social movement interlinkages, activist continue to challenge conceptions of Oakland as solely a space of Black activism. Alfredo Cruz, for example, remarked as follows when I asked him about the Chicano connections to Black Power mobilizations: "Everyone assumed that they were the only power opposing the white establishment ... the media bypassed us basically and we became the silent shadow."[4] Through their commemoration of their activism, these social movement leaders put Fruitvale on the map of translocal and transnational organizing.

The activists are mobilizing to create multiple platforms through which Fruitvale's history of activism can shine. For example, a number of activists are now affiliated with Oakland's Museum of California, where they are pushing for greater inclusion of Chicano history. Annette Oropeza sits on the committee that helps to organize the museum's annual Day of the Dead celebration. Through this work, she hopes to bring attention to the history of Chicano activism in Fruitvale. The museum recently had a retrospective on the Black Panthers. The 2016 exhibition, entitled *All Power to the People: Black Panthers at 50*, solidified the way that Oakland will forever be marked by Black Panther mobilizations. The museum now has a permanent installation that honors that work. In contrast, there is little or no mention of Chicano activism in Oakland. Most of the activists I spoke to acknowledge that the museum has had a history of minimizing the role of Chicanos in the production of Oakland. This is why they are infiltrating places like the Oakland Museum of California to incite changes in the way in which the Chicano movement and the Fruitvale neighborhood are commemorated in the city. In so doing, they are activating their cartographic memories to help shape the narrative about the past and current role of Latinos in Oakland. This is not just about getting credit for the work they did. It is about creating pride in a cultural legacy.

On October 19, 2019, the *veteranos* joined the Day of the Dead celebration at the Oakland Museum of California. The museum had a special exhibit called *El Movimiento Vivo!*, or *The Living Movement!*, that focused on the

c.1 The altar *El Movimiento Nunca Muere* commemorating Fruitvale activism. Photograph by the Fruitvale History Project.

Chicano movement in California and its role in the creation of the popular Day of the Dead celebrations throughout the United States. For weeks, the activists worked collaboratively with the museum to design an altar that commemorated activism in Fruitvale and honored many of the activists who have passed. Most prominently, the altar celebrated the ongoing legacy of this activism. The *ofrenda* (altar) was boldly titled *El Movimiento Nunca Muere*, or *The Movement Never Dies*, a message that underscores one of the major arguments of this book. It urges us to move away from analyses that emphasize the birth, rise, and fall of mobilizations and instead redirects focus to their lasting impacts on the social and spatial fabric of Fruitvale. Like their cartographic memories, the altar spatializes Chicano movement activism in Fruitvale and offers selective mappings that emphasize activists' unique contributions to community change. The name of the community— Fruitvale—stands prominently at the top of the altar, which also showcases a mini-mural by Liz Meza, who once was the primary motor of COMEXAZ (see chapters 1 and 5). Her mural tells the long history of Chicano movement activism and how it shaped Fruitvale neighborhood dynamics. Graphed

C.2 Side detail of the altar *El Movimiento Nunca Muere* commemorating Fruitvale activism. Photograph by the Fruitvale History Project.

below the mural is a representation of the neighborhood's geography, with Fruitvale Avenue and other streets cartographically situating activism in place. The lower portion of the altar visualizes the impact of many activists and organizers on Fruitvale and the Bay Area by weaving together the specific activists and organizations with Latina/o iconography such as La Virgen de Guadalupe and Fruitvale and Bay Area landmarks to demonstrate the

C.3 Members of the Fruitvale History Project stand in front of the altar *El Movimiento Nunca Muere. Left to right:* Mariano Contreras, Beatriz Pesquera, Annette Oropeza, Selia Melero, Elizabeth "Liz" Meza, Lenor de Cruz, Judy Garcia, Joel Garcia, Betsy Schultz, and Regina Chavarín. Photograph by the Fruitvale History Project.

social and spatial impacts of the activism. In doing so, space and time are intricately entwined. In order to commemorate the Chicano movement, which is popularly known as a "historical" form of collective action that occurred "in the past," activists graph its enduring impact on Fruitvale and the social relations they built in this community. Through this altar, the activists once again remind us of the importance of accounting for the spatiality and multiplicity of social movement activism. As a form of cartographic memory, the altar makes the temporal argument that this movement is not dead but alive and thriving.

The altar also explains another dimension of cartographic memory—the perspectival nature of written accounts of place. It foregrounds additional Fruitvale-based struggles that are not prominently featured in this book. For example, activists were involved in mobilizations in support of affirmative action in the wake of the monumental US Supreme Court case *Regents of the University of California v. Bakke* in 1978. Activists from Fruitvale joined a statewide movement in defense of affirmative action, a key social movement gain of the civil rights movement that they fervently fought to maintain. They also supported the struggle against police brutality that shows the historical precedents of contemporary movements like Black Lives Matter. Activists were galvanized after the death of Barlow Benavides in Fruitvale and organized a Bay Area–wide mobilization in support of the Benavides family. This included a strong coalitional movement that united Chicano and Black communities against police surveillance and violence. A significant erasure in these activists' altar, however, is any mention of Unity Council projects in the neighborhood. Although the altar is dedicated to activism in the community, the organization that is popularly known as the neighborhood's principal steward is remarkably left out (see chapter 4).

As these activists remind us, there are many stories that make up how people experience and help to produce place—especially in accordance with the multilayered process of social movement activism. To borrow from Doreen Massey, any characterization of space is just a cut across a myriad of simultaneous stories happening in a contemporaneous plurality. This is the perspectival nature of cartographic memory, and a methodology for writing about the complexities of place. I hope that this book can help in a process of telling more complex stories of Latino neighborhoods and the multilayered experiences of social movement activism. Ultimately, this book is an invitation for other perspectival renderings of this and other social movement spatialities of struggle.

Toward a Space-Time Analysis of Activism

By paying attention to the spatiality of social movements, this book has also demonstrated that movements fundamentally mobilize for the care and protection of marginalized populations. Race-based social movements in the United States have historically mobilized to combat white supremacy and the forms of georacial management that it enables (Jim Crow segregation, redlining, and border walls, for example). These movements therefore demonstrate that racial matters are also spatial matters (see McKittrick 2006). Furthermore, because of the effects of segregation in shaping US society, movements that mobilize to care for particular racialized populations are grounded in specific spatialities. Institutions like Clínica de la Raza, Centro Legal de la Raza, and the Unity Council are social movement organizations constructed to link the most marginalized groups (and their respective spatialities) to networks of care and resources. In a context of shifting neighborhood demographics, new organizations have developed to meet a new set of demands. However, these organizations have not emerged in isolation; they are guided and shaped by conditions of possibility constructed by powerful 1960s and 1970s nonprofits.

When I was first introduced to Fruitvale in 2005, it was almost forty years after the heyday of the Chicano movement. As I entered the neighborhood, however, there were numerous traces of 1960s activism that were invisible to me. It took years before I learned, through activists' cartographic memories, to pay attention to the reverberations of the past in the present. Despite being initially blind to these dynamics, I could easily see many of the same conditions found in the late 1960s and 1970s: as in the past, Fruitvale continues to be a community with an ever-changing population. Additionally, the population regenerates as the neighborhood attracts newer waves of immigrants. As a result of the Bay Area housing crisis, the neighborhood is also now attracting gentrifiers looking for cheaper housing.

As I alluded to in the introduction, this is a deeply personal book. For more than six years, I worked closely with the Street Level Health Project, a community resource center and medical clinic. I was part of a long tradition of Latino UC Berkeley students who found in Fruitvale a place where they could "give back" to their community and "put to practice" their university training. Many students volunteered at different legal clinics or health clinics throughout the neighborhood. Like generations of the past, self-identified students of color at UC Berkeley found in Fruitvale an important site to develop and test their politicization.

At Street Level I began as a volunteer, then as a work-study employee, and I assisted on many projects, including grant writing, translation, and everyday operations. I was a board member, board president, and then an adviser to the organization once I moved out of Oakland. I say this not to emphasize my methodological rigor or to authenticate the activist nature of my scholarship. I do so to underscore how I also intimately experienced—and took part in—the social movement production of space. Throughout my tenure at Street Level, I interacted with community members who utilized the community resources and came to know the everyday struggles of residents and nonprofit employees and the day-to-day challenges of running a nonprofit institution. I also witnessed the way organizations supported one another and the politics that animated how disparate institutions all worked together to care for and support Fruitvale's predominantly immigrant and Latino population (albeit with power asymmetries and conflicting interests).

C.4 Street Level Health Project reunion. *Left to right:* Kathy Ahoy, Juan Herrera, and Gabriela Galicia. Kathy Ahoy has officially retired, but she can always be found at Street Level; Gabriela Galicia has worked at the organization for a number of years and is now the current executive director. Photograph by the author.

Street-Level Care

When I first started volunteering, the office of the Street Level Health Project was located in an old hospital building that was run-down but showed signs of the grandeur of the past. As I entered the office, all I could see were people busily going about their activities. On one end of the room men were being served lunch, on another end a curtain partitioned a makeshift clinic where patients saw the doctor. There were about forty people in a room with a capacity of thirty. Volunteers carried clipboards on which they wrote patients' information. The room was permeated with the smell of food cooked on hotplates in one corner. The men talked with one another while they waited either for lunch or for their turn to see the doctor. I looked for a woman named Laura Lopez, who was then the organization's executive director. I initially did not see her but could hear her powerful voice giving orders and making sure that everyone was being helped. At five feet, Lopez is far shorter than one would expect from how her voice projects. She was clearly Street Level's main motor, and her caring nature attracted clients to the organization. Clients came there not just to access medical care. Many came solely to consult with Señorita Laura about a particular problem, and medical care ensued afterward. As an immigrant from Peru and a former undocumented worker, Lopez personally understood the fears and limitations that Street Level's clients confronted on a daily basis.

The Street Level Health Project was founded in 2002 by a group of Alameda County nurses and premed students from Mills College. At that time its services were provided mainly on the streets and the organization existed only on an irregular basis as a mobile clinic. The head organizer of the services was the energetic Kathy Ahoy, a senior Alameda County nurse who pulled strings to get the Alameda County Public Health Department to let her go out to the streets. Nobody ever said no to Kathy Ahoy because she exuded so much compassion and conviction to helping people. As a refugee from India, Ahoy understood that many recently arrived immigrants get left out of care. According to Ahoy, the "system" was not created to reach out to this population. Like nonprofit workers of the past, the charismatic Kathy Ahoy wore many hats and served as a critical nexus between the Alameda County Public Health Department as a state agency and the Street Level Health Project. Furthermore, as a product of 1970s grassroots activism in the Bay Area, Ahoy also linked past struggles to the present. All of this was embodied in the day-to-day services at Street Level and the political work of targeting primarily undocumented, recently arrived immigrants.

The Dialectical Relationship of the Past and the Present

Street Level's Kathy Ahoy embodies a long genealogy of activism. I initially thought her involvement emerged solely from her work as an Alameda County public health nurse. Ahoy, however, had a longer history of politicization that was connected to the farmworker struggles of the 1970s. As a recently arrived refugee from India in the 1970s, Ahoy was captivated by the strength of the United Farm Workers movement. For her, the movement represented much more than farmworkers' struggles. It epitomized the training of a generation of community leaders who developed a vision of helping to link poor people with networks of care. She saw firsthand the powerful role of the church in this movement and was inspired to become involved. She recalled: "There was a coalition in those days. Back in the seventies churches backed them up [the UFW] to have people come in from Salinas, all over the place. We would go into the Lucky's, Safeway, all the big grocery stores to protest grapes. So that's where the groups came

together to work in some social welfare issue and labor issue."[5] Ahoy understood the value of collective action and gained a profound desire to make
this kind of mobilizing sustainable. As she explained, it was important to
think of the longevity of the struggle. She interpreted working within the
Alameda County health system as a way of making sure that she could reach
out to the poorest individuals. The farmworkers' movement galvanized her
to become involved in this and other struggles.

Ahoy recalled how a whole generation of leaders transferred their
grassroots energy into institutions that then cared for the poorest and
most marginalized. As Ahoy nostalgically recalled: "Having a visibility
at that time Cesar Chavez was there gave people a sense of 'Hey, you can
be leaders!' This sense of momentum to start up and then to also enter
health care."[6] According to Ahoy, some of the most prominent leaders were
propelled to take on different kinds of work in Fruitvale and surrounding
communities. Joel Garcia, for example, was trained as a lawyer but gained
greater visibility in health care through his work in establishing Clínica
de la Raza and Tiburcio Vasquez Health Center (in Hayward, California),
both community health clinics that focus on reaching out to the most
marginalized.

For Chicano activists, health care was a key site of struggle. Nonprofit
leaders innovated new ways of thinking about the relationship between
health and community and how to treat people appropriately. Like Street
Level's humble beginnings sharing space with other organizations and re-
lying on an all-volunteer staff, Clínica de la Raza emerged as a completely
grassroots project; it was a community-based effort that recognized the
lack of state health services for Mexican Americans. As a former nonprofit
worker, Manuel Alcalá, recalled: "One of the things they started doing was
using culture. I remember seeing posters with sayings like 'la cultura cura'
[culture cures]."[7] Alcalá recalled the power of this new way of thinking
about health care and culture, which he argued developed into theories
and new modes of working with people. He also lamented that this period
of innovation came to a halt once health care clinics became institutionalized. According to Alcalá, expanding nonprofit institutionalization and
professionalization meant that these agencies no longer were key sites of
innovation. As he further explained: "There was a transition, from grassroots agencies to very structured organizations. And they lost something
along the way."[8]

Clínica de la Raza is now a multimillion-dollar community clinic in Fruitvale with multiple branches throughout Oakland. Its growth was facilitated

C.5 Walls at the Street Level Health Project adorned with protest posters and a reminder that culture is extremely important to curing one's ills. "La cultura cura," or "culture cures," was an important health slogan of the Chicano movement. Photograph by the author.

by its transformation in the mid-1970s into a Federally Qualified Health Center. Clínica's ability to bill Alameda County and the federal government gave it a secured flow of revenue that contributed to its continued growth. Throughout this process the federal terrain over the provision of services for undocumented people changed completely. As the Fruitvale district's population has shifted, a greater proportion of residents are now undocumented immigrants. Clínica's primary reliance on federal funds meant that it could not as easily offer services to undocumented clients. Furthermore, its increasing professionalization made it less focused on its links to the community. As a public health nurse, Ahoy always advocated for less institutionalized provision of health care because she understood that the most marginalized could not be easily reached via large institutions. She believed that instead of waiting for the poor to come to community clinics or hospitals to seek emergency care, health care institutions should actively reach out to them. That is why she and other public health nurses collaborated to establish the Street Level Health Project.[9]

The Street Level Health Project was founded in 2002 to directly link the most impoverished sectors to community health clinics like Clínica de la Raza. The project primarily targeted the growing number of day laborers in the neighborhood, who congregated on prominent street corners looking for work. However, its services soon moved to work with all members of the community who felt left out of institutionalized forms of health care. The organization worked closely with Clínica de la Raza to help expedite services for undocumented migrants, with the two organizations developing an interdependent relationship that allows them to hold each other accountable. Before Street Level, it was challenging for day laborers, and undocumented immigrants in general, to access Clínica. Many simply could not produce any form of proof of residency in Alameda County, a requirement that Clínica firmly upheld due to federal and state funding guidelines. Furthermore, in order to be seen at Clínica, new members were put on a long waiting list. Street Level created a referral system with Clínica so that its clients would be seen within a week. Through this system, Street Level clients also avoided the proof of residency requirement that many undocumented day laborers could not produce.

Clínica and Street Level have become important partner organizations, as was best evidenced on September 27, 2012, when I attended the celebration of Street Level's tenth anniversary. At this event, I was able to see the connection between 1960s organizations and the formation of newer nonprofits. As a young organization, Street Level thanked key players who had helped in the organization's formation. These players included both nonprofit allies (especially Centro Legal de la Raza and Clínica de la Raza), Alameda County officials, and philanthropic organizations. As in the past, the triangulation of municipal agencies, nonprofits, and philanthropy is a key feature in the formation of current projects in Fruitvale and shaping the direction of newer organizations. Representatives of all three sectors identified Street Level's unique contribution: unlike other more institutionalized nonprofits, it connected effortlessly with the immigrant poor. Representatives from Alameda County positioned Street Level as a model for achieving social justice in health care.

Street Level's executive director gave awards to Centro Legal de la Raza and Clínica for their continued support. Centro was instrumental in helping to give Street Level a more institutional footing. As a newly formed organization in 2002, Street Level could not yet receive private foundation money on its own. Centro came to the rescue by offering to be Street Level's fiscal sponsor. Foundation money would come to Centro, and for a nominal overhead fee, it would funnel that money to Street Level. At Street Level's tenth-anniversary celebration, Jane Garcia, Clínica's executive director, graciously accepted Street Level's award. In her acceptance speech, she portrayed Clínica de la Raza and Street Level as a sisterhood of sorts. She characterized Street Level as a younger sister and Clínica as the big sister in the relationship. And sometimes, as Garcia remarked, "big sisters need a little sister to tug at them and nudge them to do something." Garcia admitted that Street Level had awakened Clínica to the reality of its institutionalization and the fact that, as she saw it, Clínica was also now part of the "system." Like any system, she acknowledged, Clínica was difficult to navigate, especially for newly arrived immigrants. She described a relationship of reciprocity between the two organizations whereby Clínica helped to mentor Street Level and provided key openings to its medical services. At the same time, Street Level's prodding helped Clínica realize some of its pitfalls: the fact that as a community clinic, it was inaccessible to a certain kind of population. The sisterhood was a two-way relationship filled with mentorship, mutual policy suggestions, and a continuation of 1960s organizing that promoted the formation of the Chicano nonprofits in Oakland.

This insightful moment illustrates a critical transmission of information between institutionalized organizations that emerged out of 1960s activism, like Clínica, and newer grassroots nonprofits, such as the Street Level Health Project. These organizations rely on mutual interactions and exert pressures on one another that help to shape Fruitvale residents' experiences. Both Clínica and Centro emerged out of the 1960s mobilizations and were the products of the institutionalization of grassroots activism. Now, according to Clínica's executive director Jane Garcia, these formerly grassroots struggles are completely part of the "system," and they have to deal with the daily struggles of institutionalization. Garcia's comment also referred to the fact that Fruitvale residents find it difficult to navigate these rigid bureaucratic systems. The Street Level Health Project responded to these bureaucratic limits of institutionalization and the shifting composition of Fruitvale's population.

Fruitvale as an Interlinkage of Activism

Taking a neighborhood-level approach to social movements and processes of institutionalization has allowed me to see how movements adapt to changing political, economic, and spatial dynamics. Fruitvale's population has changed tremendously since the 1960s. The political climate has also rendered certain issues more salient than others. The current political conjuncture of immigrant rights activism has intersected with and reignited many of the key practices of neighborhood care set in place through Chicano movement organizing. Oakland is now ardently a sanctuary city, a status that ensures the city will not cooperate with US Immigration and Custom Enforcement agencies. In this current citywide endeavor to help and protect undocumented migrants, Fruitvale has emerged as a major spatiality for the making of immigrant rights politics.

The reality of gentrification in the Bay Area has also made housing justice a major concern for neighborhood nonprofits. In fact, Centro Legal de la Raza now has two offices. One works predominantly on immigration issues, helping people fight deportation orders and normalize their immigration status, including help with DACA applications. The other office focuses on workers' and tenants' rights. These tenants' rights clinics, which mainly work to protect clients from eviction, are so widely used that staff members expressed frustrations about not being able to give each client the proper attention. Because of the housing crisis, many landlords are pushing to evict older tenants and then rent their units at market rate to new residents. Centro also protects residents by helping to file affirmative housing lawsuits that help to ensure the well-being of both tenants and landlords.

Causa Justa/Just Cause (CJJC) is another organization that works in the realm of tenants' rights and movement-building. Officially started in 2010, CJJC merged the work of two powerful Oakland organizations that had been operating for more than thirty years to empower tenants and undocumented workers. Since its inception, CJJC has worked hard to build Black and brown coalitions in Oakland and to consolidate a movement in support of immigrants' and tenants' rights. In addition, it has been fighting gentrification by working with elected officials and other coalitions to pass several Oakland-based policies to help fight against displacement.

These coordinated efforts make Fruitvale a prime site in the fight for immigrant rights and other contemporary forms of resistance. The most salient example of this is the trajectory of immigrant rights marches in the East Bay. The immigrant rights marches that took place in the East Bay in 2006 arose from Fruitvale (see Zepeda-Millán 2017). I was then already working with the Street Level Health Project, and I enthusiastically marched with all the workers. We made protest posters and wore all white in solidarity with marchers throughout the United States. The nonprofits and political action groups assembled their members, and we convened at

Fruitvale Village, transforming plazas and walkways into spaces of protest. As we marched down International Boulevard toward downtown Oakland, marchers clustered behind their organizations' banners. Others gathered at all the different nonprofits along International Boulevard. Those of us from Street Level took turns holding a huge banner while marching and chanting in support of immigrant rights. When we passed by Street Level's offices, members joined or simply cheered us on our path to downtown Oakland. Other marchers assembled behind the CJJC banner. Centro also had an enormous contingency made up of students, parents, and day laborers. Although the path on International Boulevard is mostly flat, at one point along the trajectory the street curved upward into a small hill. As I looked back, all I could see was a sea of white-clad marchers who transformed the urban landscape both with their visual presence and with their chants and singing. As I now reflect on the immigrant rights marches of 2006, I can more fully appreciate how social movement activism of the 1960s influenced the kinds of mobilizing strategies currently deployed in defense of immigrant rights.[10] More important, these mobilizing strategies take place in space and also continue to produce Fruitvale as a site of resistance and a geography of activism.

For a recently arrived immigrant or any other person unfamiliar with this region of Oakland, Fruitvale is a classic ethnic enclave—a safe and welcoming Latino place that appears to have some sense of insularity. The existence of Chicano-themed social services such as Centro Legal de la Raza and Clínica de la Raza just seems natural. So, too, do the aesthetics of the local stores and the Latino-inspired architecture of Fruitvale Village and the recently completed addition of housing called Casa Arabella. Yet if we summon up a spatial imaginary and make use of activists' cartographic memories, we can see how the neighborhood was transformed by the stories set in place as a result of Chicano movement activism in the 1960s and 1970s. Furthermore, we can use space as a register to account for these effects. A spatial register can therefore help to open up the sphere of the political, to better understand how organizations that were created in the 1960s continue to shape neighborhood politics and resources, as well as the built environment and the social relations that constitute a distinct neighborhood identity. This kind of spatial reading also challenges the obsession with calling this neighborhood an ethnic enclave, an erroneous and essentializing spatial identity that positions this space as having always been separated and contained, instead of allowing us to think of *how* certain political, economic, and human-environment relationships created its current space-time conjuncture. Neighborhood particularity is not a product of insularity. The particularity of this neighborhood has been forged by historical processes of settler colonialism, exploitation of land and labor, *and* social movement activism.

The dynamics that I describe in this book, however, are not unique to Fruitvale. Similar human-environment relationships can be found in many other places. I had to learn to see this particular constellation of space and power. It took some time for me to learn to listen to activists' cartographic memories. Consider, for example, how Liz Meza repeated what many activists told me about the neighborhood and the very spatiality of social movement activism: "At the time the organizing in this area was just phenomenal. You couldn't go out the door without running into some little action. It was great. It was really special."[11] The Chicano movement and other race-based mobilizations of the 1960s were national movements that took root in multiple places. This means that the situations that I describe in Fruitvale can be seen in other neighborhoods throughout the United States. We need a better inventory of these spatial productions that social movements set forth. An accounting of these impacts in other places can give us a better sense of how communities continue to thrive despite the continuation of seemingly demagogic injustices that mobilize through spatial inequality. In accounting for these situated forms of activism routed through community, we can take better stock of the different kinds of politics deployed by impoverished and racialized sectors. This means broadening the definition of politics and activism and paying more rigorous attention to the spatiality of contentious politics. It also requires having a better understanding of activism in space and time in order to account for the ongoing nature of social movements and to understand their imaginative and prophetic fight for more socially just futures—waiting to be mapped.

Introduction

1   Much has changed in terms of terminology in the span of researching and writing this book. It is now more popular to use *Latinx* as a gender-neutral or nonbinary alternative to *Latino* or *Latina*. However, I maintain my use of *Latino*, *Latina*, *Chicano*, *Chicana*, *Spanish-speaking*, and even *Hispanic* as terms people used to define themselves during this research. I also researched and wrote using these terms. My intent is to show the historical making of terminology, and to show how these identities were experienced and used.

2   For a similar critique of the partitioning of the ghetto from a mainstream society, see Gregory 1999. There exists a long sociological tradition that has conceptualized ethnic enclaves in particular ways. According to Portes and Jensen (1992, 418), an ethnic enclave refers to "a concentration of ethnic firms in physical space—generally a metropolitan area—that employ a significant proportion of workers from the same minority." See also Portes and Jensen 1987; Waldinger 1993; Wilson and Portes 1980.

3   The 1960s was a period of relocation in which thousands of American Indians were forcibly moved from reservations to inner-city spaces such as Los Angeles and Oakland. See, for example, Ramirez 2007.

4   I thank anonymous reviewer two for alerting me that this dimension of the book reminded them of Kelley's (2002) seminal book *Freedom Dreams*. I had read so much of Robin Kelley's work, but for some reason I had missed this one pathbreaking book. It was only after finishing this book that I fully read Kelley (2002) and was amazed to encounter so much of what I found in my own research on Chicano movement activism in Oakland. These kinds of connections are not uncommon across social movements. My intent is to foreground the geographical imperatives of social movement activisms and how these experiences take shape in place and are also productive of spatialities.

5 By aestheticized blackness, geographer Brandi Thompson Summers (2019) draws attention to how the Black aesthetic is increasingly emplaced and valued in urban settings. According to Summers, this process by which blackness accrues value is part of the urban capitalist simulacra. However, the aesthetic appreciation of blackness does not guarantee that Black bodies are equally respected and celebrated.

6 The literature on the United Farm Workers is expansive, but I am most influenced by the following accounts: Bardacke 2012; Flores 2016; Kohl-Arenas 2015a.

7 As a result of their movement activism, Chicano activists became aware that the United States had taken lands from Mexico as part of the Treaty of Guadalupe Hidalgo. And given the alliances with Native Americans, many Chicanos understood that land had been stolen from Indigenous people to make way for the United States of America. This all occurred during a period in which African nations were fighting against colonization in unprecedented anticolonial movements. This period in history therefore constituted an entire geographic understanding of power, colonialism, empire, and racialized forms of dispossession.

8 Most scholars advance the definition developed by Berenice Fisher and Joan Tronto, who define *care* as "a species activity that includes everything that we do to maintain, continue, and repair our 'world' so that we can live in it as well as possible. That world includes our bodies, ourselves, and our environment, all of which we seek to interweave in a complex, life-sustaining web" (Fisher and Tronto 1990, 40; see also Tronto 2013, 19). This is a rather broad definition and allows for us to view different notions of care that extend to nonhuman realms. Activists were consistently concerned about caring for disenfranchised groups, all of which were located in specific places. In order to care for fellow human beings, activists also advanced a politics about caring for geographic communities.

9 I owe this to the incredible work of Jacqueline Nassy Brown (2005), which was instrumental in my understanding of the politics of place. I am also indebted to Donald S. Moore and Jake Kosek for multiple conversations we had regarding cultural politics rooted and routed through place.

10 For an analysis of the Chicano movement's complex history of overlooking women's contributions, see Cotera, Blackwell, and Espinoza 2018; see also Blackwell 2011.

11 Through my research I became intrigued by how activists conceptualized different generations. We often think of generations as the division between much older folks and youths, yet in this period an age difference of five or so years constituted a significant generational difference. Many of the older activists who were closer to thirty had different political subjectivities than more youthful activists in their early twenties.

12 As chapter 2 details, the designation Spanish-speaking was popular up until the 1960s to refer to people of Latin American descent. In fact, the book traces the development of designations such as Chicano and Mexican American as categories that came into existence largely out of social movement organizing. In the 1980s, a new umbrella category, Hispanic, came into existence based on the triangulation of a number of political factors. See Mora 2014.

13 The National Council of La Raza (NCLR) recently changed its name to UNIDOS. It first emerged, however, as the Southwest Council of La Raza (SCLR). In the book I will refer to both NCLR and SCLR (see Mora 2014).

14 The CSO was an important Mexican American civil rights organization created in the aftermath of World War II. It sought to empower the Mexican American community through different grassroots organizing efforts that privileged electoral politics. It is most well known for having trained famed leaders like Cesar Chavez and Dolores Huerta. See chapter 2 for a more detailed elaboration of how the CSO was an important precedent to Oakland-based Chicano movement activism.

15 The Cesar Chavez Lifetime Achievement Awards is a rotating ceremony that moves to different communities. It honors the legacy of Cesar Chavez and his mission of grassroots activism and empowerment.

16 A new body of literature on the Chicano movement has begun to address these concerns. For elaboration on this longue durée analysis, see Cotera, Blackwell, and Espinoza 2018; Flores 2016; Krochmal 2016.

17 Commemorations of the Chicano movement, African American civil rights mobilizations, and even Black Power, for example, are now part of the ethnic pageantry of US neoliberal multiculturalism. This is most powerfully performed through the celebration of figures such as Martin Luther King Jr., Malcom X, Cesar Chavez, and, more recently, Dolores Huerta. This kind of incorporation of social movement icons serves a crucial political function that fashions the United States as a postracial nation in which race-based mobilizations are a thing of the past (Melamed 2006, 2011).

18 In fact, activists often didn't remember exact dates. My thinking about how activists' memories emphasized place over time stems from my reading of Indigenous oral traditions that passed down information and stories from one generation to the next. William Bauer writes extensively about Native American history prior to conquest. He is especially concerned with how oral traditions emphasize how people "move across space, not time; from place to place, not from date to date" (Bauer 2012, 109).

19 As Jacqueline Nassy Brown (2005, 11) would argue, these activists made "sense of place-as-matter, a practice that includes reading landscapes and acting on the view that place acts, that it shapes human consciousness." In a similar fashion, geographer Helga Leitner, Eric Sheppard, and Kristin M. Sziarto

(2008) insist that it is important to pay close attention to the materiality of contentious politics. To do so means analyzing how agency is distributed across the more-than-human world.

20 Katherine McKittrick (2011, 969) comes to a similar conclusion regarding Black geographies during slavery and reveals how conditions of bondage incited alternative mapping practices outside the official tenets of cartography: "Fugitive and maroon maps, literacy maps, food-nourishment maps, family maps, music maps were assembled alongside 'real' maps (those produced by black cartographers and explorers who document landmasses, roads, routes, boundaries, and so forth." See also McKittrick 2006; and McKittrick and Woods 2007.

21 For a similar analysis of this concept of remapping and native space, see Barnd 2017.

22 When thinking about how people remember the past, anthropologist Lisa Yoneyama (1999, 4) argues that we must "question why and how we remember—for what purpose, for whom, and from which position we remember—even when discussing sites of memory, where to many the significance of remembrance seems obvious."

23 I am inspired by the work of historians, ethnic studies scholars, and geographers like Laura Pulido (2006) who have pushed us to think about how race is constructed in a relational fashion. See Molina, HoSang, and Gutiérrez 2019.

24 I am indebted to the work of geographer Doreen Massey for this conceptualization of space. Her life's work was to dynamize space and to capture some of the complexity of the production of space, especially in a context in which space is generally thought of as a surface upon which we simply traverse.

25 For an extensive review of the literature on the geographies of social movements, see Nicholls 2007; Oslender 2016, 1–35.

26 My analysis of a *longue durée* of movements stems from a reading of recent scholarship on the longevity of the civil rights movement and Black Power mobilizations (Clay 2012; Hall 2005; Nelson 2011). I echo sociologist Alondra Nelson by arguing for an analysis that broadens the scope for examining movements. Also helpful is Andreana Clay's insistence on thinking about how popular and scholarly writing has created representations and understandings of 1950s and 1960s activism, which are embodied in ossified repertoires of activism. These repertoires are linked to large social movements and privilege the most radical, militant, or outspoken leaders (Clay 2012, 153). For a similar analysis of social movement continuities, see also Magaña 2017. I am grateful to "Mauricio" Magaña and Maylei Blackwell for all our conversations regarding social movements and geography and for providing such a rich intellectual exchange. Magaña (2021) offers a splendid analysis of the cartographies of youth resistance in Oaxaca, Mexico, that like this book also centers a spatial and *longue durée* reading of social movement activism.

27 I am inspired here by recent work on lingering by Joshua Javier Guzmán and Christina A. Léon (2015). They ask: What if we allow Latinidad to breathe and linger? In a similar way, what if we allow "space" to linger or breathe? By taking this longue durée approach, we can understand more of the complexities that define the suturing of race and space.

28 The literature on social movements has its origins in the development of a series of concepts and theories that helped to explain how and why social movements develop (McAdam 1982; McAdam, Tarrow, and Tilly 2001; Tarrow 1998; Tilly 1986). Early scholarship focused on the political processes that shaped the transformation of a diverse and broad group of actors into a powerful force of social and political change. Analysts have paid attention to multiple kinds of counterhegemonic mobilizations and therefore also use the term *contentious politics* to emphasize how social movement activism is one kind of oppositional politics.

29 Sociologist Doug McAdam and colleagues (2001, 5) define contentious politics as "episodic, public, collective interaction among makers of claims and their objects when (a) at least one government is a claimant, an object of claims, or a party to the claims and (b) the claims would, if realized, affect the interests of at least one of the claimants." Helga Leitner and colleagues (2008, 157) critique the state centrism of this definition to define contentious politics as "concerted, counterhegemonic social and political action, in which differently positioned participants come together to challenge dominant systems of authority, in order to promote and enact alternative imaginaries." Admittedly, these definitions are broad and can encompass disparate kinds of mobilizations. Indeed, sociologist Tianna Paschel (2016) contends that scholars should broaden the register of what constitutes a social movement. She suggests that a social movement doesn't have to be massive, or even engage primarily in street protest, to count as a movement or to bring about change.

30 For examples of such analyses, see Leitner, Sheppard, and Sziarto 2008; Martin and Miller 2003; Nicholls 2007, 2009; Oslender 2016; Pulido 2006; Routledge 1993.

31 As they argue: "In determining how geography matters, we assert that *a priori* decisions (ontological or otherwise) to reduce this multi-valiancy to any single master concept can only impoverish analysis, by offering a partial viewpoint into how geography matters in contentious politics" (Leitner, Sheppard, and Sziarto 2008, 158).

32 As Routledge (1993, 36) argues: "The historical context of the terrain of resistance is also important in understanding movement agency in a particular time and place, for instance, if a particular place has a history of struggle or not, and how this may affect the character of contemporary movement agency."

33 For an analysis of the difference between a history of a temporal process and a history of place, see Limerick 1987, 26. Geographer Doreen Massey

(1994, 2) argues that space must be conceptualized integrally with time, so that it is best to think always in terms of space-time. For Massey, space-time is a configuration of social relations that must be conceived as a dynamic simultaneity.

34 For an analysis of the rise and fall of the Chicano movement, see E. Chávez 1994, 117–20. See also Cotera, Blackwell, and Espinoza 2018, 5.

35 Sociologist Victor Rios (2011, 32), for example, argues that "practices and discourses of criminalization and punishment of young people in the new millennium could be directly traced to the state repression of social movements of the 1960s." See also Murch 2010.

36 The same could be said for other movements such as the Black Panther mobilizations and even the civil rights movement. Of course, many of the organizations that represented the cultural arm of the movement remained, and they were prominently understood as movement groups. That included places like Galeria de la Raza in San Francisco and Teatro Campesino, among other organizations.

37 A number of scholars have shown the effects of this kind of postwar spatial development. Gaye Theresa Johnson (2013, 56) asserts, for example, that "between 1943 and 1949, scores of Black and Latino communities were destroyed to make way for the postindustrial, suburban spatial form that would characterize the modern U.S. city.... Black and Brown neighborhoods were demolished, even erased from maps as if no one had ever lived there." From the vast construction of freeways in neighborhoods like Boyle Heights and the building of Dodger Stadium that dispossessed a thriving Mexican American community to the destruction of a vibrant Mexican American and African American community in West Oakland due to the construction of Interstate 880, this was part of a relentless process of georacial management.

38 It is important to note that as Blackwell (2011) and other scholars have pointed out, it was Chicana women who were some of the first to be framed as "sellouts" or *vendidas* because they advanced "feminist" ideas that were seen as secondary or outside the demands of the Chicano movement.

39 Geographer Laura Pulido (2006, 19) shows that the term *radical* is profoundly relative: "While the Chicana/o movement was indeed radical, there was tremendous diversity within it, with some groups assuming far more conservative positions than others."

40 Self (2003, 217–55) argues that in an analogous fashion, Black Power was an extraordinarily plastic concept adaptable to multiple contexts. As Laura Pulido (2006, 91) argues: "The term included an array of ideologies, organizations, and personalities. Inspired by Malcom X, Black Power symbolized a deep radicalization of African Americans' (and others') struggle for equality with a focus on self-determination and self-defense."

41 Urban planner Jennifer Wolch (1990, xvi) similarly cautioned against the "deepening state penetration" into everyday nonprofit activities, which could "ultimately vitiate sectoral autonomy and capacity to pursue social change." Political scientist Joan Roelofs (2003, 21) raises similar scrutiny: "A closer look at the 'third sector' belies its frequent profession of neutral benevolence. Although all radical organizations are found within this sector, challengers to the system are rare and generally invisible. The third sector is largely devoted to activities that directly protect and promote capitalism."

42 I thank reviewer number two for this important way of framing the dynamic I was trying to name.

43 By showing the complexities and contradictions of social movement institutionalization, I also challenge framings that place tremendous emphasis on the efficacy of state and philanthropic regulatory projects. That is, within this framework, state and philanthropic forces can effectively silence dissent and obliterate contentious politics. This line of argument also presupposes that the state operates as a totalizing entity reduced to a singular logic. The state is not a monolith: it is composed of various offices, which are run by bureaucrats who hold different and often competing interests. The state is also composed of different scales shaped by contentious differences in jurisdiction and power among municipal, state, and federal agencies. It is undeniable that the institutional and fiscal architecture of the nonprofit organization implies a relationship to various state agencies, including the Internal Revenue Service. The federal government, for example, sets out the parameters through which an organization can be recognized as a tax-exempt agency. Furthermore, as chapter 3 reveals, since 1969, federal recognition as a 501(c)(3) prohibits nonprofits from engaging in formal political processes. I explore the practice of these clauses to reveal that they do not always secure a practice of depoliticization. As anthropologist Thomas Biolsi (2005, 240) has astutely argued, "The state's gaze, in other words, may be studiously non-panoptical, its sovereignty purposely not flat, full, or even across its territory but carefully zoned."

44 For a robust analysis of how community development was integral to 1960s Black activism, see Goldstein 2017.

Chapter 1. Making Place

1 I learned in 2018 that Regina and Roger are no longer married, although they are still connected and involved in neighborhood projects. Despite such changes in relationships, there are enduring commitments to places and causes that don't easily go away.

2 Regina Chavarín, interview by the author, October 21, 2012.

3 The Crusade for Justice was a Chicano movement organization that began in Denver, Colorado, in 1967. Like many other community-based movements,

the Crusade for Justice fought for the self-determination of the Chicano community. It did so by focusing on social, political, and economic justice for Chicanos. It saw itself as a vanguard organization and is an example of how the Chicano movement was spatialized throughout the US Southwest.

4 Annette Oropeza, interview by the author, January 8, 2012.

5 Sociologist Edward J. McCaughan (2012, 136) comes to a similar conclusion about Chicano artists who "promoted alternative notions of power and social change rooted in community, democratic participation, egalitarian relations, anti-materialistic values, and ... different ways of knowing in the world that transcended Western concepts of rationality and objectivity." I add to that analysis by focusing on the formation of community institutions through which activists crafted these alternative notions of power and ways of being in the world.

6 I thank the fantastic Laura Pulido for alerting me to this theoretical process that defined activists' connections to place. I owe immense gratitude to the Department of Geography at the University of Oregon for such generous engagement with my work in the spring of 2019.

7 Alfredo Cruz, interview by the author, September 20, 2012.

8 Cruz, interview.

9 Oropeza, interview.

10 Oropeza, interview.

11 Oropeza, interview.

12 Chicano movement activists constructed a mythical region called Aztlán as a way to lay claim to having originated from the US Southwest. According to Indigenous knowledge, the people who founded Indigenous cities in the land now called Mexico originated from the North. Critics have shown that these Chicano claims often viewed these lands as vacant and ignore the presence of Indigenous people in the North American continent, showing the complicity of people of color in settler colonialism (see Pulido 2017).

13 Liz Meza, interview by the author, October 20, 2012.

14 Meza, interview.

15 In adopting a strict cultural nationalism, some Chicano activists created strict boundaries of what constituted legitimate forms of activism. Chicana feminists, for example, were called *vendidas*, or sellouts, for allegedly aligning themselves too closely with "women's issues" and thus were accused of betraying the Chicano movement (see Blackwell 2011, 160–91; Nieto Gomez 1997, 86–92). In a similar fashion, activists who chose to align themselves with mainstream organizations, including state and philanthropic agencies, were often called *vendidos*. McCaughan (2012, 143) discusses the 1980 dispute between Chicano movement artists Malaquias and Leslie Montoya and art

historian Shifra Goldman regarding concerns of potential co-optation by state and mainstream arts institutions.

16　Herman Gallegos, interview by the author, July 5, 2012.

17　Gallegos, interview.

18　David Hayes-Bautista, interview by the author, December 19, 2011.

19　Meza, interview.

20　Jose Arredondo, interview by the author, November 13, 2012.

21　Andreana Clay makes a central argument about the impact of social movements on contemporary youth experiences in Oakland. I add to her analysis by emphasizing the social movement impacts on the built environment and in the creation of social services for Spanish-speaking residents. These services, in the form of nonprofit organizations, continue to deliver services and politicize both long-term residents and recently arrived immigrants.

22　Jose Martinez, interview by the author, February 19, 2012.

23　Regina Chavarín, interview.

24　Joel Garcia, interview by the author, August 24, 2019.

25　Hayes-Bautista, interview.

26　Regina Chavarín, interview.

27　Regina Chavarín, interview.

28　Although the activists I interviewed did not share a specific gendered analysis of their participation in institution-building, most of the labor described was indeed spearheaded by women. Women in the movement were instrumental in projects of community formation, especially those who went on to be mothers at the height of the mobilizations, or others who participated in projects of community mothering. For an extensive analysis of this gendered form of labor, see Bermúdez 2014; Blackwell 2011; Delgado Bernal 1997; Espinoza 2001.

29　Martinez, interview.

30　Garcia, interview.

31　Hayes-Bautista, interview.

32　Martinez, interview.

33　Garcia, interview.

34　The idea of *comadrazgo* and *compadrazgo* developed through movement organizing does not have a simple translation in English. Activists retooled the Chicano movement valorization of the family to create new kinds of political kinship ties based on a shared mission of community solidarity and support.

35　Regina Chavarín, interview.

36　Regina Chavarín, interview.

37　Oropeza, interview.

Chapter 2. The Other Minority

1 Ananya Roy and colleagues have argued that poverty became a domestic and international public policy issue in the 1960s, linking it to anxieties about racialized violence in US cities and wars of insurgency in the global South. They demonstrate that War on Poverty interventions must be analyzed within this context as state and philanthropic agencies were worried about both delinquent youths in the inner city and unruly third world people. The War on Poverty was a machinery that increased the emphasis on policing and pacification of unrest. See Roy, Schrader, and Chane 2015. See also Rios 2011.

2 The Watts riot was one of a number of urban riots that took place in the 1960s as a response to deteriorating conditions in cities. This lack of investment in the inner city was the direct effect of white flight and the overinvestment in the suburbs. Riots occurred in Birmingham, Alabama, in 1963; in Chicago and Cleveland in 1966; in sixty cities, including Detroit, Newark, and Milwaukee, in 1967; and in Chicago again in 1968. See Douglas Massey and Denton 1993, 58.

3 Consistent with the terminology of the time, I use *Spanish-speaking* to refer to people of Mexican American ancestry. Government officials, newspaper articles, and academic studies of the time commonly equated *Spanish-speaking* with being Mexican American. Mexican American activists also preferred to use *Spanish-speaking* to ally with other groups, such as Puerto Ricans and Filipinos, that also spoke the Spanish language.

4 The Treaty of Guadalupe Hidalgo was signed by the United States and Mexico on February 2, 1848, and ceded almost half of Mexican territory (which incorporated present-day states of California, New Mexico, Nevada, and parts of Colorado, Arizona, Utah, and Oklahoma) to the United States. Most notably, the treaty guaranteed US citizenship for Mexicans who inhabited the Southwest upon the US takeover of Mexican territory (Acuña 2004; D. G. Gutiérrez 1995). Activists referenced this treaty in claiming their status as rightful citizens of the United States. They positioned the Mexican American population as rights-bearing subjects who were deserving of state welfare provisions.

5 Tania Murray Li (2007, 7) uses the expression "rendering technical" to describe an ensemble of practices concerned with representing the domain to be governed as an intelligible field of action.

6 A pivotal component of this trend in relation to urbanization is the reconfiguration of the territory of government from the nation-state to the level of community and the reliance of nonstate agencies to help construct productive and entrepreneurial subjects (J. Ferguson and Gupta 2002; Ong 2006; Raco and Imrie 2000). Proponents of devolution couch the transfer of responsibility to local municipalities and nonstate agencies in a language of empowerment that portrays these localized arenas as the best sites of productive and positive action (Raco 2003).

7   Most of Oakland's Black residents were a product of the recent Great Migration from the US South. These predominantly rural southern Blacks relocated to cities like Oakland in search of job opportunities following postwar development. In fact, their labor fueled much post–World War II development in the area. Black labor was instrumental in the establishment of infrastructure and the region's rise as a global power. However, because of anti-Black racism, these Black laborers were not afforded proper housing in the inner city, nor opportunities to become homeowners.

8   As Michael B. Katz (1993, 14) explains, the War on Poverty and the expansion of related government programs in the 1960s created poverty research as a field in the social sciences because federal legislation mandated official evaluations. See also O'Connor 2001 for a complete elaboration on the history of poverty knowledge as a social scientific enterprise.

9   This culture-of-poverty analysis was influential in the work of Oscar Lewis, which focused on Puerto Rican and Mexican American families. See Lewis 1959, 1966. In a similar vein, in 1965, Daniel Patrick Moynihan wrote *The Negro Family: The Case for National Action* (known popularly as the Moynihan Report), which argued that African American poverty and family disintegration were due to a destructive ghetto culture and not structural inequalities.

10   California Division of Fair Employment Practices, "Californians of Spanish Surname: Population, Income, and Education, San Francisco, CA, May 1964," box 4, folder 12, Fred Ross Papers, Stanford University Archives.

11   Alex Zermeño, interview by the author, August 2, 2011. Gustavo Gutierrez was one of the principal founders of liberation theology in Latin America. Originally from Peru, he gained national attention with the publication of his ideas regarding the role of religion in social movement activism. His ideas became a subject of much controversy among conservative Catholic Church leaders who opposed the central tenets of liberation theology. See G. Gutierrez 1968.

12   Herman Gallegos, interview by the author, August 2, 2011.

13   Elvira Rose, interview by the author, May 2, 2011.

14   Rose, interview.

15   Gallegos, interview.

16   Zermeño, interview.

17   Address by Mr. Herman Gallegos, Former National President of the Community Service Organization, to a Meeting of the Mexican American Political Association Executive Board, December 6, 1964, box 14, folder 11, Ernesto Galarza Papers, Stanford University Archives.

18   Gallegos, interview.

19   Community Service Organization Target for Progress Voter Registration Flyer, 1956, box 13, folder 7, Ernesto Galarza Papers, Stanford University

Archives. For a detailed account of how the CSO had spearheaded a massive voter registration campaign in Southern California, see also Center for the Study of Democratic Institutions, "Memorandum," October 12, 1965, box 54, folder 5, Ernesto Galarza Papers, Stanford University Archives.

20 Letter from Henry Nava (CSO Chairman) to Miss Consuelo Salcedo, August 10, 1949, box 4, folder 9, Fred Ross Papers, Stanford University Archives.

21 Gallegos, interview.

22 Report from the Oakland Community Service Organization, March 15, 1956–July 15, 1956, box 4, folder 25, Fred Ross Papers, Stanford University Archives.

23 Rose, interview.

24 Zermeño, interview.

25 Community Service Organization (CSO) Newsletter, June 1964, box 38, folder 5, Bert Corona Papers, Stanford University Archives.

26 Gallegos, interview.

27 Zermeño, interview.

28 Zermeño, interview.

29 Community Service Organization (CSO) Newsletter, September 1963, Oakland, CA, box 38, folder 5, Bert Corona Papers, Stanford University Archives.

30 Community Service Organization (CSO) Newsletter, September 1963, Oakland, CA.

31 "El Momento Actual" (The Current Moment), in Community Service Organization (CSO) Newsletter, September 1963, Oakland, CA.

32 "El Momento Actual," translated by the author.

33 "What Is the Mexican Doing in the Civil Rights Movement?," in Community Service Organization (CSO) Newsletter, June 1964, Oakland, CA, box 38, folder 5, Bert Corona Papers, Stanford University Archives.

34 Community Service Organization (CSO) Newsletter, June 1964, Oakland, CA.

35 Community Service Organization (CSO) Newsletter, September 1963, Oakland, CA.

36 MAPA Registration Newsletter by Eduardo Quevedo, July 18, 1966, box 14, folder 10, Ernesto Galarza Papers, Stanford University Archives.

37 For consistency with the archival sources analyzed, I use the name Mexican American Unity Council to refer to this organization. By the late 1960s, however, the Unity Council officially became the Spanish Speaking Unity Council in order to make the organization more inclusive of non-Mexican groups. It now refers to itself simply as the Unity Council to continue to represent the shifting ethnic and racial composition of the neighborhood it serves. Arabella Martinez declined to be interviewed for this study. I tried multiple times but was unsuccessful in getting her to speak to me. However, I was able to find interviews that she did with other agencies through an oral history project

focused on the making of community development corporations. These interviews gave me a glimpse into her life and her tremendous accomplishments in both Oakland and Washington, DC.

38 Spanish Speaking Information Center Progress Report, April 17, 1967, box 31, folder 3, Bert Corona Papers, Stanford University Archives.

39 Letter to Mr. Anthony Barbieri, US Department of Labor, from James Delgadillo, July 16, 1965, box 14, folder 8, Ernesto Galarza Papers, Stanford University Archives.

40 Letter to Mr. Anthony Barbieri from James Delgadillo.

41 Letter to Mr. Anthony Barbieri from James Delgadillo.

42 Zermeño, interview.

43 Gallegos, interview.

44 Zermeño, interview.

45 Zermeño, interview.

46 "Mexican American Unity Council," in Community Service Organization (CSO) Newsletter, June 1964, Oakland, CA.

47 Letter from Jack Ortega to Judge Lionel Wilson, April 6, 1966, box 14, folder 8, Ernesto Galarza Papers, Stanford University Archives.

48 Letter from Jack Ortega to Judge Lionel Wilson.

49 Rose, interview.

50 City of Oakland, Department of Human Resources, Staff Report of a Mexican-American Community Development Survey and Resulting Proposal, March 1965, box 14, folder 8, Ernesto Galarza Papers, Stanford University Archives.

51 City of Oakland, Department of Human Resources, Staff Report.

52 City of Oakland, Department of Human Resources, Staff Report.

Chapter 3. Revolution Interrupted

1 For Cesar Chavez, for example, community service was a long-term strategy for radical independence, pride, and movement-building based on collective ownership and self-love (see Kohl-Arenas 2015, 817).

2 For more information on the significance of the Voting Rights Act of 1965, see Davidson and Grofman 1994.

3 For Kohl-Arenas (2016), the concept of twice-stolen money revolves around the fact that money built by capitalists first comes from the exploitation of impoverished workers. Second, instead of paying taxes on this profit, capitalists create private foundations. By creating these foundations, capitalists restrict the amount of money that goes into public state services and funds.

4 It is important to clarify how I am using the terms *activists* and *private foundation* as discrete entities with competing claims and demands. When I refer to Chicano activists, I mean a broad constituency that did not represent a single unified agenda or end goal. In a similar vein, philanthropic institutions (like the Ford Foundation) are run by manifold agents with a multiplicity of objectives. Both parties, however, were motivated by the single intention of improving conditions for impoverished communities, albeit with varying means for attaining this goal.

5 It is important to note that minority voting rights today might not hold the same urgency or weight. In the 1960s, however, issues of voting rights were fundamental to achieving social change. In fact, activism for voting rights and expanding the minority electorate could be seen as radical acts.

6 Today, SCLR is known as UNIDOS USA (previously it was named the National Council of La Raza [NCLR]). It is still regarded as one of the premier Latino advocacy organizations in the United States. I use SCLR and NCLR because those names were used during this historical period.

7 History of the Southwest Council and the National Council of La Raza by Herman Gallegos, April 22, 1977, RG 1, box 1, folder 15, National Council of La Raza Records, Stanford University Archives.

8 Mexican American scholars and leaders such as Julian Samora used this language to stress that African Americans were not the only minority in the United States. This strategic framing of Mexican Americans was a politicized indictment of the lack of social services and assistance for the poor available to this other minority population. One of the first major studies of Mexican Americans was funded by the Ford Foundation and conducted by Julian Samora, Ernesto Galarza, and Herman Gallegos. See Galarza, Gallegos, and Samora 1969.

9 Description of Ford Foundation Grant to the Special Purpose Fund of the Congress of Racial Equality for a Community Action Project in Cleveland, CORE Special Purpose Fund (06700446), 1967 July 21–1969 July 26, Ford Foundation Records, Rockefeller Archive Center.

10 Mitchell Sviridoff was vice president of national affairs for the Ford Foundation for more than three decades beginning in 1966. He was a national leader in urban social policy and philanthropy who played an important role in developing strategies for lifting people out of poverty and reviving decaying neighborhoods.

11 Letter from Mitchell Sviridoff to Mr. McGeorge Bundy, president of the Ford Foundation, July 15, 1968, CORE Special Purpose Fund (06700446), 1967 July 21–1969 July 26, Ford Foundation Records, Rockefeller Archive Center.

12 Description of Ford Foundation Grant to the Special Purpose Fund of the Congress of Racial Equality for a Community Action Project in Cleveland.

13 Letter from Mitchell Sviridoff to Mr. McGeorge Bundy.

14 One of the primary relationships was initially created because of Dr. Ernesto Galarza's work fighting the Bracero Program. The Ford Foundation contracted him to study conditions in Mexico before turning the attention to Mexican Americans in the United States. It was only by initially studying conditions of migration in Mexico that the Ford Foundation became interested in Mexican Americans in the United States.

15 Board of Directors Meeting Minutes, November 9, 1968, RG 1, box 1, folder 2, National Council of La Raza Records, Stanford University Archives.

16 History of the Southwest Council and the National Council of La Raza.

17 Board of Directors Meeting Minutes.

18 Herman Gallegos firmly believes that *hispanic* is the appropriate term to use to refer to Mexican Americans and other Latinos. He played a crucial role in encouraging use of this terminology even in the heyday of the Chicano movement, including advocating for the US Census to adopt this term. In my interview with him in 2011, Gallegos explained that *hispanic* was a more inclusive pan-ethnic term. I was surprised that other activists of the time also preferred to use this term, but I understood that in the historical context in which they organized, their use of this category also helped to differentiate them from Chicano "radicals."

19 History of the Southwest Council and the National Council of La Raza.

20 History of the Southwest Council and the National Council of La Raza.

21 Jose Angel Gutiérrez was one the initial organizers of the Mexican American Youth Organization (MAYO), a San Antonio, Texas, organization. He became one of the most active participants in the Raza Unida Party (see J. A. Gutierrez 1999).

22 115 Cong. Rec. 995 (1969).

23 Letter from Henry B. Gonzalez to Herman Gallegos, National Council of La Raza (06800564), 1968 June 10–1969 June 09, Ford Foundation Records, Rockefeller Archive Center.

24 Letter from Henry B. Gonzalez to Siobhan Oppenheimer, November 21, 1969, MAYO Conflict 1969, reel 2239, Ford Foundation Records, Rockefeller Archive Center.

25 MAYO Conflict Correspondence, National Council of La Raza (06800564), 1968 June 10–1969 June 09, Ford Foundation Records, Rockefeller Archive Center.

26 Letter from Jeannette Atkinson to Mr. Henry Ford II, April 22, 1969, National Council of La Raza (06800564), 1968 June 10–1969 June 09, Ford Foundation Records, Rockefeller Archive Center.

27 Letter from the Ford Community Affairs Committee of San Antonio, Texas, to Mr. McGeorge Bundy, May 6, 1969, National Council of La Raza (06800564), 1968 June 10–1969 June 09, Ford Foundation Records, Rockefeller Archive Center.

28 Letter from Mrs. Siobhan Oppenheimer to Mr. Samuel F. Tower, May 23, 1969, MAYO Conflict, 1969, reel 2239, Ford Foundation Records, Rockefeller Archive Center.

29 Letter from Mitchell Sviridoff, vice president of the Ford Foundation, to Herman Gallegos, executive director of the Southwest Council of La Raza, April 30, 1969, RG 1, box 1, folder 3, National Council of La Raza Records, Stanford University Archives.

30 History of the Southwest Council and the National Council of La Raza.

31 History of the Southwest Council and the National Council of La Raza.

32 Letter from Siobhan Oppenheimer to Dr. Joseph L. Carvajal, November 19, 1969, MAYO Conflict, 1969, reel 2239, Ford Foundation Records, Rockefeller Archive Center.

33 Letter from Siobhan Oppenheimer to Mrs. Arabella Springer, September 21, 1970, MAYO Conflict, 1969, reel 2239, Ford Foundation Records, Rockefeller Archive Center. (Arabella Martinez was also known in Ford Foundation correspondence by her married surname Springer.)

34 Letter from Siobhan Oppenheimer to Mike Sviridoff regarding Oakland Unity Council/Amador Contract, September 17, 1970, MAYO Conflict, 1969, reel 2239, Ford Foundation Records, Rockefeller Archive Center.

35 Letter from James Delgadillo and Mrs. Arabella M. Springer to Siobhan Oppenheimer, September 14, 1970, MAYO Conflict, 1969, reel 2239, Ford Foundation Records, Rockefeller Archive Center.

36 Monitor Report on California Grantees of SCLR from Hank Lopez, December 14, 1970, MAYO Conflict, 1969, reel 2239, Ford Foundation Records, Rockefeller Archive Center.

37 Letter from Maclovio Barraza, chairman of the Board of Directors, SCLR to Mr. Mike Sviridoff of the Ford Foundation, July 20, 1969, MAYO Conflict, 1969, reel 2239, Ford Foundation Records, Rockefeller Archive Center.

38 History of the Southwest Council and the National Council of La Raza.

39 History of the Southwest Council and the National Council of La Raza.

40 Current Interests of the Ford Foundation, 1974–1975, RG 1, box 19, folder 1, National Council of La Raza Records, Stanford University Archives.

41 Current Interests of the Ford Foundation.

42 Monitor Report on California Grantees of SCLR.

43 Inter-office Memorandum from William Grinker regarding meeting with Henry Santiestevan, the Southwest Council of La Raza Monitoring Report, June 5, 1970, Unity Council, SWCLR, reel 2239, Ford Foundation Records, Rockefeller Archiver Center.

44 Letter from Maclovio Barraza to Mr. Mike Sviridoff.

45 Spanish Speaking Unity Council, 1982 Annual Report, box 4, folder 4, National Council of La Raza Records, Stanford University Archives.

46 Historian Karen Ferguson meticulously details how the application of modernization theory developed in response to third world global postwar decolonization was used to make sense of situations affecting racial minorities in the United States. The president of the Ford Foundation at this time, McGeorge Bundy, for example, had no expertise in domestic race relations. Having served as national security adviser for Presidents Kennedy and Johnson, his expertise lay in foreign policy (K. Ferguson 2013, 9). Chicano movement and Black Power activists also fused an anticolonial critique with their activism. The internal colonial model, for example, became a key theoretical framework for understanding Black and Chicano disempowerment; see Blauner 1969; J. R. Chávez 2011; R. Gutiérrez 2004.

47 Ostrander (2005, 33) defines social justice funding as "philanthropic support for advancing progressive social change, that is, the redistribution of power and resources (economic, social, cultural, and/or political) in a more egalitarian direction."

Chapter 4. Development for the People!

1 Fruitvale Station is a national model for what is called transit-oriented development. Cities across the United States are using this model to bring about redevelopment in inner cities. This approach involves pedestrian-oriented development combined with improvements in transportation systems, primarily rail lines. Fruitvale Village has been hailed as one of the most successful of these development projects and an example that other communities are trying to emulate.

2 Oscar Grant III was killed by BART police on January 1, 2009. His unjust murder animated months of protests against police brutality in Oakland and the entire Bay Area. Many socially conscious residents of the Bay Area refer to Fruitvale Station as Oscar Grant Station.

3 According to the seminal work of Michel Foucault, pastoral power is productive in nature and therefore produces subjects in a population. It is concerned with both individuals and a totality or population, and in so doing produces governable subjects. It differs from the sovereign and disciplinary forms of power in that it evades repression and instead encourages certain forms of conduct or government. Foucault argues that this form of power emerges from the Christian pastorate and is transposed onto practices of the state for population management. In this chapter I contend that pastoral power can also be applied to nonprofit organizations like the Unity Council.

4 Gilda Gonzales, interview by the author, February 8, 2012.

5   Foucault (2007, 21) defines the target of government as being to fabricate, organize, and plan a milieu that consists of the following: "A set of natural givens—rivers, marshes, hills—and a set of artificial givens—an agglomeration of individuals, of houses, etc. The milieu is a certain number of combined, overall effects bearing on all who live on it." The milieu is not fixed but rather always in formation and contingent. Moreover, such a milieu is not planned or orchestrated by an omnipotent and violent state but rather is shaped by a diverse set of actors, bureaucracies, *and*, in my reading, also nonprofit organizations.

6   Goldstein (2017) asserts that government and philanthropic funding to community-based groups was guaranteed early on because of the state's shifts to devolve responsibility to the local level. See also chapter 2.

7   Ramon Rodriguez, interview by the author, March 12, 2012.

8   Rodriguez, interview.

9   See Goldstein 2017 for examples of how CDCs struggled throughout the United States.

10 For further information, see Orozco, Austin, and Beale 2008.

11 The National Council of La Raza began as a regional organization called the Southwest Council of La Raza. It became a national organization in 1969 and relocated to Washington, DC. See chapter 2.

12 Alex Zermeño, interview by the author, August 2, 2011.

13 Zermeño, interview.

14 The analysis that follows is inspired by Foucault's (2007) elaborations regarding security, territory, and the management of populations. The Unity Council's and other community stakeholders' preoccupations with the efficient circulation of people and resources within a given territory mirrors the concerns raised by early European officials in charge of planning the development of modern towns at the turn of the seventeenth century. As revealed in Foucault (2007), his understanding of governmentality stemmed fundamentally from a desire to appreciate the organization and politics of space and the ways in which populations are administered in historical-spatial contexts. Foucault's explorations begin with the development of modern European towns. As the once closed and walled-off European towns began to enter into new relationships with other places, "what was at issue . . . was the question of the spatial, juridical administrative, and economic opening up of the town: resituating the town in a space of circulation" (2007, 13). The problem was how to manage the type of circulation that occurred in and out of space. This was especially the case in the eighteenth century when newer towns were being constructed to facilitate greater circulation of goods and people, both within the town and on external roads where goods could be exchanged. An important problem for towns in the eighteenth century was surveillance of bad types of circulation, since rigid walls no longer fortified

the towns. Foucault contends that a different problem emerged that was not about fixing or enclosing territory, "but of allowing circulations to take place, of controlling them, sifting the good and the bad, ensuring that things are always in movement . . . in such a way that the inherent dangers of this circulation are canceled out" (65). What were needed were mechanisms by which to govern at a distance, where the focus on territory and people would no longer be sufficient, nor a possibility, and the well-being of the population needed to be secured. It also necessitated the activation of different stakeholders, both state and nonstate, to enable this new form of government. In my view, post–World War II developments in the US state put greater focus on nonprofit organizations, such as the Unity Council, to govern the inner city. I owe much of the thinking in this section to my engagement with Foucault (2007) and many conversations with students of Donald S. Moore, including Jake Kosek, among others.

15   Gonzales, interview.

16   Gonzales, interview.

17   Maria Sanchez, interview by the author, June 27, 2014.

18   Sanchez, interview.

19   Agnes Ramirez, interview by the author, July 29, 2011.

20   Ramirez, interview.

21   Guillermina Jimenez, interview by the author, July 29, 2011.

22   Jose Dorado, interview by the author, March 17, 2012.

23   Hugo Guerrero, interview by the author, March 26, 2012.

24   Guerrero, interview.

25   I employ the concept of the architectural from Eyal Weizman (2007), who argues that architecture is not an abstract construction of buildings or roads. By extension, urban planning is a highly political process cloaked in presumed objectivity. For a critique of planning and its roots in science, see also Lefebvre 2009, especially the chapters "Reflections on the Politics of Space" and "Space and the State."

26   Gonzales, interview.

27   Throughout this book, I have examined how 1960s social movement activism was fundamentally concerned with improving aggrieved and marginalized neighborhoods abandoned by the state and private investment due to racism and white supremacy. In short, most of this activism sought to "develop," or more accurately "improve," or create a new vision of a specific neighborhood. The concept of "development," however, has a profoundly complex history in our world, especially in fields such as geography created out of colonial endeavors. The term is also essential in popular master narratives that continue to divide the world into developed, developing, and underdeveloped countries. This kind of division of the world means that there is only one

way of developing and becoming a developed country. The word *development*, however, is derived from a now obsolete use of the French word *développer* that simply meant "to unfold" or "unfurl." This means that the neighborhood did not have to unfold as it did. There were alternatives to this particular unfolding.

Chapter 5. Mapping Interlinkages

1 Geographer and ethnic studies scholar Laura Pulido scrutinizes use of the name Aztlán among Chicanos. According to Pulido (2018), the concept of Aztlán contributes to the erasure of Native peoples in the United States. She argues that there is clear evidence of Mexicans and Chicano/as participating in settler colonialism.

2 For detailed analysis of the concept of Aztlán, see Acuña 2004; Anaya and Lomelí 2017.

3 Regina Chavarín, interview by the author, October 21, 2012.

4 Alfredo Cruz, interview by the author, September 20, 2012.

5 Cruz, interview.

6 Liz Meza, interview by the author, October 20, 2012.

7 Roger Chavarín, interview by the author, October 21, 2012.

8 Cruz, interview.

9 Roger Chavarín, interview.

10 Roger Chavarín, interview.

11 Ana Rojas, interview by the author, July 15, 2017.

12 Tomas Acuña, interview by the author, July 15, 2017.

13 Andres Cisneros Galindo, interview by the author, July 17, 2017.

14 Rojas, interview.

15 Acuña, interview.

16 Rojas, interview.

17 Rojas, interview.

18 Acuña, interview.

19 Rojas, interview.

20 For additional information regarding the American Indian Movement and the occupation of Alcatraz, see Smith and Warrior 1996.

21 Acuña, interview.

22 Acuña, interview.

23 Rojas, interview.

24 Acuña, interview.

25 Acuña, interview.

26 Cisneros Galindo, interview.

27 Cisneros Galindo, interview.

28 Cisneros Galindo, interview.

29 Rojas, interview.

30 Acuña, interview.

31 Acuña, interview.

32 Rojas, interview.

33 Acuña, interview.

34 Acuña, interview.

35 Acuña, interview.

36 Cisneros Galindo, interview.

37 Annette Oropeza, interview by the author, January 8, 2012.

38 Dr. Pesquera went on to become a professor at UC Davis where she taught about the Chicano movement and other radical mobilizations of the 1960s. She also headed a program that took students to Cuba for a number of years to support and learn from the Cuban Revolution.

39 Dr. Beatriz Pesquera, interview by the author, August 30, 2019.

40 Dr. Pesquera, interview.

41 Dr. Pesquera, interview.

42 Connie Jubb, interview by the author, August 30, 2019.

43 Meza, interview.

44 Cisneros Galindo, interview.

45 Oropeza, interview.

46 Oropeza, interview.

47 Oropeza, interview.

Conclusion

1 To be clear, my favorite pizza joint had stopped its lunch offerings by the time I crossed the bridge. I know very clearly the hours of Cheeseboard Pizza, so I sought out its next best kin.

2 Fruitvale History Project Brochure, Oakland, CA, 2016, author's personal archive.

3 Fruitvale History Project Brochure.

4 Alfredo Cruz, interview by the author, September 20, 2012.

5 Kathy Ahoy, interview by the author, June 10, 2011.

6 Ahoy, interview.

7 Manuel Alcalá, interview by the author, March 15, 2011.

8 Alcalá, interview.

9 She also helped establish a number of other organizations for a diverse sector of the Asian migrant population in Alameda County.

10 Genevieve Negrón-Gonzales (2018) comes to a similar conclusion regarding contemporary immigrant rights activism among undocumented youths. She argues that many of the immigrant rights gains, including those achieved through the Deferred Action for Childhood Arrivals (DACA) policy, as well as many university resources for undocumented students are the direct product of accelerated mobilizing by undocumented youth activists.

11 Liz Meza, interview by the author, October 20, 2012.

REFERENCES

Acuña, Rodolfo. 1972. *Occupied America: The Chicano's Struggle toward Liberation*. San Francisco: Canfield.

Acuña, Rodolfo. 2004. *Occupied America: A History of Chicanos*. New York: Pearson Longman.

Allen, Robert L. 1970. *Black Awakening in Capitalist America: An Analytic History*. Garden City, NY: Doubleday.

Anaya, Rudolfo, and Francisco A. Lomelí. 2017. *Aztlán: Essays on the Chicano Homeland*. Albuquerque: University of New Mexico Press.

Anzaldúa, Gloria. 1983. "Foreword to the Second Edition." In *This Bridge Called My Back: Writings by Radical Women of Color*, edited by Cherríe L. Moraga and Gloria E. Anzaldúa, iv–v. Berkeley: Third World Women.

Anzaldúa, Gloria. 2015. *Light in the Dark/Luz en Lo Oscuro: Rewriting Identity, Spirituality, Reality*. Edited by AnaLouise Keating. Durham, NC: Duke University Press.

Arredondo, Gabriela F., ed. 2003. *Chicana Feminisms: A Critical Reader. Postcontemporary Interventions*. Durham, NC: Duke University Press.

Bardacke, Frank. 2012. *Trampling Out the Vintage: Cesar Chavez and the Two Souls of the United Farm Workers*. New York: Verso.

Barnd, Natchee Blu. 2017. *Native Space: Geographic Strategies to Unsettle Settler Colonialism*. Corvallis: Oregon State University Press.

Bauer, William J. 2012. "The Giant and the Waterbaby: Paiute Oral Traditions and the Owens Valley Water Wars." *Boom: A Journal of California* 2 (4): 104–17.

Bermúdez, Rosie. 2014. "Chicana/o Movement Grassroots Leftists and Radical Electoral Politics in Los Angeles, 1970–1980." In *The Chicano Movement: Perspectives from the Twenty-First Century*, edited by Mario T. García, 97–116. New York: Routledge.

Bernardi, Gene. 1965. "Characteristics of the Spanish Surname Population in the City of Oakland." Oakland, CA: Oakland Interagency Project.

Biolsi, Thomas. 2005. "Imagined Geographies: Sovereignty, Indigenous Space, and American Indian Struggle." *American Ethnologist* 32 (2): 239–59.

Blackwell, Maylei. 2011. *¡Chicana Power! Contested Histories of Feminism in the Chicano Movement*. Austin: University of Texas Press.

Blackwell, Maylei. 2012. "The Practice of Autonomy in the Age of Neoliberalism: Strategies from Indigenous Women's Organising in Mexico." *Journal of Latin American Studies* 44 (4): 703–32.

Blauner, Robert. 1969. "Internal Colonialism and Ghetto Revolt." *Social Problems* 16 (4): 393–408.

Blish-Hughes, E. 2004. *In Transit: A Ford Foundation Report*. Accessed November 29, 2009. http://www.fhwa.dot.gov/environment/environmental_justice/case _studies/fruitvale.pdf.

Bonilla-Silva, Eduardo. 2018. *Racism without Racists: Color-Blind Racism and the Persistence of Racial Inequality in America*. 5th ed. Lanham, MD: Rowman and Littlefield.

Brasher, Arlene E. 1966. "Mexican American Recipients' Orientations towards and Modes of Adaptation to the Welfare System." PhD diss., University of California, Berkeley.

Brown, Jacqueline Nassy. 2005. *Dropping Anchor, Setting Sail: Geographies of Race in Black Liverpool*. Princeton, NJ: Princeton University Press.

Cacho, Lisa Marie. 2012. *Social Death: Racialized Rightlessness and the Criminalization of the Unprotected*. New York: New York University Press.

Certeau, Michel de. 1984. *The Practice of Everyday Life*. Translated by Steven Rendall. Berkeley: University of California Press.

Chávez, Ernesto. 1994. "Creating Aztlán: The Chicano Movement in Los Angeles, 1966–1978." PhD diss., University of California, Los Angeles.

Chávez, Ernesto. 2002. *"Mi Raza Primero!" (My People First!): Nationalism, Identity, and Insurgency in the Chicano Movement in Los Angeles, 1966–1978*. Berkeley: University of California Press.

Chávez, John R. 2011. "Aliens in Their Native Lands: The Persistence of Internal Colonial Theory." *Journal of World History* 22 (4): 785–809.

Chew, Jeff. 1991. "Fruitvale: A Neighborhood Commercial Revitalization Plan." Department of City and Regional Planning, University of California, Berkeley.

Cisneros, Sandra. 1991. *The House on Mango Street*. New York: Vintage.

Clark, Robert F. 2000. *Maximum Feasible Success: A History of the Community Action Program*. Washington, DC: National Association of Community Action Agencies.

Clay, Andreana. 2012. *The Hip-Hop Generation Fights Back: Youth, Activism, and Post–Civil Rights Politics*. New York: New York University Press.

Cosgrove, Denis E., ed. 1999. *Mappings: Critical Views*. London: Reaktion.

Cotera, Maria, Maylei Blackwell, and Dion Espinoza. 2018. *Chicana Movidas: New Narratives of Activism and Feminism in the Movement Era*. Austin: University of Texas Press.

Counts, Laura. 2004. "Fruitvale Prepares to Open Village; Businesses Are Placing the Final Touches on the New." *Tri-Valley Herald*, May 7, 2004.

Cox, Gerald F. 2006. *The Radical Peasant*. Victoria, CA: Trafford.

Craib, Raymond B. 2004. *Cartographic Mexico: A History of State Fixations and Fugitive Landscapes*. Durham, NC: Duke University Press.

Craib, Raymond B. 2009. "Relocating Cartography." *Postcolonial Studies* 12 (4): 481–90.

Cruikshank, Barbara. 1999. *The Will to Empower: Democratic Citizens and Other Subjects*. Ithaca, NY: Cornell University Press.

Davidson, Chandler, and Bernard Grofman, eds. 1994. *Quiet Revolution in the South: The Impact of the Voting Rights Act, 1965–1990*. Princeton, NJ: Princeton University Press.

Dávila, Arlene. 2004. *Barrio Dreams: Puerto Ricans, Latinos, and the Neoliberal City*. Berkeley: University of California Press.

Dávila, Arlene. 2008. *Latino Spin: Public Image and the Whitewashing of Race*. New York: New York University Press.

Delgado Bernal, Dolores. 1997. "Chicana School Resistance and Grassroots Leadership: Providing an Alternative History of the 1968 East Los Angeles Blowouts." PhD diss., University of California, Los Angeles.

Edney, Matthew H. 2005. "Putting 'Cartography' into the History of Cartography: Arthur H. Robinson, David Woodward, and the Creation of a Discipline." *Cartographic Perspectives*, no. 51, 14–29.

Elwood, S., V. Lawson, and E. Sheppard. 2016. "Geographical Relational Poverty Studies." *Progress in Human Geography* 41 (6): 745–65.

Espinoza, Dionne. 2001. "'Revolutionary Sisters': Women's Solidarity and Collective Identification among Chicana Brown Berets in East Los Angeles, 1967–1970." *Aztlan: A Journal of Chicano Studies* 26 (1): 15–58.

Fanon, Frantz. (1963) 2004. *The Wretched of the Earth*. Translated by Richard Philcox. New York: Grove.

Ferguson, James, and Akhil Gupta. 2002. "Spatializing States: Toward an Ethnography of Neoliberal Governmentality." *American Ethnologist* 29 (4): 981–1002.

Ferguson, Karen. 2007. "Organizing the Ghetto: The Ford Foundation, CORE, and White Power in the Black Power Era, 1967–1969." *Journal of Urban History* 34 (1): 67–100.

Ferguson, Karen. 2013. *Top Down: The Ford Foundation, Black Power, and the Reinvention of Racial Liberalism*. Philadelphia: University of Pennsylvania Press.

Fisher, Berenice, and Joan Tronto. 1990. "Toward a Feminist Theory of Caring." In *Circles of Care: Work and Identity in Women's Lives*, edited by Emily K. Abel and Margaret Nelson, 35–62. Albany: State University of New York Press.

Flores, Lori. 2016. *Grounds for Dreaming: Mexican Americans, Mexican Immigrants, and the California Farmworker Movement*. New Haven, CT: Yale University Press.

Ford Foundation. 1973. *Community Development Corporations: A Strategy for Depressed Urban and Rural Areas; A Ford Foundation Policy Paper*. New York: Ford Foundation.

Foucault, Michel. 2007. *Security, Territory, Population: Lectures at the Collège de France, 1977–1978*. Edited by Mechel Senellart. Translated by Graham Burchell. New York: Palgrave Macmillan.

Galarza, Ernesto, Herman Gallegos, and Julian Samora. 1969. *Mexican-Americans in the Southwest*. Santa Barbara, CA: McNally and Loftin.

Gallegos, Herman E. 1989. "Equity and Diversity: Hispanics in the Nonprofit World." Oral history conducted by Gabrielle Morris. Regional Oral History Office, Bancroft Library, University of California, Berkeley.

García, Alma M., ed. 1997. *Chicana Feminist Thought: The Basic Historical Writings*. New York: Routledge.

Garcia, Mario T. 1994. *Memories of Chicano History: The Life and Narrative of Bert Corona*. Berkeley: University of California Press.

Gilmore, Ruth Wilson. 2017. "In the Shadow of the Shadow State." In *The Revolution Will Not Be Funded: Beyond the Non-profit Industrial Complex*, edited by INCITE!, 41–52. Durham, NC: Duke University Press.

Glenn, Evelyn Nakano. 2010. *Forced to Care: Coercion and Caregiving in America*. Cambridge, MA: Harvard University Press.

Goeman, Mishuana. 2013. *Mark My Words: Native Women Mapping Our Nations*. Minneapolis: University of Minnesota Press.

Goldstein, Brian D. 2017. *The Roots of Urban Renaissance: Gentrification and the Struggle over Harlem*. Cambridge, MA: Harvard University Press.

Gómez, Alan Eladio. 2008. "Feminism, Torture, and the Politics of Chicana/Third World Solidarity: An Interview with Olga Talamante." *Radical History Review*, no. 101, 160–78.

Gómez, Alan Eladio. 2016. *The Revolutionary Imaginations of Greater Mexico: Chicana/o Radicalism, Solidarity Politics, and Latin American Social Movements*. Austin: University of Texas Press.

Gómez-Quiñones, Juan. 1978. *Mexican Students por La Raza: The Chicano Student Movement in Southern California 1967–1977*. Santa Barbara, CA: Editorial La Causa.

Gómez-Quiñones, Juan. 1990. *Chicano Politics: Reality and Promise, 1940–1990*. Albuquerque: University of New Mexico Press.

Gregory, Steven. 1999. *Black Corona: Race and the Politics of Place in an Urban Community*. Princeton, NJ: Princeton University Press.

Grillo, Evelio. 2000. *Black Cuban, Black American: A Memoir*. Houston: Arte Publico.

Gruen, Gruen & Associates. 1973. *Economic and Social Analysis of Three Oakland BART Station Areas; MacArthur, Rockridge, Fruitvale. A Report to the City of Oakland*. San Francisco, CA.

Gutiérrez, David G. 1995. *Walls and Mirrors: Mexican Americans, Mexican Immigrants, and the Politics of Ethnicity*. Berkeley: University of California Press.

Gutierrez, Gustavo. 1968. *A Theology of Liberation: History, Politics, and Salvation*. New York: Orbis.

Gutierrez, Jose Angel. 1999. *The Making of a Chicano Militant: Lessons from Cristal*. Madison: University of Wisconsin Press.

Gutiérrez, Ramón. 2004. "Internal Colonialism: An American Theory of Race." *Du Bois Review: Social Science Research on Race* 1 (2): 281–95.

Guzmán, Joshua Javier, and Christina A. Léon. 2015. "Cuts and Impressions: The Aesthetic Work of Lingering in Latinidad." *Women and Performance: A Journal of Feminist Theory* 25 (3): 261–76.

Hall, Jacquelyn Dowd. 2005. "The Long Civil Rights Movement and the Political Uses of the Past." *Journal of American History* 91 (4): 1233–63.

Harley, J. B. 1988. "Silences and Secrecy: The Hidden Agenda of Cartography in Early Modern Europe." *Imago Mundi* 40:57–76.

Harley, J. B. 1992. "Rereading the Maps of the Columbian Encounter." *Annals of the Association of American Geographers* 82 (3): 522–42.

Herrera, Juan. 2012. "Unsettling the Geography of Oakland's War on Poverty: Mexican American Political Organizations and the Decoupling of Poverty and Blackness." *Du Bois Review* 9 (2): 375–93.

Hondagneu-Sotelo, Pierrette. 1994. *Gendered Transitions: Mexican Experiences of Immigration*. Berkeley: University of California Press.

Irving, Carl. 1963. "Bay Area Warned on Race Problem." *Oakland Tribune*, May 14, 1963, 8.

Jackson, Thomas F. 1993. "The State, the Movement, and the Urban Poor: The War on Poverty and Political Mobilization in the 1960s." In *The "Underclass" Debate: Views from History*, edited by Michael B. Katz, 403–39. Princeton, NJ: Princeton University Press.

Jenkins, J. Craig, and Craig M. Eckert. 1986. "Channeling Black Insurgency: Elite Patronage and Professional Social Movement Organizations in the Development of the Black Movement." *American Sociological Review* 51 (6): 812–29.

Johnson, Gaye Theresa. 2013. *Spaces of Conflict, Sounds of Solidarity: Music, Race, and Spatial Entitlement in Los Angeles*. Berkeley: University of California Press.

Katz, Michael B. 1993. "The Urban 'Underclass' as a Metaphor for Social Transformation." In *The "Underclass" Debate: Views from History*, edited by Michael B. Katz, 3–26. Princeton, NJ: Princeton University Press.

Kelley, Robin D. G. 2002. *Freedom Dreams: The Black Radical Imagination*. Boston: Beacon.

Kirkpatrick, L. Owen. 2007. "The Two 'Logics' of Community Development: Neighborhoods, Markets, and Community Development Corporations." *Politics and Society* 35 (2): 329–69.

Kohl-Arenas, Erica. 2015. "The Self-Help Myth: Towards a Theory of Philanthropy as Consensus Broker." *American Journal of Economics and Sociology* 74 (4): 796–825.

Kohl-Arenas, Erica. 2016. *The Self-Help Myth: How Philanthropy Fails to Alleviate Poverty*. Berkeley: University of California Press.

Kramer, Ralph M. 1969. *Participation of the Poor: Comparative Communities Case Studies in the War on Poverty*. Englewood Cliffs, NJ: Prentice-Hall.

Krochmal, Max. 2016. *Blue Texas: The Making of a Multiracial Democratic Coalition in the Civil Rights Era*. Chapel Hill: University of North Carolina Press.

Lawson, Victoria. 2007. "Geographies of Care and Responsibility." *Annals of the Association of American Geographers* 97 (1): 1–11.

Lefebvre, Henri. 2009. *State, Space, World*. Minneapolis: University of Minnesota Press.

Leitner, Helga, Eric Sheppard, and Kristin M. Sziarto. 2008. "The Spatialities of Contentious Politics." *Transactions of the Institute of British Geographers* 33 (2): 157–72.

Lekus, Ian Keith. 2004. "Queer Harvests: Homosexuality, the US New Left, and the Venceremos Brigades to Cuba." *Radical History Review* 89 (1): 57–91.

Levinson, Sandra, and Carol Brightman, eds. 1971. *Venceremos Brigade: Young Americans Sharing the Life and Work of Revolutionary Cuba*. New York: Simon and Schuster.

Lewis, Oscar. 1959. *Five Families: Mexican Case Studies in the Culture of Poverty*. New York: Basic Books.

Lewis, Oscar. 1966. *La Vida: A Puerto Rican Family in the Culture of Poverty*. New York: Random House.

Li, Tania Murray. 2007. *The Will to Improve: Governmentality, Development, and the Practice of Politics*. Durham, NC: Duke University Press.

Limerick, Patricia Nelson. 1987. *The Legacy of Conquest: The Unbroken Past of the American West*. New York: Norton.

Lipsitz, George. 2006. *The Possessive Investment in Whiteness: How White People Profit from Identity Politics*. Philadelphia: Temple University Press.

Lopez, Alberto V. 1996. "Application of Three Dimensional Modeling and Urban Design Exercises in Citizen Participation (A Planning Exercise in the Fruitvale, Oakland CA)." Professional report (Master of City Planning). University of California, Berkeley.

Los Angeles Daily News. 1954. "New National Organization Dedicated to Equal Rights." March 24, 1954, 3.

Magaña, Maurice. 2017. "Spaces of Resistance, Everyday Activism, and Belonging: Youth Reimagining and Reconfiguring the City in Oaxaca, Mexico." *Journal of Latin American and Caribbean Anthropology* 22 (2): 215–34.

Magaña, Maurice Rafael. 2021. *Cartographies of Youth Resistance: Hip-Hop, Punk, and Urban Autonomy in Mexico*. Oakland: University of California Press.

Magat, Richard. 1979. *The Ford Foundation at Work: Philanthropic Choices, Methods, and Styles*. New York: Plenum.

Marquez, Benjamin. 2003. "Mexican American Political Organizations and Philanthropy: Bankrolling a Social Movement." *Social Science Review* 77 (3): 329–46.

Marris, Peter, and Martin Rein. 1967. *Dilemmas of Social Reform: Poverty and Community Action in the United States*. Chicago: Aldine.

Martin, Deborah, and Byron Miller. 2003. "Space and Contentious Politics." *Mobilization: An International Quarterly* 8 (2): 143–56.

Martinez, Arabella. 1976. "The Spanish Speaking Unity Council, INC., and Bay Area Foundations." *Bay Area Foundation History V*. Regional Oral History Office, Bancroft Library, University of California, Berkeley.

Martinez, Arabella. 1991. An Interview Conducted by James Briggs Murray. Community Development Corporation Oral History Project. New York Public Library, Schomburg Center for Research in Black Culture.

Marwell, Nicole P. 2004. "Privatizing the Welfare State: Nonprofit Community-Based Organizations as Political Actors." *American Sociological Review* 69 (2): 265–91.

Massey, Doreen B. 1994. *Space, Place, and Gender*. Minneapolis: University of Minnesota Press.

Massey, Doreen B. 2004. "Geographies of Responsibility." *Geografiska Annaler: Series B, Human Geography* 86 (1): 5–18.

Massey, Doreen B. 2005. *For Space*. London: Sage.

Massey, Doreen B. 2007. *World City*. Cambridge: Polity.

Massey, Douglas S., and Nancy A. Denton. 1993. *American Apartheid: Segregation and the Making of the Underclass*. Cambridge, MA: Harvard University Press.

McAdam, Doug. 1982. *Political Process and the Development of Black Insurgency, 1930–1970*. Chicago: University of Chicago Press.

McAdam, Doug, Sidney G. Tarrow, and Charles Tilly. 2001. *Dynamics of Contention*. New York: Cambridge University Press.

McCaughan, Edward. 2012. *Art and Social Movements: Cultural Politics in Mexico and Aztlán*. Durham, NC: Duke University Press.

McKittrick, Katherine. 2006. *Demonic Grounds: Black Women and the Cartographies of Struggle*. Minneapolis: University of Minnesota Press.

McKittrick, Katherine. 2011. "On Plantations, Prisons, and a Black Sense of Place." *Social and Cultural Geography* 12 (8): 947–63.

McKittrick, Katherine. 2013. "Plantation Futures." *Small Axe* 3 (42): 1–15.

McKittrick, Katherine, and Clyde Woods, eds. 2007. *Black Geographies and the Politics of Place*. Toronto: South End.

Melamed, Jodi. 2006. "The Spirit of Neoliberalism: From Racial Liberalism to Neoliberal Multiculturalism." *Social Text* 24 (4) (89): 1–24.

Melamed, Jodi. 2011. *Represent and Destroy: Rationalizing Violence in the New Racial Capitalism*. Minneapolis: University of Minnesota Press.

Miranda, Marie "Keta." 2003. *Homegirls in the Public Sphere*. Austin: University of Texas Press.

Molina, Natalia, Daniel HoSang, and Ramón A. Gutiérrez, eds. 2019. *Relational Formations of Race: Theory, Method, and Practice*. Oakland: University of California Press.

Montaña, Susana. 1981. "Fruitvale Neighborhood Commercial Revitalization (NCR) Project Development Program." Berkeley, CA: Department of City and Regional Planning.

Mora, Griselda Cristina. 2009. "De Muchos, Unos: The Institutionalization of Latino Panethnicity, 1960–1990." PhD diss., Princeton University.

Mora, G. Cristina. 2014. *Making Hispanics: How Activists, Bureaucrats, and Media Constructed a New American*. Chicago: University of Chicago Press.

Moynihan, Daniel P. 1969. *Maximum Feasible Misunderstanding: Community Action in the War on Poverty*. New York: Free Press.

Muñoz, Carlos. 2007. *Youth, Identity, Power: The Chicano Movement*. London: Verso.

Murch, Donna. 2010. *Living for the City: Migration, Education, and the Rise of the Black Panther Party in Oakland, California*. Chapel Hill: University of North Carolina Press.

Negrón-Gonzales, Genevieve. 2018. "Illegality, Poverty, and Higher Education: A Relational Perspective on Undocumented Students and Educational Access." In *Relational Poverty Politics: Forms, Struggles, and Possibilities*, edited by Victoria Lawson and Sarah Elmwood, 61–76. Athens: University of Georgia Press.

Nelson, Alondra. 2011. *Body and Soul: The Black Panther Party and the Fight against Medical Discrimination*. Minneapolis: University of Minnesota Press.

Nicholls, Walter. 2007. "The Geographies of Social Movements." *Geography Compass* 1 (3): 607–22.

Nicholls, Walter. 2009. "Place, Networks, Space: Theorising the Geographies of Social Movements." *Transactions of the Institute of British Geographers* 34 (1): 78–93.

Nichols, William L. 1966. *Poverty and Poverty Programs in Oakland: A Report to the Department of Human Resources of the City of Oakland*. Berkeley: Survey Research Center, University of California.

Nieto Gomez, Anna. 1997. "Sexism in the Movimiento." In *Chicana Feminist Thought: The Basic Historical Writings*, edited by Alma M. Garcia, 97–99. New York: Routledge.

Oakland Tribune. 1962. "City Council Approves Top Posts for Ford Foundation." February 16, 1962, 1.

Oakland Tribune. 1966. "Demands Made of City by Mexican Americans." April 15, 1966, 4.

O'Connor, Alice. 1996. "Community Action, Urban Reform, and the Fight against Poverty: The Ford Foundation's Gray Areas Program." *Journal of Urban History* 22 (5): 586–625.

O'Connor, Alice. 1999. "Swimming against the Tide: A Brief History of Federal Policy in Poor Communities." In *Urban Problems and Community Development*, edited by Ronald F. Ferguson and William T. Dickens, 77–138. Washington, DC: Brookings Institution Press.

O'Connor, Alice. 2001. *Poverty Knowledge: Social Science, Social Policy, and the Poor in Twentieth-Century U.S. History*. Princeton, NJ: Princeton University Press.

Office of Economic Opportunity. 1965. *Workbook: Community Action Program*. Washington, DC: US Department of Health, Education, and Welfare, National Institute of Education.

Olguín, Ben V. 2007. "Venceremos Is Plural for Victory: 37th Contingent of Venceremos Brigade Successfully Challenges Inhumane U.S. Embargo of Cuba." *La Voz de Esperanza* 20 (6): 9–16.

Ong, Aihwa. 2006. *Neoliberalism as Exception: Mutations in Citizenship and Sovereignty*. Durham, NC: Duke University Press.

Oropeza, Lorena. 2005. ¡Raza Si! ¡Guerra No!: Chicano Protest and Patriotism during the Viet Nam War Era. Berkeley: University of California Press.

Orozco, Manuel, Michael Austin, and Elaine Beale. 2008. "The Unity Council: Brief History of a Pioneering Community Development and Service Organization." Oakland, CA. Accessed August 9, 2010. http://www.unitycouncil.org/download /The%20Unity%20Council%20History.pdf.

Oslender, Ulrich. 2016. The Geographies of Social Movements: Afro-Colombian Mobilization and the Aquatic Space. Durham, NC: Duke University Press.

Ostrander, Susan, A. 2005. "Legacy and Promise for Social Justice Funding: Charitable Foundations and Progressive Social Movements, Past and Present." In Foundations for Social Change: Critical Perspectives on Philanthropy and Popular Movements, edited by Daniel R. Faber and Deborah McCarthy, 33–60. New York: Rowman and Littlefield.

Paoli, Richard. 2003. "Village People: Oakland's Fruitvale Project a Long Time in the Making." San Francisco Chronicle, September 28, 2003.

Paschel, Tianna S. 2016. Becoming Black Political Subjects: Movements and Ethnoracial Rights in Colombia and Brazil. Princeton, NJ: Princeton University Press.

Pérez, Emma. 1999. The Decolonial Imaginary: Writing Chicanas into History. Bloomington: Indiana University Press.

Portes, Alejandro, and Leif Jensen. 1987. "What's an Ethnic Enclave? The Case for Conceptual Clarity." American Sociological Review 52 (6): 768–71.

Portes, Alejandro, and Leif Jensen. 1992. "Disproving the Enclave Hypothesis: A Reply to Sanders and Nee." American Sociological Review 57 (3): 418–20.

Pressman, Jeffrey L. 1975. Federal Programs and City Politics: The Dynamics of the Aid Process in Oakland. Berkeley: University of California Press.

Pulido, Laura. 2000. "Rethinking Environmental Racism: White Privilege and Urban Development in Southern California." Annals of the Association of American Geographers 90 (1): 12–40.

Pulido, Laura. 2006. Black, Brown, Yellow, and Left: Radical Activism in Los Angeles. Berkeley: University of California Press.

Pulido, Laura. 2017. "Geographies of Race and Ethnicity II: Environmental Racism, Racial Capitalism and State-Sanctioned Violence." Progress in Human Geography 41 (4): 524–33.

Pulido, Laura. 2018. "Geographies of Race and Ethnicity III: Settler Colonialism and Nonnative People." Progress in Human Geography 42 (2): 309–18.

Raco, Mike. 2003. "Governmentality, Subject-Building, and the Discourses and Practices of Devolution in the UK." Transactions of the Institute of British Geographers 28 (1): 75–95.

Raco, Mike, and Rob Imrie. 2000. "Governmentality and Rights and Responsibilities in Urban Policy." Environment and Planning A 32 (12): 2187–204.

Ramírez, Margaret M. 2020. "City as Borderland: Gentrification and the Policing of Black and Latinx Geographies in Oakland." Environment and Planning D: Society and Space 38 (1): 147–66.

Ramirez, Renya K. 2007. *Native Hubs: Culture, Community, and Belonging in Silicon Valley and Beyond*. Durham, NC: Duke University Press.

Record, Wilson. 1963. "Minority Groups and Intergroup Relations in the San Francisco Bay Area." In *The San Francisco Bay Area: Its Problems and Future*, edited by Stanley Scott, 1–48. Berkeley: Institute of Governmental Studies, University of California.

Rhomberg, Chris. 2004. *No There There: Race, Class, and Political Community in Oakland*. Berkeley: University of California Press.

Rios, Victor M. 2011. *Punished: Policing the Lives of Black and Latino Boys*. New York: New York University Press.

Rodriguez, Dylan. 2017. "The Political Logic of the Non-profit Industrial Complex." In *The Revolution Will Not Be Funded: Beyond the Non-profit Industrial Complex*, edited by INCITE!, 21–40. Durham, NC: Duke University Press.

Roelofs, Joan. 2003. *Foundations and Public Policy: The Mask of Pluralism*. Albany: State University of New York Press.

Rothstein, Richard. 2017. *The Color of Law: A Forgotten History of How Our Government Segregated America*. New York: Liveright.

Routledge, Paul. 1993. *Terrains of Resistance: Nonviolent Social Movements and the Contestation of Place in India*. Westport, CT: Praeger.

Roy, Ananya. 2017. "Dis/possessive Collectivism: Property and Personhood at City's End." *Geoforum* 80 (March): A1–A11.

Roy, Ananya, Stuart Schrader, and Emma Shaw Chane. 2015. "'The Anti-poverty Hoax': Development, Pacification, and the Making of Community in the Global 1960s." *Cities* 44 (April): 139–45.

Salzman, Ed. 1963. "Castlemont's Laboratory of Life: City Reaps Core Area Study Benefits." *Oakland Tribune*, February 18, 1963, D19.

Sandoval, Gerardo Francisco. 2021. "Planning the Barrio: Ethnic Identity and Struggles over Transit-Oriented, Development-Induced Gentrification." *Journal of Planning Education and Research* 41 (4): 410–24.

Scott-Heron, Gil. 1971. "The Revolution Will Not Be Televised." On *Pieces of a Man*. Flying Dutchman Productions.

Scully, Jason. 2005. "Fruitvale Village I." *ULI Development Case Studies* 35 (4): 1–17.

Self, Robert O. 2003. *American Babylon: Race and the Struggle for Postwar Oakland*. Princeton, NJ: Princeton University Press.

Sherman, G. W. 1953. "Around the U.S.A.: A People Comes of Age." *Nation*, March 28, 1953, 256–57.

Smith, Paul Chaat, and Robert Allen Warrior. 1996. *Like a Hurricane: The Indian Movement from Alcatraz to Wounded Knee*. New York: New Press.

Sparke, Matthew. 2005. *In the Space of Theory: Postfoundational Geographies of the Nation-State*. Minneapolis: University of Minnesota Press.

Summers, Brandi Thompson. 2019. *Black in Place: The Spatial Aesthetics of Race in a Post-chocolate City*. Chapel Hill: University of North Carolina Press.

Tarrow, Sidney G. 1998. *Power in Movement: Social Movements and Contentious Politics*. Cambridge: Cambridge University Press.

Tijerina, Pete. 1968. *Mexican American Legal Defense and Educational Fund Annual Report to the Ford Foundation*. San Antonio: Mexican American Legal Defense and Educational Fund.

Tilly, Charles. 1986. *The Contentious French*. Cambridge, MA: Belknap Press of Harvard University Press.

Tronto, Joan C. 2013. *Caring Democracy: Markets, Equality, and Justice*. New York: New York University Press.

Turner-Lloveras, Mario X. 1997. "The Neighborhood Main Street Initiative in the Barrio: Commercial Revitalization in the Fruitvale District, Oakland, California." Master's thesis, Massachusetts Institute of Technology.

Unity Council. 2016. "News: Google Opens Computer Science Program in Fruitvale." October 7, 2016. https://unitycouncil.org/2016/10/google-opens -computer-science-program-in-fruitvale/.

Unity Council. 2018. "Who We Are." Accessed June 15, 2018. https://unitycouncil .org/who-we-are/about-us/.

Wadhwani, Anita. 1999. "Unique BART Plan Renewing Fruitvale." *SF Gate*, July 11, 1999. https://www.sfgate.com/bayarea/article/Unique-BART-plan-renewing -Fruitvale-3075599.php.

Waldinger, Roger. 1993. "The Ethnic Enclave Debate Revisited." *International Journal of Urban and Regional Research* 17 (3): 444–52.

Weir, Margaret. 1988. "The Federal Government and Unemployment: The Frustration of Policy Innovation from the New Deal to the Great Society." In *The Politics of Social Policy in the United States*, edited by Margaret Weir, Ann Shola Orloff, and Theda Skocpo, 149–90. Princeton, NJ: Princeton University Press.

Weizman, Eyal. 2007. *Hollow Land: Israel's Architecture of Occupation*. New York: Verso.

Williams, Harry E. 1975. "OEO and Political Activation: The Experience of Community Action Participants in Oakland and San Francisco." PhD diss., University of California, Berkeley.

Wilson, Kenneth, and Alejandro Portes. 1980. "Immigrant Enclaves: An Analysis of the Labor Market Experience of Cubans in Miami." *American Journal of Sociology* 86 (2): 295–319.

Wolch, Jennifer R. 1990. *The Shadow State: Government and Voluntary Sector in Transition*. New York: Foundation Center.

Wood, Jim. 1968. "In Spanish or in English, Poverty Problem Lives." *Oakland Tribune*, June 23, 1968, A8.

Yoneyama, Lisa. 1999. *Hiroshima Traces: Time, Space, and the Dialectics of Memory*. Berkeley: University of California Press.

Zepeda-Millán, Chris. 2017. *Latino Mass Mobilization: Immigration, Racialization, and Activism*. Cambridge: Cambridge University Press.

Banga, Ajay, 127
Barbieri, Anthony, 82
Barrazo, Maclovio, 97
Barrio Logan, San Diego, 12
Barrio Youth Alternatives, 3
BART. *See* Bay Area Rapid Transit
Bauer, William, 199n18
Bay Area Rapid Transit (BART): Fruitvale
    Station, 115, 119–21, 129, 140, 175,
    213nn1–2; Fruitvale Transit Village and,
    10, 29, 89, 114, 127, 133; Fruitvale Village,
    8–9, 115, 117–18; parking, 119, 121, 128
Beale, Elaine, 81
Bedford-Stuyvesant Restoration Corpora-
    tion, 108
Benavides, Barlow, 185
Beresford, Susan, 127
Bernardi, Gene, 69
Biolsi, Thomas, 203n43
Birmingham riots (1963), 206n2
Black, Brown, Yellow, and Left (Pulido), 19
Black Corona (Gregory), 61
Black geographies, 200n20
Black identity, 95
Black Lives Matter, 185
Black militancy, 69, 94, 96
blackness, 65, 68–70, 198n5
Black-owned property, 13
Black Panther Party (BPP), 4, 25, 99, 156–58,
    181, 202n36
Black Power movement, 80, 96, 200n26,
    213n46; AIM, Chicano movement, and,
    149; influence, 3, 75; militancy and, 94;
    mobilization, 122, 181; multiculturalism,
    199n17; radicalism and, 202n40
Blackwell, Maylei, 14, 22, 202n38
Black-white relations, 5, 69
Boalt Law School, 53
boycotts, UFW, 32, 152, 153, 158
Boyle Heights, Los Angeles, 12, 202n37
BPP (Black Panther Party), 4, 25, 99, 156–58,
    181, 202n36
Bracero Program, 211n14
Bradshaw, Twinkie Flores, 39
Bridge Called My Back, The (Anzaldúa), 144
Brown, Claude, 164
Brown, Jacqueline Nassy, 1, 7, 137, 199n19
Brown, Jerry, 32, 127
Brown Berets, 42, 99, 100, 156

Bundy, McGeorge, 94, 96, 103–4, 213n46
Burgos, Claudia, 134

CAAs (community action agencies), 67–68
California State Department of Labor, 81
CAP (Community Action Program), 67–68,
    81
capitalists, private foundations and, 209n3
Carmen Flores Culture Center, 38–39
Carter, Jimmy, 127
cartographic memory, 176, 178; activism
    and, 8, 31–39, 41–56, 58–60, 63; ana-
    lytical and methodological framework,
    13–18; place-making and, 8, 15, 31–35,
    50, 60, 112–13
Casitas, Las, 124
Castillo-Speed, Lilian, 167–68
Castlemont district, Oakland, 65–66
Catholic Church, 54, 70–72, 207n11
CAUSA, La, 153–56
Causa Inc., La, 98, 125
Causa Justa/Just Cause (CJJC), 193–94
CDCs. *See* community development
    corporations
Census, US, 86, 211n18
Center for Community Change, 108
Central Valley, 5, 61, 71
Centro Infantil, 48, 49, 131, 145, 178
Centro Legal de la Raza, 2–3, 16, 29–30;
    activism and, 8–9, 179–80, 185, 191,
    193–94; founding, 53–57, 178; Fruitvale
    History Project and, 144; institutional-
    ization of, 62; place-making and, 34
Certeau, Michel de, 41
Cesar Chavez Lifetime Achievement Awards,
    10, 37–38, 59, 199n15
Cesar Chavez Park, 37–38
César E. Chávez Branch, Oakland Public
    Library, 116
Cesar E. Chavez Education Center, 175
Chavarín, Regina, 145–47, 203n1; Fruitvale
    History Project and, 177, 180, 184; mem-
    ory and activism, 31–33; social relations
    of community care and, 52, 54–55,
    57–58; UFW and, 152
Chavarín, Roger, 31–33, 57–58, 153–55,
    203n1
Chavez, Cesar, 52, 199n17; Catholic Church
    and, 71–72; Cesar Chavez Lifetime

Achievement Awards, 10, 37–38, 59, 199n15; community service and, 209n1; CSO and, 74, 199n14; UFW and, 32, 50, 83, 97, 105, 152, 189

Chávez, Ernesto, 21

Cheeseboard Pizza, 217n1

Chicago riots (1966), 206n2

¡Chicana Power! (Blackwell), 22

Chicanismo, 8

Chicano, as designation, 199n12

Chicano militancy, 21

Chicano movement, 8, 24, 52, 199n17, 204n12, 213n46; activism, 3, 10–11, 21–22, 50–51, 101–8, 116, 122; AIM, Black Power movement, and, 149; artists, 50, 204n15; as boot camp, 57–59; cartographic memory and, 13, 14, 34; Crusade for Justice, 32, 203n3; Fruitvale and erasure from, 4–5, 33; Mexican Americans and, 6, 21–22; radicalism and, 49, 202n39; in San Francisco Bay Area, 4, 151, 179; space and, 3, 4, 38, 42; women and, 22, 205n28

Chicano studies, 3, 53, 151, 153–57, 159, 168

Chinese Americans, 69

church-based mobilizations, 70–71

Cisneros, Sandra, 31

Cisneros Galindo, Andres, 46, 58, 157, 159–61, 164–65

City of Oakland Housing Authority, 77

civil rights: CSO and, 199n14; movement, 4, 5, 78–79, 88, 116, 178, 185, 200n26, 202n36

CJJC (Causa Justa/Just Cause), 193–94

Clay, Andreana, 200n26, 205n21

Cleveland riots (1966, 1968), 206n2

Clínica de la Raza, 16, 47, 48, 116, 132; activism and, 185, 189–91; first location of, 54, 55; founding, 57, 178; Fruitvale Village and, 20–21; institutionalization of, 62

Club Social Puertoriqueño, 81

coalitional politics, 75–80

Code Next, 140, 141

COINTELPRO (Counterintelligence Program), FBI, 91

Colombia, 19

colonialism, 213n46

comadrazgo, 57, 205n34

Comité de México y Aztlán (COMEXAZ), 43–46, 58–59, 156, 159, 177; news monitoring service, 160–64, 168–69; solidarity movements and, 166–67

communities: building, 52–57; care, 35, 48, 60, 129; improvement, 22–27, 121–40; kinship networks and, 4, 8, 57; voice for, 130–34. *See also* social relations, of community care

community action agencies (CAAs), 67–68

Community Action Program (CAP), 67–68, 81

Community and Human Resources Agency, 107

Community Coalition, South Central, 3

Community Development Block Grant, 138

community development corporations (CDCs), 27, 47, 92, 141; Ford Foundation and shift to, 106–11; Mexican American, 123–25

community mothering, 119, 121, 130, 137, 205n28

Community Programs Office (CPO), UCLA, 3

Community Service Organization (CSO), 10, 54, 70–79, 81–85, 97, 199n14

compadrazgo, 57, 205n34

Compean, Mario, 105

concilios (councils), 97

Congress of Racial Equality (CORE), 77, 95–96, 98, 100, 105

contentious politics, 201nn28–29, 201n31

Contreras, Mariano, 184

Cooperative Puertorriqueña, 81

CORE (Congress of Racial Equality), 77, 95–96, 98, 100, 105

Corona, Bert, 82, 97

corporatized agencies, 47

Cosgrove, Denis, 31, 150, 168

councils (*concilios*), 97

Counterintelligence Program (COINTEL-PRO), FBI, 91

Cox, Gerald (Father), 70

CPO (Community Programs Office), UCLA, 3

Craib, Raymond, 41–42

Cruikshank, Barbara, 87–88

Crusade for Justice, 32, 203n3

Cruz, Alfredo, 37–38, 39, 42–43, 45, 152–55, 181

Cruz, Leonor de, 167, 184

human-environment relationships, 4, 174, 194–95

identity, Black, 95
identity-based movements, 19
Iglesias, Chris, 140, 141
IIMA (Instituto de Investigaciones de México y Aztlán), 160–61
immigrants, 2, 218n9; Clínica de la Raza and, 20–21; rights, 6, 12, 193–94, 218n10; Street Level Health Project and, 16, 186, 194
Indians, 69, 158
Indigenous people, 13, 19, 174, 198n7; Aztlán and, 204n12; Guatemalan Mayas, 175; Native Americans, 3, 6, 69, 109, 149, 156, 158, 167, 175, 197n3, 199n18
Industrial Areas Foundation, 72
inequality: racial, 14, 65, 88; racism and, 6
institutionalization: as contested process, 90; Mexican American presence, 80–87; of neighborhood projects, 61–62, 90; nonprofit organizations, 93; of social movements in 1960s, 25, 203n43
Instituto de Investigaciones de México y Aztlán (IIMA), 160–61
interlinkages, mapping: COMEXAZ and translocal projects, 159–63; Merritt College and social movement activism, 148–49, 156–59; social movement activism and, 149–59; solidarity movements and transnational connections, 164–67
Internal Revenue Service (IRS), 106, 107, 203n43
International Boulevard (East Fourteenth), 2, 129, 135, 194; Fruitvale Avenue and, xvi, 17, 33–34, 42–43, 175–76; merchant sector along, 138–39
Interstate 880, 5, 202n37
IRS (Internal Revenue Service), 106, 107, 203n43
Italians, 5, 51, 134
Itliong, Larry, 105

Japanese Americans, 69
Jensen, Leif, 197n2
Jim Crow segregation, 23, 66
Jimenez, Guillermina, 133
Jingle Town, 175

Johnson, Gaye Theresa, 202n37
Johnson, Lyndon, 63, 213n46
Josie de La Cruz Park (Sandborn Park), 38
Jubb, Connie, 165
Jungle Hill, 32

Kaiser Industries, 109
Katz, Michael B., 207n8
Kelley, Robin D. G., 171, 197n4
Kennedy, John F., 213n46
King, Martin Luther, Jr., 45, 96, 199n17
kinship networks, 4, 8, 57
Kohl-Arenas, Erica, 83, 91, 92–93, 109, 209n3
KPFA Radio, 45
Kramer, Ralph, 68

labor laws, 23
La Garza, Eligio de, 105
land, 19, 101
LA Times (newspaper), 161
Latin American Library, 81, 85
Latinidad, 2, 8, 117, 122, 134–42, 201n27
Latinx, as term, 197n1
League of United Latin American Citizens (LULAC), 71
Lefebvre, Henri, 124
"Legacy of Organizing in the Fruitvale," 179
legal services, 2, 34, 55, 56, 63. See also Centro Legal de la Raza
Leitner, Helga, 20, 199n18, 201n29
Léon, Christina A., 201n27
Lewis, Oscar, 207n9
Li, Tania Murray, 206n5
liberation theology, 70, 97, 207n11
Limerick, Patricia Nelson, 201n33
Lopez, Alberto V., 121, 133, 139
Lopez, Laura, 187–88
Los Angeles, 3, 19, 98; Boyle Heights, 12, 202n37; Watts uprising, 63, 206n2
Los Angeles Daily News (newspaper), 73
Lozada, Froben, 156
"lucha continúa!, la" (the struggle continues!), 12
LULAC (League of United Latin American Citizens), 71

Magaña, "Mauricio," 200n26
Main Street Program, 139
Malcolm X, 45, 164, 199n17, 202n40

space-time: analysis of activism, 185–92; analysis of social movements, 18–22; compression, 19; with Fruitvale as interlinkage of activism, 192–95; with remembering past, 177–86; social movement place-making and, 174–77

Spanish-speaking, as term, 199n12, 206n3

Spanish Speaking Citizens Foundation, 50–51, 82

Spanish Speaking Unity Council, 29, 77, 178; activism and, 185; CDCs and, 27, 110, 141; community improvement, 121–40; as community voice, 130–34; as corporatized agency, 47; development for people, 122–26; educational programming, 109–10; fiscal expedience, 127–28; as 501(c)(3) nonprofit organization, 85; Ford Foundation and, 91–92, 99, 107, 123, 125; founding, 89–90, 116; on Fruitvale Avenue, 85, 126; Fruitvale Village and, 9, 11, 117, 127–42; influence, 89; institutionalization of, 62; Main Street Program, 139; Mexican Americans and, 83–85, 124; as Mexican American Unity Council, 64, 81, 104, 208n37; minigrants, 100; "people are our business" and, 111–13; report, 85–86; SCLR and, 98; social movement place-making and, 177; space of circulation, 128–30; Street Level Health Project and, 16

Spanish surnames, 68, 69

Sparke, Matthew, 149

spatial practices, of remembering, 37–42

spatial technologies, of remembering, 50

Special Purpose Funds, Target City, 95

Staff Report of a Mexican American Community Development Survey and Resulting Proposal, 85–86

Stanford University, 15

St. Elizabeth's Church, 137, 153

Stokes, Carl, 96, 105–6

Street Academy, 39

Street Level Health Project, 29, 192; care, 187–88; entryway to, 17; founding of, 188–91; immigrants and, 16, 186, 194; with protest posters, 190, 193; reunion, 187

struggle, social movement space and, 157

"struggle continues!, the" (la lucha continúa!), 12

Summers, Brandi Thompson, 198n5

Supreme Court, US, 184

Sviridoff, Mitchell "Mike," 96, 104, 210n10

Sziarto, Kristin M., 199n18

TAAC (Target Area Advisory Committee), 84

Talamante, Olga, 166, 167

Target Area Advisory Committee (TAAC), 84

Target City, 95

Tarrow, Sidney G., 21

Tax Reform Act (1969), 91, 113; Ford Foundation and shift to CDC, 106–11; MAYO conflict, 101–8; revolution and, 100–111

Teatro Campesino, 202n36

Third World Liberation Front, 52

Third World News Bureau, 45, 58

Third World Strike, 52–53, 157

Tiburcio Vazquez Health Center, 179, 189

Tijerina, Reies Lopez, 98–99, 101

Tilly, Charles, 21

time, social movement continuity, 18, 22, 37

torture, 166

translocal projects, COMEXAZ and, 159–63

transnational connections, solidarity movements, 164–67

Treaty of Guadalupe Hidalgo, 64, 198n7, 206n4

Tri-Valley Herald (newspaper), 116

Tronto, Joan, 198n8

Trump, Donald, 173

Turner-Lloveras, Mario X., 120–21, 139

twice stolen money, 91, 209n3

UC Berkeley, 48, 52, 69, 154, 161, 186; activism, 156, 157; Boalt Law School, 53; Centro Legal de la Raza and, 55; Ethnic Studies Library, 167, 168–69; Frente, 99; Mexican Americans at, 5; National Transit Access Center, 133

UCLA, 3

UC Santa Barbara, 154

UFW. *See* United Farm Workers

UNIDOS USA, 199n13, 210n6

United Farm Workers (UFW), 10, 39, 83, 158; activism, 105, 151–53; civil rights movement and, 5; flags, 32, 37, 50; influence, 97, 188–89